D1030399

The Unfinished Enlightenment

The Unfinished Enlightenment

Description in the Age of the Encyclopedia

Joanna Stalnaker

Cornell University Press
Ithaca and London

First published 2010 by Cornell University Press

Printed in the United States of America

Library of Congress Cataloging-in-Publication Data

Stalnaker, Joanna.
    The unfinished Enlightenment : description in the age of the
encyclopedia / Joanna Stalnaker.
        p. cm.
    Includes bibliographical references and index.
    ISBN 978-0-8014-4864-5 (cloth : alk. paper)
    1. French literature—18th century—History and criticism.
2. Description (Rhetoric)—History—18th century.   3. Encyclopedias
and dictionaries, French—History and criticism.   4. Natural history—
France—History—18th century.   5. Enlightenment—France.
6. France—Intellectual life—18th century.   I. Title.
    PQ265.S72   2010
    840.9'005—dc22   2009036987

Cornell University Press strives to use environmentally responsible
suppliers and materials to the fullest extent possible in the publishing of
its books. Such materials include vegetable-based, low-VOC inks and
acid-free papers that are recycled, totally chlorine-free, or partly
composed of nonwood fibers. For further information, visit our website at
www.cornellpress.cornell.edu.

Cloth printing   10 9 8 7 6 5 4 3 2 1

To Eric

Contents

Figures

PREFACE

This is not a book about description in the novel. On the contrary, its premise is that our modern tendency to view description as the inevitable (and subservient) partner of narration has obscured the central place of description in Enlightenment discourse. The modern association between description and the novel was already firmly anchored in French culture by the 1870s, when Gustave Flaubert wrote in his *Dictionnaire des idées reçues:* "Descriptions: There are always too many of them in novels."[1] But just a century earlier, in the rich and diverse network of articles on description in Denis Diderot and Jean d'Alembert's *Encyclopédie* and in the works derived from it, there was not a single mention of the novel. Instead, we find articles on description in natural history, geometry, belles-lettres (the category where one might expect to find some reference to the novel), and

---

1. Gustave Flaubert, *Dictionnaire des idées reçues,* in *Bouvard et Pécuchet,* ed. Claudine Gothot-Mersch (Paris: Gallimard, 1979), 506. Unless otherwise noted, all translations throughout the book are my own.

poetry. Only the article on poetry makes any reference to narration, but it is to chastise the popular new genre of descriptive poetry for not respecting the narrative framework of epic poetry. In other words, narration is evoked not because it is relevant to the Enlightenment practice of description, but to deplore its irrelevance to that practice.

Thus when I started working on this project many years ago, I was puzzled to find the theoretical and practical problem of description popping up everywhere in Enlightenment discourse, but almost no secondary literature on the topic.[2] There was of course a large body of criticism on description in the novel, much of it inspired by structuralism and narratology, but none of it seemed helpful to me in accounting for the kinds of theoretical and practical issues I was encountering in Enlightenment texts. It took me many years to understand that I was looking in the wrong places: to a large degree, the secondary literature that has informed my project comes out of the history of ideas and the history of science. This has started to change, notably with the work of Cynthia Wall, John Bender, and Michael Marrinan, for reasons that I address in the introduction.[3] Just as historians of science have become increasingly aware of the rhetorical and literary issues that shape scientific writing, literary scholars have become more reluctant to make the kinds of artificial distinctions between literature and reality that long made it impossible to engage with the central issues of Enlightenment description. At this critical juncture, the time is ripe for an interdisciplinary dialogue around the epistemological and literary problems posed by description in the age of encyclopedia.

That said, this book is very much a literary study, even though I pay close attention to epistemological context and take a broad view of the kinds of texts that merit literary analysis. For reasons that will become clear only by the end of the book, it is my contention that certain historical questions about the Enlightenment relationship to knowledge, and about

---

2. One notable exception was Denis Reynaud, "Pour une théorie de la description au XVIIIe siècle," *Dix-huitième siècle* 22 (1990): 347–66.

3. See Cynthia Sundberg Wall, *The Prose of Things: Transformations of Description in the Eighteenth Century* (Chicago: University of Chicago Press, 2006); and John Bender and Michael Marrinan, eds., *Regimes of Description: In the Archive of the Eighteenth Century* (Stanford: Stanford University Press, 2005). Bender and Marrinan are also coauthoring a forthcoming book on the articles on description in Diderot and d'Alembert's *Encyclopédie* and on the epistemological status of the diagram in Enlightenment thought.

the epistemological status of description, cannot be fully answered without sustained attention to language, style, and literary form. Since the trajectory of my own work has been from text to context, it is perhaps not surprising that I still tend to favor literary analysis. At the same time, one of the most important things I have learned about the Enlightenment practice of description is that it inevitably draws its readers into the eighteenth-century world of ideas, objects, and culture. This, as I will suggest in the chapters that follow, is precisely what its practitioners intended it to do.

Before proceeding further, a few caveats should be mentioned here: as a literary scholar, and especially as someone who works on a language that is foreign to my native culture (both because it is French and because it is from the eighteenth century), I am especially sensitive to the importance of subtle linguistic nuances in textual interpretation. It may therefore seem paradoxical that I have translated quotations from French into English and have only provided brief parenthetical references to the original French when necessary. This was undoubtedly a sacrifice, but it was one I made consciously, both because I wanted the book to be accessible to a wide audience, and because of the necessary constraints imposed by university presses in today's challenging climate for academic publishing. The second caveat concerns my focus on French works, despite the widespread exchange of ideas and cultural practices across Europe (and especially across the Channel) during the Enlightenment. Although I suspect that the massive impact of Diderot and d'Alembert's *Encyclopédie* and George-Louis Leclerc de Buffon's *Histoire naturelle* on French intellectual culture added a particular intensity to the epistemological and literary tensions surrounding description in France, I do not mean to suggest that description was not undergoing similar transformations in neighboring cultures. As Cynthia Wall has shown in her book *The Prose of Things,* the practice of description in the English novel was transformed over the course of the eighteenth century. Nonetheless, the interdisciplinary context for Enlightenment description, and the unwieldy nature of the works in which it was practiced, obliged me to make choices. Limiting my corpus was particularly vital because I wanted to pay close attention both to epistemological context and to literary form. The chapters that follow are thus by no means intended as an encyclopedic account of Enlightenment description. Rather, they are an attempt to do justice to the subtle equilibrium between words and things that Enlightenment describers sought to achieve.

Acknowledgments

Many people helped me write this book, and it is difficult to find sufficient words of thanks for all of them. I am particularly grateful to Anne Deneys-Tunney for encouraging me to stick with a difficult topic and for helping me make key choices about my corpus and methodology, and to Richard Sieburth for his infectious enthusiasm and ability to see the big picture. Over the years, I have always kept Michel Beaujour's hardest question ("So what?") in mind, and all of my thinking about literature is deeply indebted to him. The support and friendship of Philippe Roger have been invaluable to me over the past decade, and I hope that he will find signs of his inspiration in the pages that follow.

This book owes its existence, quite literally, to Elisabeth Ladenson. I thank her for tearing the proposal out of my hands, for commenting on several chapters, and, above all, for her example and her incomparable friendship. Dorothea von Mücke's incisive comments on a draft of the introduction were instrumental in helping me conceptualize the book, and the support and advice of Vincent Debaene kept me going throughout the revision process. Pierre Force has been a valuable source of practical and intellectual advice since I joined the faculty at Columbia University, and I thank him for making the Department of French and Romance Philology a hospitable environment for teaching and research.

This book has benefited incalculably from the astute and generous comments of Cynthia Wall, whose own book on description served as a model for my project. David Bates gave me one of the most precious gifts a scholar can receive: a reading that transformed both my conception of the book and its tiniest details. I am especially grateful to him for the continuing intellectual inspiration that our conversations and his work have provided. I thank Michael Marrinan and John Bender for putting Enlightenment description on the map, and for a lively discussion Chez Prune in Paris at the formative stage of my project. Martin Puchner and Jenny Davidson generously offered both practical advice on publishing and intellectual guidance on the book's overall conception and argument, and Jeff Loveland gave helpful comments on a version of chapter 1. I consider myself very lucky to have had the expert guidance of Peter Potter at Cornell University Press; I have also greatly appreciated the help of Ange Romeo-Hall, Marian Rogers, and Rachel Post throughout the publishing process.

I would like to express my gratitude to the Schoff Fund at the University Seminars at Columbia University, and to Bob Belknap in particular, for their assistance. This book has benefited from discussions in the University Seminars on Early Modern France and on 18th-Century European Culture; special thanks go to Pierre Force, Benjamin Young, and Elizabeth Powers for fostering the intellectual exchange that makes these seminars so special. The book also profited from a most stimulating (and challenging!) discussion at The Heyman Center for the Humanities at Columbia University; I thank the colleagues who participated in that discussion, and in particular Akeel Bilgrami for his invitation and willingness to read my work.

Special thanks go to Isabelle Chagnon for finding me an ideal research assistant, and to Rebecca Sopchik for being one, and especially for tracking down several of the illustrations in the book. I would also like to thank Katalin Escher of the Musée des Plans-Reliefs in Paris for her assistance and for permission to reproduce the photograph in chapter 6, the Bibliothèque nationale de France for its wonderful digital library and the images in chapters 1 and 3, and Anne-Lise Grobéty of the Bibliothèque de

Neuchâtel for permission to publish the image in chapter 2. An earlier version of chapter 1, entitled "Painting Life, Describing Death," appeared in *Studies in Eighteenth-Century Culture,* vol. 32, ed. Ourida Mostefai and Catherine Ingrassia (Baltimore: Johns Hopkins University Press, 2003), 193–227; an earlier version of chapter 6, entitled "The New Paris in Guise of the Old," appeared in *Studies in Eighteenth-Century Culture,* vol. 35, ed. Jeffrey Ravel and Linda Zionkowski (Baltimore: Johns Hopkins University Press, 2006), 223–42; and part of chapter 2 was published as "The Post-Enlightenment Sketch," in *Landau-Paris Studies on the Eighteenth Century,* vol. 2, ed. Peter Wagner, Frédéric Ogée, and Achim Hescher (Trier: WVT, 2008), 97–105. I gratefully acknowledge the publishers for permission to reprint these articles in modified form.

I am indebted to Mary Bartlett and Lizzy Straus for providing the kind of love and care to my children that allowed me to focus on my work, and for their insight and good conversation day in and day out. My two intense and lovely little boys, Léon and Félix Leveau, cannot yet read these words, but someday I hope they will know how much I appreciate the boundless joy and learning they bring to my life. Other members of my family— Donna Younger, Tom and Aimee Stalnaker, Philippe and Maggy Leveau, and the entire Leveau family—have offered precious love and support over the years. I offer heartfelt thanks to my parents, Nan and Bob Stalnaker, for the two complementary intellectual models they have provided, and most of all for their love and teaching from day one. This book is dedicated to my husband, Eric Leveau, who has been with me from its first word to its last. His devotion to my work and our family is a model of love and generosity. I hope that he will accept this dedication not as compensation for debts that cannot be repaid, but as a simple acknowledgment of all that he has done for me.

INTRODUCTION

In 1788, Louis Sébastien Mercier traced the twelve volumes of his *Tableau de Paris,* a sprawling description of Paris and its social mores, to an identity he had forged in his childhood. In the last volume of this late eighteenth-century best seller, he recounted his memories of a dancing teacher whose appearance and manners were so hilarious that the ten-year-old Louis Sébastien would describe him to his young friends whenever he wanted to make them laugh. "In the evening," he wrote, "I made for my comrades the description of M. Cupis from head to toe; without him I wouldn't have been a describer [descripteur]; he developed in me the seed that has since made the *Tableau de Paris.* I had to paint his grotesque physiognomy, his short arms, his pointy head; and since that time I have amused myself with describing."[1] Although it might escape the notice of a modern reader, Mercier's self-identification as a *descripteur* was remarkable in the context of the Enlightenment.

1. Louis Sébastien Mercier, *Tableau de Paris,* ed. Jean-Claude Bonnet (Paris: Mercure de France, 1994), 2:1479.

For Mercier's contemporaries, the term was a neologism. In Jean-François Féraud's *Dictionnaire critique de la langue française* (1787–88), the entry "Descripteur" notes not only that "Describer and descriptive are two neologisms," but also that "M. Mercier appears to be the author of the first."[2] Coining new words was characteristic of Mercier, who believed that authors must transform language to reflect changing times, and who published his own dictionary of revolutionary neologisms, *La néologie,* in 1801.[3] Yet the term *descripteur* was not strictly speaking a neologism: the first attested use of the term in the French language dates to 1464, and other occurrences can be found throughout the Renaissance and the seventeenth century. What was new was Mercier's use of the term. Whereas its previous usage had designated a limited aspect of an author's identity (as in the example cited in the modern *Grand Robert* dictionary: "This writer has great talents as a describer"), Mercier used the term to define his authorial identity in a way that set him apart from traditional authorial categories.[4] He was neither a poet nor a historian nor a philosopher, but a describer.[5] It was this identity, which Mercier traced to a formative childhood experience divorced from literary tradition and even from writing itself, that provided the impetus (or planted the seed) for the *Tableau de Paris,* a work that lay outside traditional generic categories, just as Mercier set himself apart from traditional authorial categories.

But Mercier's identity as a describer was not unique to him. Like all authorial categories, it was as much the product of a particular cultural, historical, and, in this case, epistemological context as it was an expression of

---

2. Jean-François Féraud, *Dictionaire* [sic] *critique de la langue française* (Marseille: Mossy, 1777–78), 1:739.

3. See Philippe Roger, "'Libre et despote': Mercier néologue," in *Louis Sébastien Mercier (1740–1814): Un hérétique en littérature,* ed. Jean-Claude Bonnet (Paris: Mercure de France, 1995), 327–47; and Daniel Rosenberg, "Louis-Sébastien Mercier's New Words," *Eighteenth-Century Studies* 36, no. 3 (2003): 367–86.

4. "Descripteur," *Le grand Robert de la langue française,* 2nd ed. (Paris: Dictionnaires Le Robert, 1985), 3:414.

5. As Jeremy Popkin puts it, "Claiming for the *Tableau de Paris* a place on a level with the acknowledged masterpieces of writing about Paris requires a redefinition of the canon of French literature. The *Tableau de Paris* fits into none of the established categories of literature: it is not a novel, not a history, not a work of philosophy." Jeremy Popkin, editor's preface to *Panorama of Paris: Selections from "Tableau de Paris,"* by Louis-Sébastien Mercier (University Park: Pennsylvania State University Press, 1999), 2.

his personal experiences and talents.[6] This same context produced descriptive poetry, a self-consciously modern poetic genre that revolved around the central figure of the describer, even though, unlike romantic poetry, it eschewed lyric self-expression. This book shows how the authorial category of the describer and the descriptive genre emerged from the descriptive practices of Enlightenment natural history and encyclopedism, briefly enjoyed a position of prominence in French letters, and then quickly fell into obsolescence. To understand the prominence and subsequent obscurity of the category and the genre, we must both scrutinize and step outside the modern configuration of scientific and literary description that postdates the Enlightenment. New trends in literary studies and the history of science have made it possible to do so.

Science versus Literature

Two books, with strikingly similar jacket illustrations, indicate that literary studies and the history of science share an interest in the problem of description. The first, *The Prose of Things* by Cynthia Wall, traces a path, in the British tradition, from the spare, object-studded descriptions of the seventeenth-century novel to the rich, contextual descriptions of the late eighteenth-century novel. The second, *The Science of Describing* by Brian Ogilvie, ties the invention of natural history, which Ogilvie dates to the Renaissance, to the new practices of botanical field observation and description that were developed during that period.[7] Both studies are symptomatic of a critical preoccupation with material culture, and with the ways that literature and science stem from concrete practices. Wall, for example, shows how interior design, domestic tours, and country-house guides "define and make visible narrative space," while Ogilvie argues that "the problems of classification that characterized later natural history were

---

6. On the relationship between changing categories of authorship and evolutions in the life sciences at the end of the Enlightenment, see Dorothea von Mücke, "Goethe's Metamorphosis: Changing Forms in Nature, the Life Sciences, and Authorship," *Representations* 95 (2006): 27–53.

7. Brian W. Ogilvie, *The Science of Describing: Natural History in Renaissance Europe* (Chicago: University of Chicago Press, 2006).

a consequence of the attempt to describe the world" in more limited, local contexts during the Renaissance.[8]

The two studies also share an implicit, subtle resistance to the cordoning off of literature from science, whose origins can be traced to the late Enlightenment. During the heyday of structuralism, the strategies adopted by literary critics with respect to this division were largely defensive: on the one hand, they developed a scientific discourse of literary criticism, while, on the other, they reinforced the absolute divide between science and literature by asserting that literature was all about language. Roland Barthes's 1967 article "De la science à la littérature" reflected upon these strategies and marked Barthes's transition from a science of literary criticism to a self-conscious awareness of his own writing practice (a transition that can be mapped onto his move from structuralism to poststructuralism). In this brief and rhetorically powerful essay, Barthes defined science (disparagingly) in terms of its instrumental use of language, and literature (glowingly) in terms of its self-conscious awareness of its status as language. But his intention was not to reinforce the divide between science and literature. Instead, he sought to annul that divide by proposing that literature's self-conscious use of language become the model for the previously "scientific" discourse of structuralism: "The logical prolongation of structuralism can only be to rejoin literature no longer as 'object' of analysis, but as activity of writing."[9] Thus the most radical strategy of all was to deny science its special status as science, by turning scientific discourse, including literary criticism, into a self-conscious writing practice analogous to literature itself.

Whether or not they followed Barthes's move from science to literature, critics influenced by structuralism were aware that description posed a particular challenge to their claim that literature should not be interpreted in terms of its connections to reality (a term that some literary critics continue to enclose in quotation marks to this day). Michael Riffaterre's response to this challenge was emblematic of the flurry of studies on literary description that marked the 1970s and 1980s (although his focus on eighteenth-century poetry was entirely atypical, for reasons that will soon become clear). In a 1972 article, Riffaterre took descriptive

---

8. Wall, *Prose of Things,* 5; and Ogilvie, *Science of Describing,* 8.

9. Roland Barthes, "De la science à la littérature," in *Le bruissement de la langue* (Paris: Éditions du Seuil, 1984), 17. First published in 1967 in the *Times Literary Supplement.*

poetry, a long-neglected poetic genre invented during the eighteenth century, as a test case for his more general argument about the self-sufficiency of literary texts. "The descriptive genre," he wrote, "more than any other literary form, appeared to open out necessarily onto reality. This is not at all the case: all forms of mimesis in this genre do nothing else than to create an *illusion* of reality."[10] For scholars of the Enlightenment familiar with descriptive poetry, there are two problems with this interpretation: first, it runs directly counter to the manner in which descriptive poets such as Jacques Delille and Jean-François de Saint-Lambert conceived of their poetic enterprise, and second, it ignores the strange back-and-forth between artful verse and scientific prose notes that makes their poetry so difficult to read today. Indeed, Riffaterre chose descriptive poetry as his test case precisely because it appeared (and strived) to turn the encyclopedic and scientific knowledge of its day into poetry, whereas he wanted to demonstrate that poetry had principally to do with language. If he could prove that *descriptive* poetry was not about the world, in some important sense, he could prove the same thing about poetry more generally.

In the history of science, on the other hand, poststructuralism led to an increasing emphasis on the rhetorical nature of scientific language. In its worst excesses, this trend reduced science to mere rhetoric, thereby remaining trapped within the dichotomy between reality and language that marked Riffaterre's treatment of descriptive poetry. But this trend was also productive in allowing scholars, as Jeff Loveland puts it, "to undercut the myth of science's independence from human activity" and "to establish rhetoric as a far from irrational means of persuasion and to cleanse it of its modern image as ornament or trickery."[11] The development of historical epistemology, in the wake of Michel Foucault's *Les mots et les choses* (1966), has enriched our appreciation for the historical contingency of specific scientific practices, from observation to image making. And just as the emphasis on material culture, in Wall's work, for example, has led to a reappraisal of literary description, the emphasis on scientific rhetoric and historical epistemology has led to a reappraisal of scientific description. The work of Lorraine Daston, who has shown how epistemological

---

10. Michael Riffaterre, "Système d'un genre descriptif," *Poétique* 9 (1972): 30.

11. Jeff Loveland, *Rhetoric and Natural History: Buffon in Polemical and Literary Context,* Studies on Voltaire and the Eighteenth Century 2001:3 (Oxford: Voltaire Foundation, 2001), 19–20.

and cultural configurations inform both scientific descriptions and images, illustrates how much potential there is for dialogue between historians of science and literary scholars around the question of description.[12]

Given this critical conjuncture, it now seems appropriate to probe the origins of the modern polarity between literary and scientific description. While no single study can locate or explain those origins completely (and as readers of the Enlightenment we may be suspicious of the search for origins in the first place), this book isolates a constitutive moment in the long, complicated history of that divide.[13] Although we generally think of the Enlightenment as a time when the sciences (rather than science) and belles-lettres (rather than literature) were not yet distinct discourses, I argue that in the late Enlightenment it became necessary to think about description in terms of competing truth claims that would eventually resolve themselves in our modern distinction between literature and science. Description was theorized and practiced like never before during the second half of the eighteenth century because it had become the site of growing tensions between epistemology and poetics, and Enlightenment writers were struggling to keep what Michel Beaujour has called the two "Janus-like" faces of description from coming apart.[14]

But those two faces did come apart. As a result, the works that participated in the Enlightenment's descriptive project quickly came to appear unreadable. This was in part due to formal and generic qualities of the works themselves: confirming the most ferocious Enlightenment critiques of descriptive excess, they are multivolume, detail laden, digressive, convoluted, and open ended. They also lie outside classical and modern literary genres: the invention of descriptive poetry, conceived as a modern poetic genre

---

12. See Lorraine Daston and Peter Galison, *Objectivity* (New York: Zone Books, 2007); Lorraine Daston, "Description by Omission: Nature Enlightened and Obscured," in Bender and Marrinan, *Regimes of Description,* 11–24; and Lorraine Daston and Katharine Park, *Wonders and the Order of Nature, 1150–1750* (New York: Zone Books, 1998). An interdisciplinary dialogue around the question of eighteenth-century description was initiated at a conference organized by Bender and Marrinan, the proceedings of which were published in *Regimes of Description.*

13. On the Enlightenment search for origins, and our own relationship to it, see Catherine Labio, *Origins and the Enlightenment: Aesthetic Epistemology from Descartes to Kant* (Ithaca, N.Y.: Cornell University Press, 2004).

14. Michel Beaujour, "Some Paradoxes of Description," in "Towards a Theory of Description," ed. Jeffrey Kittay, special issue, *Yale French Studies* 61 (1981): 28. See Wall, *Prose of Things,* 13, who quotes and comments on Beaujour's Janus image, which I modify here for my own purposes.

consistent with the encyclopedic aspirations of its time, is symptomatic of the generic experimentation that characterizes all the works discussed in this book. But the obsolescence of these works was also, and principally, due to the polarization of scientific and literary description that severed the competing truth claims that gave meaning to Enlightenment description. To cite just one example, Jacques-Henri Bernardin de Saint-Pierre has been remembered as the first great describer in modern French literature for his exotic pastoral novel *Paul et Virginie* (1788), even as the work of natural history in which he developed his descriptive technique, the *Études de la nature* (1784–88), quickly fell into oblivion.[15] A growing number of modern critical editions, however, indicates a renewed interest in descriptive works that belong neither to literature nor to science in their modern acceptations. In addition to the *Études de la nature,* Mercier's multivolume descriptions of Paris, the *Tableau de Paris* (1781–88) and *Le nouveau Paris* (1798 or 1799), have been published in their entirety, and the naturalist Georges-Louis Leclerc de Buffon has entered the prestigious Pléiade collection.[16] Still, the anatomical descriptions of quadrupeds written by Buffon's collaborator Louis-Jean-Marie Daubenton have been excised from that edition (thereby separating the "scientific" anatomical descriptions from the "literary" descriptions of animals in their natural habitats), and descriptive poetry, with its voluminous prose notes and distinctly nonlyrical tone, continues to be deemed unworthy of modern editions. Whether or not descriptive poetry is ever resuscitated, the long neglect to which all of the works considered here have been subjected is closely tied to the struggle this book documents, and Enlightenment describers were not entirely unaware of the potential fate of their enterprise. It is for this reason above all that I have written this book, as a testament to their persistent efforts to describe the world in the face of epistemological and cultural transformations that would soon make their descriptions obsolete.

---

15. See Daniel Mornet, *Le sentiment de la nature en France de Jean-Jacques Rousseau à Bernardin de Saint-Pierre: Essai sur le rapport de la littérature aux moeurs* (1907; repr., Geneva: Slatkine Reprints, 2000), 435.

16. These modern critical editions are Jacques-Henri Bernardin de Saint-Pierre, *Les études de la nature,* ed. Colas Duflo (Saint-Étienne: Publications de l'Université de Saint-Étienne, 2007); Louis Sébastien Mercier, *Tableau de Paris,* ed. Jean-Claude Bonnet, 2 vols. (Paris: Mercure de France, 1994); id., *Le nouveau Paris,* ed. Jean-Claude Bonnet (Paris: Mercure de France, 1994); Georges-Louis Leclerc de Buffon, *Oeuvres,* ed. Stéphane Schmitt, Bibliothèque de la Pléiade 532 (Paris: Gallimard, 2007).

The place of Foucault with respect to the obsolescence and resurgence of Enlightenment description is particularly interesting. Historical episte-mology, which is heavily indebted to Foucault, is one of the critical trends that has made it possible for scholars such as Daston to shed new light on techniques of scientific observation and description that were "bodily, instrumental, literary, and moral."[17] The recognition that observation and description are not natural phenomena but historically contingent prac-tices that, as Patrick Singy expresses it, "form what we might call a *regime of perception*" grows directly out of Foucault's archaeology of the human sciences.[18] And in his chapter on classification in *Les mots et les choses*, Fou-cault himself offered an account of natural history that made it clear why description was so central to the field: it was the particular means by which the naturalist brought language and nature into close proximity, bridging the new gap that had opened up between words and things in the classical episteme.

But Foucault gave a rather limited and selective reading of natural history description in the classical episteme, neglecting the constitutive tensions between epistemology and poetics that made description both a central theoretical preoccupation and a highly variable and experimental set of practices during the Enlightenment. For Foucault, description in the classical episteme was essentially, to borrow a phrase coined by Das-ton, "description by omission."[19] The naturalist stripped nature of most of its qualities—notably taste, smell, and texture—and imposed a taxonomic structure that transformed nature into a language even before describing it. Although Foucault's archaeology of the human sciences was predicated on a rejection of the history of proper names, he in fact took the Swed-ish botanist and taxonomist Carl Linnaeus as the prototypical describer for the classical episteme. The following characterization of Linnaeus's descriptive method (which reflects an ideal rather than an actual prac-tice) came to symbolize description across the classical episteme for Fou-cault: "Faced with the same individual, each person will be able to write

---

17. Lorraine Daston, "The Disciplines of Attention," in *A New History of German Literature*, ed. David E. Wellbery (Cambridge, Mass.: Harvard University Press, 2004), 437; and Michel Fou-cault, *Les mots et les choses: Une archéologie des sciences humaines* (Paris: Gallimard, 1966).

18. Patrick Singy, "Huber's Eyes: The Art of Scientific Observation before the Emergence of Positivism," *Representations* 95 (2006): 57.

19. Daston, "Description by Omission," 11.

the same description; and conversely, on the basis of a given description, each person will be able to recognize the individuals that correspond to it. In this fundamental articulation of the visible, the first confrontation between language and things can be established in a manner that excludes all uncertainty."[20] Description, in this view, was not an occasion for individual writers to wrestle with the incommensurability between language and nature, or to experiment with new approaches to writing in order to communicate the messy empirical data of firsthand observation. It was a system, and as such, it excluded not only uncertainty but also any experimental dimension or individual idiosyncrasies. Foucault even went so far as to group the two quarreling giants of Enlightenment natural history under the same descriptive tent: "Buffon and Linnaeus impose the same grid [Buffon et Linné posent la même grille]; their gaze occupies on things the same surface of contact; the same black squares contain the invisible; the same blanks, clear and distinct, offer themselves to words."[21] With this rapprochement, Foucault turned his generally subtle concept of the episteme into a reductive system that curiously mirrors his account of the grid Buffon and Linnaeus allegedly imposed on the diversity and heterogeneity of nature. How, within such an inflexible and deterministic view of the episteme, can we account for Buffon's critique of systems, his quarrel with Linnean taxonomy, and his lasting engagement with the competing claims of epistemology and rhetoric in his descriptive practice? More generally, how can we understand why description became such a central epistemological and literary problem during the Enlightenment, even within the field of natural history?

If I have insisted on Foucault's effacement of individual idiosyncrasies in descriptive practice, it is not in order to reassert the naïve humanism he was trying to combat. Rather, it is to take seriously the historically contingent category of the describer, which Foucault's own work has made it possible to unearth. This category, I argue, was forged in the context of Enlightenment natural history and encyclopedism, two central manifestations of the classical episteme for Foucault, but its emergence blurs the clean break between the classical and modern epistemes on which *Les mots et les choses* is predicated. If, as Foucault argued in his famous chapter

---

20. Foucault, *Mots et choses,* 146.
21. Ibid., 148.

on Diego Velázquez's *Las Meninas,* the representational regime characteristic of the classical episteme depends upon the effacement of the figure
responsible for its representation, the classical episteme should end with
the emergence of the describer.[22] But a closer look at the Enlightenment
describers who adopted that identity demonstrates how inextricable it was
from the representational practices and epistemological grounding Foucault took to be characteristic of the classical episteme. In this sense, my
book marks a departure from the Foucauldian tradition.

What I do share with that tradition, however, is an interest in the fragmentary and partial nature of descriptions. In their introduction to *Regimes
of Description,* an interdisciplinary collection of essays indebted to Foucault, John Bender and Michael Marrinan develop a comparison between
eighteenth-century descriptive modes and the computerized mapping of
the human genome achieved at the beginning of the twenty-first century.[23]
Their purpose in making this comparison is by no means to argue that
Enlightenment description is the source of modern, "objective" descriptions of nature, but to underline that today's knowledge, all knowledge, is
built on gaps that we are perpetually filling as our (technological) means
of description change, only to create and discover new gaps in the process. In citing the philosopher and mathematician Nicolas de Condorcet's
dream of "a language of science that grew towards perfection with no
gaps or errors," Bender and Marrinan surmise that Condorcet "probably
never imagined that knowledge could be erected on gaps."[24] What remains
unclear in their brief introduction, however, is whether they think other
Enlightenment writers, and describers in particular, imagined knowledge
could be built on gaps. In the chapters that follow, I offer some answers
to that question, and to the related question of how acknowledged gaps
in knowledge transformed the status of description and led to the emergence of new approaches to writing. Of particular interest to me is the
way Enlightenment describers tackled the problem of incompleteness, and
even self-consciously integrated the inevitable fragmentation of description into the form of their works. This fragmentation in turn affected the
place of the describer, who emerged as the sole principle of unity in works

---

22. Ibid., 19–31.
23. Bender and Marrinan, introduction to *Regimes of Description,* 2–4 and 6–7.
24. Ibid., 3.

otherwise subject to the disorderly (and disorienting) effects of digression, detail, and stylistic and formal experimentation. The emergence of the describer might itself be perceived as quintessentially Foucauldian, mirroring the emergence of man that for Foucault marked the birth of the modern episteme, if it were not for the fact that such an interpretation would deny the epistemic breaks that were so crucial to Foucault's archaeology of the human sciences. Whether or not we accept his account of those breaks, Foucault's work laid the necessary groundwork for a cross-disciplinary approach to Enlightenment description.

Natural History, Geometry, and Belles-Lettres

Diderot and d'Alembert's *Encyclopédie* (1751–72) is the logical place to start if one wishes to get a sense of the interlocking network of disciplines in which description was theorized and practiced in the Enlightenment. But it is difficult to give a concise account of the articles on description in the *Encyclopédie* and in the works derived from it. This is in part because these articles share many of the essential and complex features of the *Encyclopédie* itself: they are the work of multiple authors from various fields of knowledge, they create relationships among three different branches of the tree of knowledge (natural history, geometry, and belles-lettres), and they reflect the changing landscape of human knowledge between 1754 (when the first three articles on description were published in the fourth volume of the *Encyclopédie*) and 1782 (when those articles were supplemented and reconfigured in the *Encyclopédie méthodique*). Most importantly, they are traversed by internal contradictions and methodological tensions that eventually resulted in the polarization of scientific and literary description.

Of the three articles that initially figured in the *Encyclopédie,* the first appeared under the heading "Description, s.f. (*Hist. nat.*)." Its author was Daubenton, the physician and anatomist who wrote anatomical descriptions for Buffon's *Histoire naturelle,* and who also contributed a variety of articles on botany and zoology to the *Encyclopédie.* What this article demonstrates, above all, is that description posed deep and potentially insoluble methodological problems for Daubenton (and, as we shall see in chapter 1, for Buffon). This may seem surprising given that, as Ogilvie's study shows, the techniques of observation and description that constituted the science of describing had already been firmly established by Renaissance naturalists. But, despite a shared emphasis on empirical observation and precise description, Daubenton and Buffon could no longer define their descriptive approach with reference to that tradition. First, they were primarily concerned with zoological description, whereas the Renaissance science of describing was rooted in the study of botany.[25] Second, partly as a result of their focus on animals, they rejected the systematic approach of Linnean taxonomy that according to Ogilvie grew directly out of the Renaissance science of describing.[26] As Scott Atran has shown, the methodological challenges posed by zoology are markedly different from those of botany, and these differences have important implications for descriptive technique. Notably, the most important differences between plants can be discerned in their exterior structure, whereas comparative zoology demands an appreciation of internal anatomy. As Atran remarks, in an implicit critique of Foucault, "The separation between external morphology and internal anatomy, which eased conception of a vast tableau spanning the plant world, would thus prove much more problematic in the case of animals."[27] As a comparative anatomist who also contributed botanical articles to the *Encyclopédie,* Daubenton was in a good position to appreciate this difference. Like his collaborator Buffon, he ferociously attacked the "nomenclaturists" and Linnaeus in particular for what he viewed as their arbitrary systems and imperfect descriptions.

It is thus somewhat misleading for Daston to group Daubenton with Linnaeus as part of a broader trend in scientific description toward what she calls "description by omission." Citing both Daubenton's *Encyclopédie* article on description and Linnaeus's critique of the detailed descriptions of Parisian botanists, Daston identifies "a far broader transformation in the ideals and practices of scientific description that occurred between 1660 and 1730."[28] Whereas earlier naturalists had favored minutely detailed

---

25. As Ogilvie notes, "Renaissance naturalists studied animals and minerals, but the core of Renaissance natural history was *res herbaria,* the study of plants." Ogilvie, *Science of Describing,* 24. Ogilvie devotes some attention to the problem of describing animals, especially exotic ones, in his fifth chapter, 209–64.

26. Ogilvie, *Science of Describing,* 8, 209–64.

27. Scott Atran, *Cognitive Foundations of Natural History: Towards an Anthropology of Science* (Cambridge: Cambridge University Press, 1990), 191.

28. Daston, "Description by Omission," 12.

descriptions of individuals, a practice that reflected their belief in the variety and inconstancy of nature, Linnaeus and his followers favored pared-down descriptions that better served their classificatory aims. Associating this shift in descriptive practice with a broader mutation in the category of the natural fact, Daston characterizes the change as follows: "The texture of descriptions of nature changed accordingly, from long accounts bristling with particulars to concise reports made deliberately bland by summary, repetition, and omission of details." The new approach to description was, according to Daston, part of the process of nature becoming "universal and eternal" by the mid-eighteenth century.[29]

Daston's concept of "description by omission" is rich in implications, because it underlines the extent to which description can involve not only a confrontation with the diversity and heterogeneity of nature, but also a strong drive toward the idealization or abstraction of empirical data. But it does not accurately reflect Daubenton's concept or practice of description. A closer look at Daubenton's article reveals on the contrary the extent to which his descriptive priorities diverged from those of Linnaeus. It is true that like Linnaeus, Daubenton acknowledged the need to impose strict limits on natural history description. "Descriptions," he wrote, "would have no limits whatsoever if we extended them indiscriminately to all the beings in nature, to all the varieties of their forms, & to all the details of their conformation or their organization."[30] But for Daubenton the main problem with long, detailed descriptions was not that they posed an obstacle to classification, but that they made it impossible for readers to visualize the animals he described: "A book containing so many & such long descriptions, far from giving us clear & distinct ideas of the bodies that cover the earth & of those of which it is composed, would only present to the mind formless & gigantic figures dispersed without order & traced without proportions" (4:878). Paradoxically, for Daubenton, the accumulation of detail served to distort rather than to define the anatomical structure the naturalist was

---

29. Ibid., 13.

30. Louis-Jean-Marie Daubenton, "Description, s.f. (*Hist. nat.*)," in *Encyclopédie, ou Dictionnaire raisonné des sciences, des arts et des métiers,* ed. Denis Diderot and Jean le Rond d'Alembert, University of Chicago: ARTFL Encyclopédie Project, Winter 2008 ed., gen. ed. Robert Morrissey, http://encyclopedie.uchicago.edu/. Subsequent references to the *Encyclopédie* appear parenthetically in the main text and use the original volume and page numbers as provided by ARTFL; for this reference, 4:878.

seeking to convey. At the same time, Daubenton's rejection of Linnean taxonomy was predicated on complete description as the only means of avoiding arbitrary systems in the study of nature. Hence Daubenton faced a serious methodological problem: how could he preserve representational coherence, while still maintaining the high level of detail he required to define natural beings in all their individuality?

Readers versed in eighteenth-century aesthetics will recognize this as a familiar problem. According to Alex Potts, it was one that surfaced in various epistemological and aesthetic contexts during the Enlightenment and can be characterized as follows: "In elaborating a full description of an empirical phenomenon, does the accumulation of detail come together naturally to give a coherent picture of the whole, or does the successive definition of individual parts operate at a tangent to apprehending a phenomenon in its totality—and perhaps even get in the way of this?"[31] This question pertained in similar ways in natural history and aesthetics, and in fact there was significant overlap between the two fields. When Diderot posed the problem of descriptive detail in his *Salon de 1767,* noting that too much detail would inevitably distort his reader's mental image of the paintings he described, he made an analogy to natural history description: "There is a sure way to make our listener take an aphid for an elephant; it is simply a matter of pushing to an excess the detailed anatomical description of the living atom."[32] This analogy underlines the extent to which Diderot inscribed his art criticism into the broader epistemological problem of describing nature, rather than associating it exclusively with the ancient tradition of *ekphrasis,* in which the verbal description of works of art was not necessarily based on empirical observation.[33]

---

31. Alex Potts, "Disparities between Part and Whole in the Description of Works of Art," in Bender and Marrinan, *Regimes of Description,* 136.

32. Denis Diderot, *Salon de 1767,* in *Oeuvres,* ed. Laurent Versini, vol. 4, *Esthétique-Théâtre* (Paris: Robert Laffont, 1996), 704.

33. *Ekphrasis* initially had a broader meaning, referring to the description of objects, and then narrowed to mean the verbal description of works of visual art. See James A. W. Heffernan, *Museum of Words: The Poetics of Ekphrasis from Homer to Ashbery* (Chicago: University of Chicago Press, 1980), 191. Potts notes that in the classical tradition "the point of ekphrasis as originally conceived was to offer a demonstration of the rhetorical power of language, not to provide an accurate verbal representation of things observed. Indeed, ekphrasis was often quite detached from the observation of any actual works of art." Potts, "Disparities between Part and Whole," 137.

But the problem found its most eloquent and extended discussion in Gotthold Ephraim Lessing's *Laocoön* (1766). This influential treatise sought to establish firm boundaries between painting and poetry, by defining painting as the simultaneous arrangement of forms in space, and poetry as the successive arrangement of actions in time. What is often forgotten, however, is that Lessing wrote his treatise in response to what he viewed as the excesses of descriptive poetry, an Enlightenment genre that was primarily engaged with the representation of nature, not paintings, and that looked to natural history and encyclopedism for poetic inspiration. This context helps to explain why Lessing's aesthetic concerns were so close to Daubenton's methodological concerns. Lessing's rejection of descriptive poetry rested in part on the idea that the accumulation of detail in an extended verbal description did not allow the reader (or the listener, as Lessing generally characterized him) to develop a perception of the whole: "That which the eye takes in at a single glance [the poet] counts out to us with perceptible slowness, and it often happens that when we arrive at the end of his description we have already forgotten the first features."[34] This meant that Lessing's strict boundaries between poetry and painting, to which the art critic and historian Michael Fried has traced the origins of modernism, were rooted in the methodological problems surrounding empirical description in the Enlightenment.[35] Although Lessing rejected extended verbal descriptions (except in the narrative form exemplified by Hephaestus's dynamic creation of Achilles' shield in the *Iliad*), he shared Daubenton's theoretical preoccupation with the uneasy relationship between part and whole in a description, and with the dangers that detail posed to representational coherence.

But Daubenton's methodological concerns were not limited to the problem of representational coherence. He was also engaged in a project of comparative anatomy, seeking to establish connections between anatomical structures across species. Long, detailed descriptions posed a threat to this project, because they undermined the readers' attempts to perceive

---

34. Gotthold Ephraim Lessing, *Laocoön: An Essay on the Limits of Painting and Poetry,* ed. and trans. Edward Allen McCormick (1962; repr., Baltimore: Johns Hopkins University Press, 1984), 86.

35. See Michael Fried, foreword to *Laocoön,* by Lessing, vii–viii.

connections between individuals in nature. Any work of natural history that did not limit its descriptions, Daubenton warned, "would be an enormous, confused heap formed from the debris of a multitude of machines; one would only recognize detached parts, without seeing the relationships & the assemblage" (4:878). The task of natural history, for Daubenton, was not only to observe and describe individual animals but also to achieve a broad understanding of animal economy. In this sense, he was, as Daston suggests, closer to Linnaeus than to the early Renaissance naturalists who devoted such fine-grained attention to the field observation and description of individual specimens in local context.[36] At the same time, even within the context of his comparative project, Daubenton still insisted on the necessity of complete descriptions. This made his anatomical comparisons much more difficult to systematize than the selective studies of organs of fructification that served as the basis for Linnaeus's taxonomic system. Hence Daubenton faced a second serious methodological problem: how could he help his readers achieve a global understanding of animal economy, while still maintaining the level of detail necessary to avoid arbitrary systems in the study of nature?

Similar methodological tensions can be seen in the second *Encyclopédie* article, which appeared under the heading "Description (*Terme de Géométrie*)." The author of this article was d'Alembert, the mathematician and philosopher who served as Diderot's coeditor in the early years of the *Encyclopédie*. Despite its brevity and apparent irrelevance to verbal description, d'Alembert's article articulated a choice between two methods of describing curves, in a manner not unrelated to the methodological challenges facing the naturalists. The first method, which "traced" a curve through continuous movement with an instrument like the compass, can be seen as an artisanal method grounded in actual, mechanical practice and leading to the creation of a "real" circle. The second method, which "constructed" a curve by linking several points established by geometrical calculations, can be seen as a conceptual method grounded in abstract calculation and leading to the creation of an "ideal" circle (although the necessity of linking those points through approximation brings this method closer to the

---

36. On the relationship between the Renaissance naturalists and the subsequent taxonomical tradition, see Ogilvie, *Science of Describing*, 8, 209–64.

messiness and materiality of the "real" circle).[37] So what relevance did this have for verbal description, whether in natural history or in belles-lettres?

As I have suggested, Daston's concept of description by omission under- lines the extent to which natural history description can involve an idealiza- tion or abstraction of empirical data, as exemplified by Linnean taxonomy. Buffon and Daubenton's critique of Linnaeus was indeed predicated on the idea that his descriptive method was too abstract to be useful within what Buffon called the "real sciences."[38] Within the realm of belles-lettres, on the other hand, the competing claims of real and ideal descriptions had long served to define different authorial categories: Aristotle's distinction between the historian and the poet, for example, was founded on the oppo- sition between the real, particular facts of history and the probable, general truths of poetry, in a way that had important implications for descriptive practice.[39] As long as such distinctions remained operative, poetic descrip- tion could remain impervious to the methodological challenges facing the naturalists. But as those distinctions started to break down, poetic descrip- tion was transformed in a way that disrupted both classical poetics and rhetorical doctrine. Signs of this transformation can be seen in the third *Encyclopédie* article on description.

The third article, which appeared under the heading "Description (*Belles-Lettres*)," is by far the most difficult to characterize, for a variety of reasons. First, it was the work of several authors and was subject to several additions over a period of three decades. Second, the category of belles- lettres was much broader, and more vague, than those of natural history and geometry and was undergoing significant changes during the three decades that separated the original article from its most expanded version. According to John Bender and David Wellbery, it was "the overriding unity of rhetorical doctrine, which governed all of verbal production" that gave coherence to the broad categories of literature and belles-lettres, be- fore the emergence of our more restrictive, modern category of literature

---

37. Jean d'Alembert, "Description (*Terme de Géométrie*)," in *Encyclopédie*, ARTFL, 4:878.

38. Georges-Louis Leclerc de Buffon and Louis-Jean-Marie Daubenton, *Histoire naturelle, générale et particulière, avec la description du Cabinet du Roy* (Paris: Imprimerie Royale, 1749), 1:54–55.

39. Aristotle, *Poetics*, in *Ancient Literary Criticism: The Principal Texts in New Translations,* ed. D. A. Russell and M. Winterbottom, trans. M. E. Hubbard (Oxford: Oxford University Press, 1972), 9.1451a38-b33.

as imaginative aesthetic production.[40] In tracking the decline of rhetoric, Bender and Wellbery identify two distinct historical moments: first the Enlightenment "banished rhetoric from the domain of theoretical and practical discourse" through appeals to neutrality and objectivity, and then romanticism achieved a similar feat in the domain of "imaginative or aesthetic discourse" through appeals to originality and subjectivity.[41] This two-phase historical model illustrates how difficult it is to step outside the modern dichotomy between science and literature: in Bender and Wellbery's account, the first phase is clearly (although not exclusively) associated with scientific discourse, while the second is associated with literature in its modern acceptation. This account is to a certain extent confirmed by the *Encyclopédie* articles on description: while Daubenton's article appears relatively impervious to rhetorical doctrine, the belles-lettres article is infused with traditional rhetorical definitions and concerns. At the same time, we can witness in the evolution of this article a gradual shift from traditional rhetorical doctrine to more modern considerations concerning the aesthetic reception of descriptions. This evolution suggests a deeper entanglement between the decline of rhetoric in "scientific" and "literary" description than Bender and Wellbery's two-phase model implies.

The article's original author was Edmé Mallet, a theologian who contributed many of the articles on grammar, poetry, and eloquence in the early years of the *Encyclopédie*. Mallet's contribution to the article reflects two important tendencies in the traditional rhetorical treatment of description: first, the widespread suspicion surrounding description and the corresponding emphasis on constraints; and second, the treatment of description as a figure of discourse and the corresponding emphasis on taxonomy.[42] Mallet opened his article by asserting the epistemological inferiority of description with respect to definition: "Description: imperfect & inexact definition, in which one attempts to make a thing known by way of a few

---

40. John Bender and David E. Wellbery, eds., *The Ends of Rhetoric: History, Theory, Practice* (Stanford: Stanford University Press, 1990), 15.

41. Ibid., 5.

42. On the rhetorical status of description, see Philippe Hamon, *Du descriptif,* 4th ed. (Paris: Hachette, 1993), 9–36. First published in 1981 as *Introduction à l'analyse du descriptif.* See also Philippe Hamon, "Rhetorical Status of the Descriptive," in Kittay, "Towards a Theory of Description," 1–26; and Perrine Galand-Hallyn, *Le reflet des fleurs: Description et métalangage poétique d'Homère à la Renaissance* (Geneva: Droz, 1994), 7–20.

properties & circumstances that are particular to it, and that are sufficient to give an idea of it & distinguish it from others, but that do not at all develop its nature & its essence."[43] This characterization of description, which echoes Antoine Furetière's 1690 *Dictionnaire universel,* makes clear why natural history required its own separate article on description: whereas for Buffon and Daubenton particulars were essential to the definition of living beings, for Mallet description was epistemologically inferior to definition precisely because it was grounded in particulars. Mallet's negative definition of description was consistent with traditional rhetorical doctrine, which tended to view description with a high level of suspicion and to focus on containing its excesses rather than explaining its mechanisms.

Mallet then went on to characterize description as "the favorite figure of orators & poets" (4:879). His more restrictive treatment of description as a figure of discourse was again consistent with traditional rhetorical doctrine: first, he provided a typical taxonomy of different kinds of descriptions that might figure in a judicial context (for example, topography as the description of places, and portraiture as the description of people). Second, he offered a traditional definition of the classical figure of *enargeia:* "Descriptions of things must present images that render the objects as if present" (4:879).[44] This classic definition of the vivid depiction of absent objects was sufficiently vague to have potential relevance for natural history; as we have seen, Daubenton was similarly concerned with presenting clear and distinct images to his readers. But the example Mallet chose to illustrate *enargeia* underscored the gulf that separated his conception of poetic description from the empirical context of natural history. In his sole example, he cited not a description of a material object, but an allegorical description of indolence from the neoclassical poet Nicolas Boileau-Despréaux's poem "Le lutrin":

> La mollesse oppressée
> Dans sa bouche à ce mot sent sa langue glacée,
> Et lasse de parler, succombant sous l'effort,
> Soupire, étend les bras, ferme l'oeil & s'endort.
> (4:879)

---

43. Edmé Mallet and Louis de Jaucourt, "Description (*Belles-Lettres*)," in *Encyclopédie, ARTFL,* 4:878. Subsequent references appear parenthetically in the main text.

44. On *enargeia* in the classical tradition, see Galand-Hallyn, *Reflet des fleurs,* 37–39.

[Indolence oppressed
In her mouth at this word feels her tongue frozen,
And weary of speaking, succumbs to the effort,
Sighs, stretches out her arms, closes her eyes, and falls to sleep.]

This example, which we would probably refer to today as allegory or personification rather than description, underscores the gulf between natural history description and description in the realm of belles-lettres: whereas Daubenton was concerned with his readers' ability to envision concrete objects on the basis of his descriptions, Mallet was concerned with the poetic representation of abstract concepts. The example thus suggests that our modern conception of literary description owes more to natural history than to classical poetics.

Although it was published with Mallet's original article in 1754, Louis de Jaucourt's addition marked a distinct shift from traditional rhetorical doctrine to the emerging discipline of aesthetics as a framework for understanding description. In part, this shift reflected the provenance of the text: it was almost entirely lifted from the English poet Joseph Addison's papers titled "The Pleasures of the Imagination," which were published in *The Spectator* in 1712. By focusing on the pleasures elicited by different kinds of description, Addison drew attention to the aesthetic reception of description rather than its rhetorical function. According to Barbara Warnick, this shift was characteristic of the belletristic rhetoric of the seventeenth century in France and the Scottish Enlightenment, in which the traditional focus on *inventio* (identifying the relevant means of persuasion) was displaced by what she calls the "sixth canon," a concern for "aesthetics and the development of receptive competence."[45] Many critics, however, would interpret this shift as a symptom of rhetoric's decline, as it was gradually supplanted by the modern discipline of aesthetics; as Bender and Wellbery observe, "Aesthetics is not a theory of the production of effective or persuasive discourse; it is a theory of 'sensate cognitions' and of the signs that convey them. Its frame of reference is not a notion of social interaction within a hierarchical space, but the soul conceived as a faculty of representation."[46]

---

45. Barbara Warnick, *The Sixth Canon: Belletristic Rhetorical Theory and Its French Antecedents* (Columbia: University of South Carolina Press, 1993), xi.

46. Bender and Wellbery, *Ends of Rhetoric,* 18.

To the extent that Addison (and Jaucourt borrowing from him) focused on how description elicited pleasure by stimulating the imagination, his theory made room for an autonomous aesthetic practice of description divorced from rhetorical context.

Nevertheless, Jaucourt's addition, like Mallet's original article, left little room for any real overlap between poetic and empirical description, because it relied heavily on the doctrine of *la belle nature,* thereby emphasizing the idealizing function of poetic description: "Since the imagination can represent for itself things that are greater, more extraordinary, & more beautiful than those that nature offers ordinarily to the eyes, it is permissible, it is worthy of a great master to gather in his descriptions all possible beauties" (4:879). According to Jean-Paul Sermain, this emphasis was typical of rhetorical doctrine in the first half of the eighteenth century, when Addison's papers were published: "The theoreticians of the first half of the century remain in the framework of an imitation of *'belle nature',* understood not as a reflection, but as a generic or typical knowledge."[47] In the doctrine of *la belle nature* we can see the persistence of Mallet's proscription of the particular and accidental from the realm of belles-lettres, in a way that underlines the continuing gulf between poetic and empirical description.

When the bookseller Charles-Joseph Panckoucke published a four-volume *Supplément* to the *Encyclopédie* in 1776–77, the original article on description in belles-lettres appeared with an addition by the belletristic theorist Jean-François Marmontel that more than doubled the article's length. Whereas Mallet had relied heavily on traditional rhetorical doctrine, and Jaucourt had emphasized the aesthetic pleasures elicited by description, Marmontel centered his addition on the comparison between painting and poetry, relying on the tradition of *ut pictura poesis,* which took its name from Horace's phrase: "As is painting, so is poetry." In the Renaissance, the phrase was understood above all to mean that painting should borrow its subjects and motifs from poetic tradition.[48] As Svetlana Alpers has shown, the tradition of Italian painting favored narrative genres such

47. Jean-Paul Sermain, "Le code du bon goût (1725–1750)," in *Histoire de la rhétorique dans l'Europe moderne, 1450–1950,* ed. Marc Fumaroli (Paris: Presses Universitaires de France, 1999), 907.

48. See Rensselaer W. Lee, *Ut Pictura Poesis: The Humanistic Theory of Painting* (New York: W. W. Norton, 1967).

as history painting, at the expense of what Alpers calls "the art of describing," an alternative tradition exemplified by seventeenth-century Dutch still life.[49] In the Enlightenment, however, the evolution toward modern aesthetics made room for a reevaluation of the *ut pictura poesis* doctrine: on the one hand, as Diderot's art criticism attests, there was an increased appreciation for still life and genre paintings, while, on the other, there was an increased interest in the specific aesthetic properties of painting and poetry. This interest culminated in Lessing's *Laocoön,* which can be read as an explicit refutation of the *ut pictura poesis* doctrine. Nonetheless, Lessing shared the widespread Enlightenment interest in the aesthetic functioning of descriptions, as his extended analysis of Homer's *ekphrasis* demonstrates.

Marmontel's addition reflects this context, opening with a definition of description as painting that implicitly refuted Mallet's earlier characterization of description as an imperfect definition: "Description does not limit itself to characterizing its object; it often presents a painting of it in its most interesting details and in all its breadth."[50] We can see here how the concept of description as painting made room for the gradual incursion of detail into the realm of poetry; whereas neoclassical poetics had emphasized the proscription of detail—most famously in a line from Boileau's *Art poétique,* "Et ne vous chargez point d'un détail inutile" (And don't weigh yourself down with a useless detail)—Marmontel emphasized the interest that well-chosen details could spark in the reader.[51] Even more significant, however, was his emphasis on the "spectator's" point of view with respect to a description: "The point of view is relative from the object to the spectator" (1.594). In keeping with his analogy between painting and poetry, Marmontel insisted that the poet choose a single moment and "the point of view most favorable to the effect that one is proposing" (1.594). Nonetheless, he emphasized the mobility of nature and the multiple details that could be used to depict any given object or scene: "Since almost all of nature is mobile, & everything is composed, imitation can vary infinitely in

49. Svetlana Alpers, *The Art of Describing: Dutch Art in the Seventeenth Century* (Chicago: University of Chicago Press, 1983).

50. I cite Marmontel's addition from *Grammaire et littérature,* in *Encyclopédie méthodique* (Paris: Panckoucke, 1782), 1:594. Subsequent references appear parenthetically in the main text.

51. Nicolas Boileau, *Art poétique,* in *Satires, Épîtres, Art poétique,* ed. Jean-Pierre Collinet (Paris: Gallimard, 1985), 1.60.

its details" (1.594). In this way, Marmontel allowed for the possibility of a more dynamic and shifting conception of the descriptive *tableau* (literally "painting" in French, but often used with a broader figurative meaning), during the same decade that Mercier's multivolume description of Paris became a best seller. Although Mercier's elaboration of a single *tableau* across twelve volumes and over the course of eight years was certainly more innovative than Marmontel's classical theory permitted, both writers understood description as an art of perspective and recognized that any given object could be described from multiple vantage points.

Marmontel's addition thus reflected the evolution from rhetorical doctrine to aesthetics and gestured toward a more experimental approach to the descriptive *tableau*. But despite these innovations, Marmontel adhered to rhetorical doctrine in his emphasis on the proper limits that must be placed on description (limits that both Mercier and the descriptive poets felt free to abandon). Description, for Marmontel, could not be an end in itself; it had to be justified by its relevance to a specific poetic or rhetorical context: "In general, if the description is not very important, touch lightly; if it is essential, describe more fully" (1.596). In narrative poetry, this meant that poets should limit detailed "paintings" to occasions when there was a lull in narrative: "An essential rule, & one from which I exhort poets never to depart, is to reserve detailed paintings for moments of calm & repose: in those where the action is lively & quick, one cannot rush too quickly to paint in bold touches what is spectacle & decoration" (1:596). As Perrine Galand-Hallyn notes in her study of classical description from Homer to the Renaissance, the concept of description as a digression can be seen both in classical rhetorical doctrine and in modern, structuralist theories of description.[52] It was this concept of description as a digression from a dominant narrative framework that made descriptive poetry so unacceptable for Marmontel, and so incomprehensible from the vantage point of structuralism.

In 1782, the third article on description in belles-lettres appeared in the volumes of *Grammaire et littérature* in the *Encyclopédie méthodique,* an adaptation of the original *Encyclopédie* organized by subject matter. The article was supplemented by an entirely new article, by Marmontel, under the heading "Descriptif, -ive, adj. (*Belles-Lettres, Poésie*)." In this new article,

---

52. Galand-Hallyn, *Reflet des fleurs,* 8–9.

exclusively devoted to descriptive poetry, Marmontel rejected descriptive poetry, espousing the widely held belief that it was a modern genre with no ancient antecedents: "What today is called the descriptive genre in poetry was unknown to the ancients. It is a modern invention of which, it seems to me, neither reason nor taste approves" (1:592).[53] Marmontel's characterization of descriptive poetry as a modern invention (which mirrored the claims of the descriptive poets' themselves) depended on a clear distinction between descriptive and didactic poetry, the latter of which had a long and venerable classical tradition illustrated by Lucretius and Vergil. Clearly, there was some overlap between the two genres: to cite just one example, the most popular and prolific of the French descriptive poets, Jacques Delille, first gained fame for his translation of Vergil's *Georgics,* and then went on to label his own *L'homme des champs, ou Les géorgiques françaises* a descriptive poem. Modern critics, notably Riffaterre, have thus tended to view the descriptive genre as a broad category encompassing didactic poetry.[54] But this view neglects the Enlightenment understanding of the genre and makes it difficult to account for the virulent eighteenth-century reaction against descriptive poetry. In order to make sense of this reaction, we must understand what made descriptive poetry fundamentally different from didactic poetry for eighteenth-century poets and theorists.

Marmontel's critique of descriptive poetry reflects the eighteenth-century overlap between rhetorical and poetic doctrine, and normative Enlightenment conceptions of nature. First, he claimed that while didactic poetry was consistent with the way people actually use description to convince or persuade their listeners in "natural," everyday conversation, descriptive poetry used description in a way that was fundamentally unnatural:

> Poetic imitation is the art of doing in a more pleasing fashion what is done in nature. Well, it happens to all men to describe while speaking to make more apparent the objects that interest them; and description is connected with a story that introduces it, with an intention to instruct or to persuade, with an interest that serves as its motive. But what happens to no one, in any

---

53. In 1787, Marmontel published the article (along with his supplement to the belles-lettres article) in his personal compendium of belletristic theory. See Jean-François Marmontel, *Éléments de littérature,* ed. Sophie Le Ménahèze (Paris: Desjonquères, 2005), 387–94.
54. Riffaterre, "Système," 15.

situation, is to describe for the sake of describing, and to describe again after having described, moving from one object to another, with no other cause than the mobility of the gaze and of thought. (1:592)

We can see here that Marmontel's account of the "natural" use of description is grounded in traditional rhetorical doctrine: in everyday exchanges, as in classical rhetoric or poetics, description is always motivated by an overriding rhetorical, didactic, or narrative purpose. As we saw in Marmontel's addition to the article "Description (*Belles-Lettres*)," this purpose determined when and at what length it was appropriate to describe. For Marmontel, the problem with descriptive poetry was that it abandoned this purpose; as a result, there was no basis on which to check the incursion of description into poetic discourse. At the same time, by taxing the genre as unnatural, Marmontel suggested that descriptive poetry used language in a way that artificially separated it from other forms of discourse. From a modern perspective, Marmontel's critique thus suggests that descriptive poetry was an early symptom of the emergence of literature as an autonomous category of discourse.

Second, Marmontel attacked the descriptive poets for abandoning the "reasonable" classical principles of poetic composition: "Any reasonable composition must form an ensemble, a whole, in which the parts are linked, in which the middle corresponds to the beginning, and the end to the middle: that is the precept of Aristotle and Horace. But in the descriptive poem, no ensemble, no order, no correspondence: there are beauties, I well believe it, but beauties that destroy each other by their monotonous succession, or their discordant assemblage" (1:592–93). To underscore his claim that descriptive poetry was not only unnatural but also unreasonable, Marmontel cited the English poet and physician Mark Akenside's poem *The Pleasures of the Imagination* (1744), which was translated into French by the philosophe Paul-Henri Dietrich d'Holbach in 1759: "But if we ask the descriptive poet, the author, for example, of the *Pleasures of the Imagination,* what is his purpose, he will respond: it is to dream, and to describe my dreams for you. But a volume of dreams cannot be interesting" (1:592). Since the vast majority of descriptive poetry did not, in fact, focus on dreams but rather on the workings of nature, Marmontel appears to have chosen this particular example to support his claim that descriptive poetry was marked by a loss of poetic reason, and perhaps also to recall Horace's famous analogy between a bad poem and a sick man's dreams.[55] Like his argument concerning the natural use of description, Marmontel's criticism of descriptive poetry as unreasonable suggested that the compositional principles of classical poetics were grounded in nature and not merely in tradition.

Third, Marmontel criticized the descriptive poets for abandoning serious poetic purpose or design to revel in the pure pleasure of describing: "But that a poem without object, without design, be a series of descriptions introduced by nothing; that the poet, looking around himself, describe everything that presents itself for the sole pleasure of describing, if he does not find it tiresome himself, he can be sure that his readers will soon find it so" (1:592). For Annie Becq, Marmontel's resistance to the pleasure of describing as an end in itself marks the descriptive genre as "one of the possible sites for the emergence of the modern conception of a poem."[56] One might add that Marmontel's critique also underscores the emergence of the poet as sole origin of his poetic discourse. As we shall see in chapter 4, descriptive poetry did not favor self-expression, and romantic poets and critics criticized it harshly in part for that reason. Nonetheless, Marmontel's critique suggests that it was "the mobility of the gaze and of thought" that replaced the framework of rhetorical doctrine and the reasonable principles of classical poetics. If we accept the terms of his critique, descriptive poetry appears as an innovative attempt to place the poet's vision and reflection at the center and origin of poetic creation. It should thus come as no surprise that descriptive poetry reached the height of its popularity in France during the same decade that Mercier used the term *descripteur* to define his authorial identity.

* * *

The rich and diverse network of articles on description in the *Encyclopédie* and in the *Encyclopédie méthodique* demonstrates how central description was to Enlightenment discourse and illustrates the kinds of

---

55. Horace, *The Art of Poetry,* in *Ancient Literary Criticism,* lines 1–8.

56. Annie Becq, "La réflexion sur la poétique en France au XVIIIe siècle," in *Histoire des poétiques,* ed. Jean Bessière, Eva Kushner, Roland Mortier, and Jean Weisgerber (Paris: Presses Universitaires de France, 1997), 237.

epistemological and literary challenges it posed for its practitioners. The first part of this book focuses on the specific problems surrounding description in the field of natural history, as manifested in Buffon and Daubenton's monumental *Histoire naturelle* and in Bernardin de Saint-Pierre's fragmented and experimental *Études de la nature*. The second part of the book addresses the place of description in Enlightenment encyclopedism, broadly conceived, by looking first at Diderot and d'Alembert's *Encyclopédie* and then at the encyclopedic dimension of descriptive poetry. The third part of the book takes up moral and political topographies and the issue of change, both temporal and historical, in description, as exhibited in the two descriptions of Paris Mercier wrote before and after the French Revolution, the *Tableau de Paris* and *Le nouveau Paris*. Whereas the figure of the describer serves both as a unifying principle and as an agent of change in Mercier's earlier description of Paris, in *Le nouveau Paris* he becomes a self-conscious historical subject whose fragmented perceptions and limited viewpoint can only ever provide a kaleidoscope of perspectives, in a way that marked a definitive break with the Enlightenment's descriptive project.

PART I

NATURAL HISTORIES

1

BUFFON AND DAUBENTON'S TWO HORSES

George-Louis Leclerc de Buffon's *Histoire naturelle, générale et particulière* (1749–89) was initially conceived in far more modest terms than its
eventual thirty-six volumes, which included theories of the earth, reproduction, and man, twelve volumes on quadrupeds that combined comparative anatomy with studies of animal habits and habitats, nine volumes on
birds, five on minerals, an anthropological account of racial and cultural
diversity, and one of the first historical accounts of the earth's transformations over time.[1] Although our knowledge of the work's origins remains
sketchy, Buffon appears to have started his project intending merely to
write a descriptive catalog of the king's cabinet of natural curiosities, for

---

1. I focus mainly on the first fifteen volumes of this work, on which Buffon and Daubenton
collaborated. Because subsequent editions often did not include Daubenton's anatomical descriptions, I refer to the original edition of the work: Georges-Louis Leclerc de Buffon and Louis-Jean-
Marie Daubenton, *Histoire naturelle, générale et particulière, avec la description du Cabinet du Roy*,
15 vols. (Paris: Imprimerie Royale, 1749–67). References to this work appear parenthetically in
the main text.

which he served as intendant from 1739 until his death in 1788.[2] This descriptive catalog, eventually written by Buffon's collaborator the anatomist Louis-Jean-Marie Daubenton, represents a relatively brief and insignificant chapter in the Enlightenment's most ambitious work of natural history; yet we still find a trace of its initial importance in the work's subtitle, *Avec la description du Cabinet du Roy* (With the Description of the King's Cabinet).

Description was thus part of Buffon's project from the very beginning, in the schematic form of a catalog of the various stuffed specimens, skeletons, anatomical parts, and monstrosities held in the royal collection. As his project developed, however, Buffon's concept of description became increasingly complex and took on a philosophical dimension. In fact, description became the focus of methodological and epistemological tensions that impacted the shape and evolution of the *Histoire naturelle* and even Buffon's view of natural history. There were many reasons for these tensions, but two broad tendencies in Buffon's approach to natural history were particularly significant. The first was his idiosyncratic attempt to combine a highly detailed, empirical approach to natural history with broad theories of nature that relied on hypotheses to generalize the particular.[3] The second was his growing emphasis, over the course of his career, on historical modifications in nature. Both tendencies posed methodological problems and set Buffon apart from his contemporaries, as scholarship in the history of science has shown.[4] But they also posed specific problems for Buffon as a describer of nature. On the one hand, Buffon's insistence on the diversity of nature, and his corresponding rejection of Linnean taxonomy, made him critical of the schematic descriptions favored by the naturalists he referred

    2. John Lyon and Phillip R. Sloan, eds., *From Natural History to the History of Nature: Readings from Buffon and His Critics* (Notre Dame: University of Notre Dame Press, 1981), 6.

    3. Peter Hanns Reill has emphasized this aspect of Buffon's work, which he views as symptomatic of a broader "creative tension" in Enlightenment thought. Peter Hanns Reill, *Vitalizing Nature in the Enlightenment* (Berkeley and Los Angeles: University of California Press, 2005), 238–39.

    4. See Reill, *Vitalizing Nature;* James L. Larson, *Interpreting Nature: The Science of Living Form from Linnaeus to Kant* (Baltimore: Johns Hopkins University Press, 1994); Virginia P. Dawson, "The Limits of Observation and the Hypotheses of Georges Louis Buffon and Charles Bonnet," in *Beyond History of Science,* ed. Elizabeth Garber (London: Associated University Presses/Lehigh University Press, 1990), 107–25; Phillip R. Sloan, "The Buffon-Linnaeus Controversy," *Isis* 67 (1976): 356–75; and Lyon and Sloan, *Natural History.*

to as "nomenclaturists." On the other hand, his insistence on broad theories and hypotheses in the study of nature led him to reject the particularized, wonder-infused descriptions characteristic of naturalists working in the tradition of physico-theology. Most importantly, because Buffon conceived of nature as a dynamic system subject to gradual modifications over time, he required an approach to description that could incorporate change, movement, and even vitality into its fold.

The methodological and epistemological problems surrounding description in the *Histoire naturelle* had important implications for the concept of literary style Buffon elaborated in his reception speech to the Académie française, the *Discours sur le style* (1753), and in his little-known essay *De l'art d'écrire*. The latter essay, an unpublished fragment that has not been dated precisely, provides the missing link between Buffon's natural philosophy and his conception of literary style. It thus allows us to avoid the tendency in Buffon scholarship to emphasize the naturalist's style at the expense of his scientific contribution, or his science at the expense of his style.[5]

One notable exception to this tendency is Jeff Loveland's nuanced treatment of Buffon's natural philosophy in a rhetorical and polemical context.[6] Loveland has given a convincing account of how rhetorical considerations impacted Buffon's presentation of his philosophical and scientific ideas in various contexts and has emphasized how Buffon skillfully manipulated his much vaunted literary style to attract readers and situate himself with respect to rivals and critics. Among other contributions, Loveland's book helps explain certain apparent philosophical contradictions between different parts of the *Histoire naturelle* and provides a model for thinking about the ways scientific discourse can be shaped by rhetorical and polemical considerations, without reducing science to mere rhetoric.

Yet Loveland does not go far enough in asserting the deep and pervasive significance of literary style in Buffon's work. His account relies on a traditional conception of literary style as an ornamental manipulation of rhetorical figures that can be added or removed depending on the polemical context. For example, Loveland emphasizes the extent to which

---

5. Phillip R. Sloan addresses this tendency in "Buffon Studies Today," *History of Science* 32 (1994): 469–77.

6. Loveland, *Rhetoric and Natural History.*

Buffon's opening discourses and paragraphs are marked by more "stylish writing" than other sections geared toward specialists.[7] Although his analyses are convincing, his emphasis on chunks of stylish writing makes Buffon's style appear as if it were simply a matter of fancy, Ciceronian periods, and the skillful manipulation of rhetorical figures. Yet Buffon's essay on style was influential precisely because it made style inextricable both from the writer's individual perspective and from the world he sought to represent. The famous phrase "Le style est l'homme même" (Style is man himself), often misinterpreted as a pre-romantic assertion of literary subjectivity, instead expressed Buffon's belief that style was a fundamental means of communicating the writer's empirical experience of nature.[8] Thus in order to avoid the dichotomy between style and substance (and between literature and science) that has marked Buffon scholarship, we need an account of his concept of literary style that is grounded in his natural philosophy.[9] Description, inasmuch as it is central to both Buffon's writings on style and his natural philosophy, can serve as a basis for such an account.

Dissecting and Measuring Animals

Description served several different functions in natural history as it was practiced when Buffon, a mathematician by training and a relative outsider to the field, was named Intendant to the King's Garden and Natural History Cabinet in Paris in 1739. In the tradition of physico-theology, exemplified by Noël-Antoine Pluche's best-selling *Spectacle de la nature* (1732–50), description was an occasion to detail the wonders and beauties of nature in praise of God's creation. Because popular naturalists such as Pluche were less concerned with explaining nature than with illustrating the richness, intricacy, and immensity of the created world, the accumulation of descriptive detail did not pose a threat to the purpose at hand;

---

7. Ibid., 25, 39–41, and 51.

8. Georges-Louis Leclerc de Buffon, *Discours sur le style, suivi de "L'art d'écrire" du même et de "Visite à Buffon" d'Hérault de Séchelles* (Paris: Climats, 1992), 30.

9. For a rich, albeit brief, account of Buffon's style in terms of his attitudes toward taxonomy and systematic approaches to natural history, see Julie Candler Hayes, *Reading the French Enlightenment: System and Subversion* (Cambridge: Cambridge University Press, 1999), 30–39.

indeed, Pluche's subtitle, *Entretiens sur les particularités de l'histoire naturelle* (Dialogues on the Particulars of Natural History), implied that his work was uniquely concerned with the details of nature. In the tradition of Linnean taxonomy, on the contrary, description served the purpose of isolating a limited number of essential traits that would become the basis for classificatory systems. As Lorraine Daston has shown, the move toward Linnean taxonomy was accompanied by a corresponding shift in descriptive technique as descriptions were simplified and schematized in order to serve classificatory aims. Daston's account of this new descriptive regime, "description by omission," is consistent with the account she and Peter Galison have given of scientific atlas illustrations prior to the emergence of objectivity.[10] Within what they call the "truth to nature" paradigm, illustrators proceeded by selecting the most representative natural specimens and by correcting any imperfections or idiosyncrasies in them. Linnaeus was the prototypical naturalist for both the "description by omission" and the "truth to nature" paradigms, just as he was central to Foucault's account of the classical episteme in *Les mots et les choses.*

Yet these paradigms cannot adequately account for the methodological problems surrounding description in Buffon's work. In the opening chapter of the *Histoire naturelle,* the "Discours sur la manière d'étudier & de traiter l'histoire naturelle" (Discourse on the Manner of Studying & Treating Natural History), Buffon set the tone for a markedly different approach to natural history in general and to description in particular. Several themes in this methodological chapter had crucial implications for the theory and practice of description in the *Histoire naturelle.* The first was Buffon's distinction between the mathematical sciences and what he called the "real sciences," an important distinction for him given his training and early work as a mathematician. As Jacques Roger and Peter Hanns Reill have shown, the belief that mathematical principles could not adequately account for physical reality was fundamental to Buffon's natural philosophy.[11] This belief was accompanied by a reevaluation of the epistemological relationship between definitions and descriptions. In his opening chapter,

10. See Daston, "Description by Omission"; and Daston and Galison, *Objectivity.*

11. See Jacques Roger, *Buffon: Un philosophe au Jardin du Roi* (Paris: Fayard, 1989), 30–40; and Reill, *Vitalizing Nature,* 33–42. Loveland has convincingly argued in *Rhetoric and Natural History,* 127–52, that Buffon exaggerated his critique of mathematics for rhetorical effect.

Buffon characterized mathematical truths as exact and definitive, but also abstract and arbitrary, because they were based on man-made definitions: "It is sufficient for us to have proved that mathematical truths are nothing but truths of definition...and that they are only truths with respect to those same definitions we have made; it is for this reason that they have the advantage of always being exact and demonstrative, but abstract, intellectual, and arbitrary" (1:54). In the "real sciences," on the contrary, the abstract definitions proper to mathematics were replaced by empirical observations of the physical world: "One moves from definition to definition in the abstract sciences, one advances from observation to observation in the real sciences" (1:54–55). The contrast between abstract definitions and concrete observations allowed Buffon to give epistemological weight to description in the "real sciences," as the only appropriate means of defining natural beings in all of their individuality and particularity. For the naturalist, Buffon concluded, "nothing is well defined but that which is exactly described" (1:25).

This claim was significant because it reversed a traditional epistemological hierarchy according to which description was nothing but an imperfect definition. As we have seen, this hierarchy was in evidence both in Furetière's *Dictionnaire universel* and in Diderot and d'Alembert's *Encyclopédie,* in which the article on literary description began as follows: "Description *(Belles-Lettres.)* An imperfect and imprecise definition."[12] Description was an imperfect definition, Mallet went on to explain, because it did not communicate the essence of its object, but only particular qualities. It was inexact because, unlike a definition, it gave only a vague idea of its object, sufficient to distinguish it from other objects but not sufficient to make it known. Because it focused on qualities that were "exterior and accidental" to the object described, description could represent only individuals, not species or types.[13] Hence the article implied that belles-lettres was fundamentally concerned with types and essences, not with individuals and their particular qualities. If description had little or no epistemological weight in belles-lettres at mid-century, it was because it recorded particulars that lay outside the purview of literature.

---

12. Edmé Mallet and Louis de Jaucourt, "Description *(Belles-Lettres)*," *Encyclopédie,* ARTFL, 4:878.
    13. Ibid.

Yet this epistemological devaluing of description could subsist only as long as belles-lettres' claims to truth did not involve concrete individuals. Indeed, the very fact that the *Encyclopédie* offered different articles on description for belles-lettres and natural history underlined the opposing epistemological priorities of the two fields. Daubenton's article on natural history description, like Buffon's opening discourse, made it perfectly clear that in natural history, description had epistemological weight. It was through description that we could "know" the animal world, "discover" plant mechanisms, and "conceptualize" mineralization. Moreover, in contrast to the belles-lettres article, there was nothing vague, imperfect, or superficial about description as defined by Daubenton: it established clear contours, "tracing" its object, and at the same time reached beyond the surface, "painting" its object inside and out.[14] Whereas in belles-lettres, description was an imperfect definition, in natural history it was the only possible means of defining natural beings.

The second important theme in Buffon's opening discourse was his opposition to Linnean taxonomy and what he viewed as arbitrary systems in the study of nature. Like his distinction between the mathematical and "real" sciences, Buffon's critique of Linnaean taxonomy was centered on the notion that arbitrary definitions had no place in the natural sciences. Daubenton echoed this critique in his own methodological chapter, "De la description des animaux," when he characterized the definitions of the "nomenclaturists" as imperfect sketches based on a limited number of purportedly essential traits: "Thus the methods of nomenclature, and the definitions they contain, are nothing but highly imperfect sketches of the painting of nature, which can only be expressed through complete descriptions" (4:115–16). Just as Buffon taxed mathematical definitions with arbitrariness, Daubenton criticized the "nomenclaturists" for imposing their own a priori definitions on nature with no prior basis in knowledge: "They want to define the different productions of nature before having described them well: that is to want to judge before having understood, and to teach others what one doesn't know oneself" (4:115). This critique of nomenclature reflects the epistemological modesty characteristic of Buffon and Daubenton, for whom "a definition is nothing more than the result of

---

14. Louis-Jean-Marie Daubenton, "Description (*Hist. nat.*)," *Encyclopédie,* ARTFL, 4:878. Subsequent references appear parenthetically in the main text.

our knowledge, which is always limited, and even faulty" (4:115).[15] It also demonstrates the extent to which Daubenton (and Buffon) diverged from Foucault's characterization of natural history description in the classical episteme. Whereas Foucault claimed that naturalists as diverse as Buffon and Linnaeus "impose[d] the same grid," Daubenton criticized the nomenclaturists precisely because they favored a rigidly systematic approach to description.[16] Instead of deciding which traits were essential and then describing them, he asserted, the naturalist must begin by describing as completely as possible in order to develop an empirical knowledge of nature. Whether or not Daubenton realized this in his own descriptions, it is significant that he upheld a descriptive ideal of openness to the messy process of observing nature and criticized any approach to description that gave precedent to preformed systems over empirical observation.

In criticizing the nomenclaturists, both Daubenton and Buffon stressed the importance of complete descriptions in natural history. Only by means of such descriptions could the naturalist avoid the arbitrariness of Linnean taxonomy, since every trait was potentially significant. Thus the ideal of natural history description, as Buffon and Daubenton saw it, was to provide the fullest possible account of the naturalist's actual empirical observations. Yet the high level of descriptive detail required by such an antisystematic approach posed serious methodological and practical problems. As we have seen, Daubenton touched on several of these problems in his *Encyclopédie* article on natural history description: first, lengthy descriptions led inevitably to representational incoherence and distortion, and second, they prevented readers from gaining an understanding of natural economy. A work of natural history with overly long descriptions, Daubenton wrote, "would present to the mind only shapeless and gigantic forms dispersed without order and traced without proportion: the greatest efforts of the imagination would not be sufficient to perceive them" (4:878). Such descriptions would also give an inaccurate impression of the animal's size, calling to mind "gigantic figures...traced without proportion...an enormous heap" (4:878). At the same time, Daubenton claimed that long

---

15. On the Enlightenment's epistemological modesty, and its relationship to the epistemology of error, see David W. Bates, *Enlightenment Aberrations: Error and Revolution in France* (Ithaca, N.Y.: Cornell University Press, 2002).

16. Foucault, *Mots et choses*, 148.

descriptions ran counter to the most important epistemological function of natural history, which was to uncover the underlying natural economy. Instead of perceiving natural order, readers would imagine "an enormous and confused heap made up of the debris of multiple machines; they would only recognize detached parts, without seeing their relationships or arrangement" (4:878). Hence the central problem in natural history description was posed: how could the naturalist circumscribe his descriptions to preserve both the form of natural beings and the natural order that connected them, while at the same time incorporating sufficient detail to define each being as an individual?

The question of natural order was crucial for Daubenton, because the anatomical descriptions he wrote for the *Histoire naturelle* were part of his project in comparative anatomy. This project required an approach to description that facilitated anatomical comparisons across species. It was with these priorities in mind that Daubenton introduced a drastically simplified approach to description, as a basic set of measurements, in his methodological chapter, "De la description des animaux": "The description of the external parts of an animal is simply the exposition of the different dimensions of its body; it is true there is some choice to be made in the manner of taking them, but the simplest are the best, for example, the length, the width, the thickness, the diameter, the circumference, etc." (4:135). Daubenton was not the first in the field of natural history to define description in terms of measurement. As early as 1676, Claude Perrault took a similar approach in his *Mémoires pour servir à l'histoire naturelle des animaux.* For Perrault, anatomical descriptions were essentially proportional comparisons, with man serving as the yardstick against which all other beings were compared.[17] For Daubenton, too, measurements served to facilitate morphological comparisons between different species and provided the basis for a global understanding of animal economy: "Such an account of the bodies of animals can furnish, through the comparisons that can be made between them, important results for animal economy, which is the principal object of natural history" (4:135). In order to facilitate such

---

17. See Claude Perrault, *Mémoires pour servir à l'histoire naturelle des animaux* (Paris: Imprimerie Royale, 1676). Perrault explains his comparative method as follows: "One compares the size, the shape, and the situation of [the animal's] parts, both external and internal, with those of man, which we establish as the ruler of the proportions of all animals" (n.p.).

comparisons, Daubenton presented his measurements in numerical tables that he integrated into his prose articles. These tables allowed the reader to make comparisons between two different quadrupeds quickly and efficiently, by consulting the same line on two tables and comparing values.

With the comparative function came a specific form, above and beyond the strange juxtaposition of numerical tables and descriptive text. In order to facilitate proportional comparisons, Daubenton was obliged to follow the very same outline in all of his descriptions. If he began his description of the horse with its length from nose to tail, he was required to do the same in his description of the mouse, such that the reader could easily determine which animal was longer and by how much:

> As soon as one is fully convinced that descriptions must be compared, one cannot doubt that it is absolutely necessary to do all of them according to the same outline. A descriptive outline is the method one intends to follow in observing animals; each observer can come up with one to his own liking; it will always be good if it is constantly the same in all descriptions, because one can compare such descriptions in all their points and draw results from these comparisons. (4:130)

The standard of descriptive uniformity upheld by Daubenton was not simply a basic sequence (front to back, head to tail, for example). It required that the exact same measurements be made on all quadrupeds, regardless of extreme differences in size or structure: "The outline of these descriptions is the same for all animals, such that the description of the mouse is just as extensive as that of the horse, because the mouse's body is indeed made up of about the same number of viscera and bones as that of the horse, and they must be compared with each other" (4:138). In fact, Daubenton's measurement tables were far from a "simple" set of measurements: they were so detailed that only animals with similar numbers of viscera or bones could be properly compared. The question of how to compare two animals with vastly dissimilar structures was never addressed. Even though a horse's hoof might seem incomparable with a mouse's paw, the measurement tables were set up to facilitate a proportional comparison between the two.

Yet the comparative function of anatomical description was clearly incompatible with the goal of visualization underlined in Daubenton's

Encyclopédie article on description. In fact, the measurement-based descriptions frustrated any attempt at visualization, for two reasons. First, they threatened descriptive coherence by breaking each quadruped down into an immensely detailed sequence of measurements. In his "Description du chien," for example, Daubenton provided some forty measurements for various breeds of dogs, the last five of which were as follows: "Length from the heel to the tip of the toenails / Width of the front foot / Width of the back foot / Length of the longest toenails / Width at the base" (5:262). Thus conceived, description became the textual equivalent of Daubenton's dissections, presenting discrete measurement segments successively, but never linking them together. If such a description could claim to provide a "tracing" of a dog (the ideal expressed in Daubenton's *Encyclopédie* article), it was at best a connect-the-dots drawing in which the dots had not yet been connected.

Second, in his one attempt to provide an overall measurement, which he called the "principal dimension," Daubenton found himself obliged to distort each animal's individual form; for regardless whether the subject was a horse or a mouse, the principal dimension was always to be measured along a straight line: "This dimension is measured in a straight line, from the tip of the muzzle to the anus, the head and the neck being stretched out as much as possible in the direction of the portion of the spine" (4:136). So distortive was this comparative yardstick, in fact, that it could be established only with great difficulty on live animals. In his "Description du cheval," Daubenton thus warned his readers that the principal measurement might be inaccurate because he was working on a live specimen: "Because the animal was alive, it wasn't easy to make it raise its muzzle high enough to erase as much as possible the curve of the occiput, as one can do with dead animals to take this principal measurement, which must extend in a straight line from the extremity of the lips to the anus, and which is the surest one that can be used to make comparisons" (4:301). Rather than tracing an outline of the actual horse, Daubenton's description proceeded by erasing the curve of the horse's neck, in an attempt to translate the animal into a geometrical figure composed of straight lines and measurable surfaces.

In his influential interpretation of Enlightenment philosophy, Ernst Cassirer insisted on the gap between the mathematical description of nature proper to Newtonian physics, and the qualitative description of nature proper to the life sciences: "As we go from physics to biology, the postulate of pure description takes on a different meaning. It is no longer a question of transforming directly observed reality into an aggregate of quantities, into a network of numbers and measures; it is now rather a matter of retaining the specific form of empirical reality."[18] By attempting to translate living beings into a set of measurement tables, Daubenton's descriptions appeared to deny this crucial distinction and thus coexisted uneasily with Buffon's natural philosophy. Buffon insisted on the fact that the naturalist must not transform living beings into mathematical abstractions:

> One is obliged in all cases to make suppositions that are always contrary to nature, to strip the subject of most of its qualities, to turn it into an abstract being that no longer resembles the real being, and when one has reasoned and calculated at length on the relationships and properties of this abstract being, and when one has come to a conclusion that is just as abstract, one believes one has found something real, and one carries this ideal result over to the real subject, which produces an infinite number of false consequences and errors. (1:61)

Buffon's critique of mathematical abstractions in the natural sciences underscored one of the weaknesses of Daubenton's descriptive method: if readers of the *Histoire naturelle* compared a giraffe and a horse solely in terms of their principal dimensions, they would end up with a grossly inaccurate impression of the giraffe's size (especially when one considers that most readers of the *Histoire naturelle* had never seen a giraffe; Buffon himself first saw this exotic animal in a drawing sent to him by the navigator Louis-Antoine de Bougainville in 1761).[19] It was precisely because this process of abstraction was inappropriate in the natural sciences that Buffon placed description at the heart of natural history. The goal of description, for him, was to provide a textual counterpart to the corporeal presence of an actual being. If description distorted the individual form and qualities of that being, it became just as reductive as the definitions of nomenclature it was intended to replace. In this sense, Daubenton's measurement-based

---

18. Ernst Cassirer, *The Philosophy of the Enlightenment,* trans. Fritz C. A. Koelln and James P. Pettegrove (1951; repr., Princeton: Princeton University Press, 1979), 76.

19. See Michèle Duchet, *Anthropologie et histoire au siècle des Lumières* (1971; repr., Paris: Albin Michel, 1995), 51.

descriptions were fundamentally incompatible with Buffon's natural philosophy: rather than a full and complex portrait of beings in life, they provided a limited and distorted representation of beings in death, a highly imperfect definition.

The Naturalist as Painter

Daubenton himself was aware that measuring a dead horse with its neck stretched out in an unnatural position did not fulfill the goal he had set for himself in his *Encyclopédie* article on description, to give his readers "clear and distinct ideas of the beings that cover the earth" (4:878). He acknowledged this limitation in his "Description du cheval," noting that while measurements were useful for making comparisons, they conveyed only a vague and imperfect idea of the animal's appearance: "All these dimensions are elements that will enter into the comparison we will make between the horse and other animals, but they can only represent strokes [traits] that are too vague and imperfect to give a distinct idea of this animal; we must therefore try to bring them together and express their union to achieve a sketch" (4:304). Daubenton's emphasis on the need for a descriptive sketch suggests that he was aware of the limitations of his measurement-based approach to description. The purpose of such sketches was to unify the disparate elements of his measurement-based descriptions and to allow the reader to form a clear mental image of the animal.

The idea of a descriptive sketch was further developed in "De la description des animaux," when Daubenton introduced a second approach to description. This approach, which likened description to a painting, coexisted with the measurement-based approach, despite apparent contradictions between the two. The concept of description as painting took Daubenton far afield from the styleless, technical descriptions of his comparative system and led him to engage with properly aesthetic questions concerning the relationship between painting and written expression: Given the successive nature of language, how could the writer achieve the spatial simultaneity and coherence of a painting? More generally, to what extent could readers imagine a complex arrangement of visual forms on the basis of a description? Although these questions were central to the aesthetic debates on the relationship between painting and poetry, Daubenton's grounding in natural history gave him an original perspective on them, one that has often been neglected in discussions of eighteenth-century aesthetics.

The notion that description could "paint" nature was crucial to the success of the *Histoire naturelle* as a didactic project, since Buffon viewed observation as the primary basis for learning about nature. In natural history, he wrote in his opening chapter, "one must start by seeing a lot and seeing again often" (1:6). Daubenton echoed this principle, noting that "we can only know of nature's productions what we have seen, and we can only judge them to the extent we have observed them" (4:113). One important implication of this founding principle was that in order to learn about nature, readers of the *Histoire naturelle* needed some visual experience of natural beings. According to Buffon, firsthand observation, in nature or in a natural history cabinet, was preferable, since actual beings "strike us with more force and truth than the most exact descriptions and the most perfect illustrations" (3:2). Nevertheless, descriptions could provide a substitute for firsthand observation, especially for those readers who did not have access to live beings or stuffed specimens. In fact, in many cases Buffon and Daubenton themselves learned about animals solely through descriptions, since they worked with a vast network of traveling correspondents whose written accounts of inaccessible specimens were incorporated into the *Histoire naturelle* (as in the case of the giraffe).[20]

Daubenton's discussion of description as painting suggests that this approach, unlike the measurement-based approach, was specifically conceived to facilitate visualization in nonspecialist readers. The basis for an effective description was word choice, or "l'expression des mots." The naturalist was to avoid obscure, technical terms, which were like muddy colors in a painting: "Any description conceived in obscure or ambiguous terms is worthless for most readers, because there are few readers who want to study and guess at things that should be clear and easy, or who are in a position to compensate for the deficiency in expression: description is a painting, if the colors are false and muddy they don't express any true and defined image; one sees but a cloud, and one distinguishes nothing"

---

20. Although he insists upon his thorough observations of most beings under study, Daubenton admits that he did not have access to all the animals discussed in the *Histoire naturelle*. See Buffon and Daubenton, *Histoire naturelle,* 4:138.

(4:120). In developing this comparison between word choice and colors, Daubenton clearly had the needs and limitations of nonspecialist readers in mind. The naturalist, he stipulated, must choose only the clearest and simplest terms to convey clear pictures to readers who do not have access to actual specimens.

Daubenton pursued his painterly metaphor in developing a theory of descriptive composition, which he called "l'expression de la chose": "There should also be in descriptions another kind of expression that is quite different from that of words: it is the expression of the thing, the composition of the painting, which is much more difficult than that of the colors" (4:121). Descriptive composition was the angle from which the describer presented his subject "so that the description is in keeping with its subject" (4:121–22). Like the painter, the naturalist had to choose the composition most suited to his subject: "This total form, this whole, and this description of the exterior can be expressed in many different ways; it is the expression of the thing, which must vary for different objects in accordance with the difference between them" (4:122). Here, we see a clear divergence between Daubenton's two approaches to description: whereas the measurement-based approach required a uniform sequence to facilitate quantitative comparisons, the pictorial approach depended on compositional variety to express qualitative differences.

Daubenton expressed his theory of compositional variety in pictorial terms, comparing the beginning of a description to the painter's first brushstroke: "If we compare a horse and a pig, a stag and a rhinoceros, we will easily see that the first brushstroke must not be the same for the one and the other" (4:122). Yet in developing this pictorial metaphor, Daubenton ignored a crucial difference between pictorial and textual representation: whereas the first words of a text are generally those first encountered by the reader, there is no reason to believe that the first brushstroke is what first captures the beholder's eye. Nevertheless, Daubenton took the first brushstroke to mean the aspect of an animal that is initially emphasized in a description. Unlike the principal dimension, the first brushstroke was to reflect the specificity of the animal's form, to express its individuality in the very first words of the description.

Descriptive composition was also charged with reproducing the describer's empirical experience of observing a living being. In typically Buffonian fashion, Daubenton criticized classificatory systems for focusing on a limited number of traits in a way that was antithetical to our lived experience of observing an animal:

> But what notion do we have of horses, simply because we know the number and position of half of their teeth and their teats, the shape of their hooves, and the lay of the hair on their tails? Let us look at a horse among other animals, and observe which characteristics allow us to distinguish it from the others: it is certainly not the teeth or the teats, we don't see them, and yet no one has ever made a mistake in identifying a horse: what characterizes an animal in our eyes is its whole aspect, its attitude, its bearing, its gait, and the proportions of the different parts of its body. This is what allows us to recognize it as soon as we catch a glimpse of it. (4:118)

These remarks could easily be interpreted as a critique of Daubenton's own measurement-based descriptions, since it is certainly not on the basis of a proportional comparison between their hooves and paws that we distinguish between a horse and a mouse. Yet Daubenton also criticized his fellow anatomists for beginning their descriptions with the trait that most struck them in their observations: "Each one described his object in terms of the aspect that most struck him, and only considered the object itself, without worrying about the comparison that could be made with other objects of the same kind" (4:133). Such contradictions reflect the incompatibility between Daubenton's two descriptive methods, the insoluble conflict between the comparative function and the goal of visualization.

It should by now be apparent that Daubenton's metaphor of description as painting created several contradictions and internal tensions within his theory of description. First, there was the question of the order in which the various elements of a description were presented—in visual terms its composition, which for Buffon formed the basis of literary style. As we have seen, description as measurement required that the same order be followed in all descriptions. As Daubenton explained in his *Encyclopédie* article on description, "It is absolutely necessary [that the outline] be uniform within the same realm, to make a precise and ordered comparison of each animal, or plant or mineral, with those that most resemble or differ from it" (4:878). The less artistry the better: in fact, Daubenton devised his numerical tables as the most styleless and efficient form of comparative description possible. Description as painting, on the contrary, required the describer to make multiple compositional and stylistic choices. With his first brushstroke, he had to capture the animal's physiognomy, that subtle quality that makes each animal unlike any other: "It is the physiognomy of animals, understood in this sense, that is very difficult to capture and render; the expression of this portrait requires a subtle and delicate execution; thus we see most draftsmen and painters perfectly express all the traits of a man or animal's face, yet without capturing the character of its physiognomy" (4:125). By claiming that an animal's physiognomy was contained neither in one particular trait nor in all of them taken together, Daubenton underscored the weakness of his own measurement-based descriptions, which presented animals as the sum of their measured parts. At the same time, he emphasized the aesthetic subtlety and genius required for natural history description, thereby asserting the central place of his articles in the *Histoire naturelle*.

Second, there was the issue of descriptive length. In his *Encyclopédie* article on description, Daubenton explicitly stipulated that the more complex the object described, the longer its description must be: "The more complicated a body is, the more necessary it is to describe the details of its organization, to expose its functioning and workings. Descriptions of animals must therefore be more extensive than those of plants, while descriptions of minerals, which are the crudest of objects, must be shorter than those of plants" (4:878). Within one realm of nature, however, the comparative system required that all descriptions be the same length regardless of extreme differences in size or complexity. This principle conflicted with the idea that the size of the being imagined by the reader was proportional to the length of its description. If the describer chose to describe the mouse and the horse in the same detail and following the same outline, the comparative function would be fulfilled, but the reader would have a wildly disproportional mental image of the mouse. If the describer reduced the description of the mouse to a length more appropriate to its size, the reader might have a more accurate mental image but would be unable to make a direct comparison with the horse. Thus the comparative function was always at odds with visualization, and vice versa.

Finally, there was the question of whether description should entertain or merely instruct, a crucial question given the diverse readership of the *Histoire naturelle*. As Buffon was well aware, the majority of readers were likely to find a total lack of descriptive variety tiresome. Daubenton's response to this issue was mixed: at times, as we have seen, he expressed concern for readers who wanted natural history to remain "clear and easy." At other times, he chided readers who found detailed descriptions tiresome, accusing them of seeking pleasure at the expense of their instruction: "The description of an animal, viewed at rest, will be interesting only to those who want to study nature, because this description is inseparable from a certain dryness in the details, always displeasing to those who are only touched by what is agreeable, and who neglect their own instruction" (4:126). Here, Daubenton downplayed the aesthetic genius and subtlety required for portraiture, suggesting on the contrary that the natural history describer need not concern himself with stylistic issues or the reader's pleasure. This attitude, similarly reflected in Daubenton's periodic attempts to relegate all aesthetic concerns to Buffon's histories, was clearly in conflict with the important stylistic and aesthetic implications of his own theory of description as painting.

The issues Daubenton faced in elaborating his concept of description as painting were central to the aesthetic debates on the relationship between painting and poetry that culminated in the publication of Lessing's *Laocoön* in 1766. Critical readings of the *Laocoön* have observed that Lessing's argument—that poetry cannot reproduce the simultaneity of painting and should thus avoid an excess of description—depended upon his erroneous assumption that paintings are perceived instantaneously.[21] This assumption seems particularly incongruous in light of the impact of empiricism in general, and natural history description in particular, on the Enlightenment understanding of aesthetic experience. As Diderot's analogy of the over-described aphid turning into an elephant in his *Salon de 1767* demonstrates, there was significant overlap between natural history and aesthetics when it came to description.[22] Because they emphasized the richness and complexity of empirical observation, naturalists had the potential to change the terms of the *ut pictura poesis* debate, by questioning the opposition between simultaneous visual forms and successive verbal language.

21. See W. J. T. Mitchell, *Iconology: Image, Text, Ideology* (Chicago: University of Chicago Press, 1986), 95–115. On the Enlightenment understanding of the temporal dimension of viewing paintings, see René Demoris, "La peinture et le 'temps du voir' au siècle des Lumières," in *L'ordre du descriptif,* ed. Jean Bessière (Paris: Presses Universitaires de France, 1988), 47–61.

22. Diderot, *Salon de 1767,* 704.

Unlike Lessing, Daubenton characterized observation as a complex and multilayered process that occurred in several stages over a period of time. Our first glimpse of an animal, captured by the first brushstroke, is instantaneous, but "upon observing it more closely, we follow the detail of its various parts, and we know it well only after having seen the whole thing, as much as it is possible for us to see" (4:118). Descriptive composition was to imitate this progression, with the first brushstroke followed by an exploration of the subsequent stages of observation: "With the first glance we take of something, we perceive its whole and entirety before distinguishing its parts; thus in the description of an animal we cannot dispense with following the natural order, which is to start by expressing the animal's whole form before detailing the parts of its body" (4:122). The notion that empirical observation occurred over time changed the terms of the *ut pictura poesis* debate, because it meant that the gradual unfolding of descriptive language could capture, rather than distort, visual experience. In fact, inasmuch as painting and poetry emulated the empiricist orientation of Enlightenment thought, the poet would have a natural advantage over the painter, even in the representation of visual forms.

The question of temporal progression in description became all the more crucial when Daubenton established a distinction between portraiture, the description of animals at rest, and history painting, the description of animals in movement:

> The description of an animal, viewed at rest, includes an account of all the parts of its body, and the expression of the makeup of its entire form; it must be a *portrait,* in which we can recognize the body's habitual state and the animal's features: the description of the same animal, seen in movement, becomes a *history painting* that represents it in the various positions proper to it, and in all the degrees of movement it engages in by its natural inclination, when it is excited by its needs or agitated by its passions. (4:123)

Daubenton's distinction between portraiture and history painting mirrored the structure of the quadruped volumes, in which Buffon's "histories" were presented separately from Daubenton's "descriptions."[23] Yet

---

23. Denis Reynaud interprets the distinction between history painting and portraiture as a reference to the division of labor between Buffon and Daubenton in the *Histoire naturelle.* He cites Daubenton's claim that portraiture requires greater genius than history painting as an example

Daubenton did not appear to be referring to Buffon's histories when he discussed history painting: on the contrary, he explicitly assigned the task of describing animals at rest and in movement to the describer and referred to portraiture and history painting as two related forms of description. His distinction between portraiture and history painting was instead grounded in the problem of visualization. Because the description of an animal in movement involved a complex process of visualization that built upon an initial mental image of the animal at rest, history painting necessarily followed portraiture and could not stand alone: "One should always start by describing an animal at rest; this is the basis for the description of the animal in movement, because in the latter, one cannot perceive the various parts of the body distinctly enough, one can only see their movement, and one already has enough difficulty recognizing the succession of movements and attitudes" (4:123). At the same time, history painting engaged the describer in the representation of action. It thus brought him closer to the task generally reserved for Buffon in the *Histoire naturelle,* that of representing an animal's habits and natural context. This made the division of labor between Buffon and Daubenton, and the corresponding distinction between history and description, much more ambiguous than the structure of the *Histoire naturelle* implied.

The History-Description Divide

In the original Imprimerie Royale edition of the *Histoire naturelle,* the twelve volumes devoted to quadrupeds, published between 1753 and 1767, were organized around a distinction between history and description. For each quadruped, the reader found a "history" of the animal by Buffon, a "description" by Daubenton, several illustrations by Jacques de Sève, and, finally, various descriptions of the relevant specimens in the king's cabinet by Daubenton. The separation of history and description, implicit in the division of labor between Buffon and Daubenton, was highlighted in the *Histoire naturelle*'s two separate tables of contents, which rather than presenting the articles in their actual order (history, description, illustrations),

---

of the frequent competitive exchanges between Buffon and Daubenton in the *Histoire naturelle.* Reynaud, "Pour une théorie," 355.

listed Buffon's and Daubenton's contributions separately in two successive columns.

Buffon and Daubenton's theoretical writings also reflected this fundamental distinction between history and description. In his opening methodological chapter, Buffon declared that "the only true means of advancing science is to work on the description and history of the different things that are its object" (1:25). He then went on to define these two distinct forms of inquiry according to their varying functions and contents. The function of description was to help the reader recognize the animal described, and it should thus consist of "the form, the size, the weight, the colors, the positions at rest and in movement, the arrangement of the parts, their relationships, their shape, their action and all the external functions: if one can add to all this an account of the internal parts, the description will be even more complete" (1:29–30). The function of history, on the other hand, was to help the reader perceive relationships among various species. The history of each species should thus include "their generation, the period of their impregnation, that of birth, the number of offspring, the care of the fathers and mothers, their type of education, their instincts, their dwellings, their food, the manner in which they procure it, their habits, their tricks, their hunting, and finally the services they can offer us and all the uses and commodities we can draw from them" (1:30). These definitions established a clear basis for the parallel structure of the *Histoire naturelle*: Daubenton was responsible for form (how quadrupeds looked), and Buffon for function (how quadrupeds lived, and how they might be useful to man). Daubenton underlined this parallel structure by writing his own methodological chapter, "De la description des animaux," in which he asserted the dignity and theoretical complexity of description.[24]

Yet the distinction between history and description was anything but clear, especially as the term *histoire* in natural history traditionally denoted description. In the *Dictionnaire de l'Académie française* (1694), we find the following among other definitions for *histoire*: "It is also used to designate all sorts of descriptions of natural things, like plants, minerals, etc. *The Natural History of Pliny. The history of animals. The history of plants. History of*

---

24. "De la description des animaux" appeared in the fourth volume of the *Histoire naturelle,* published in 1753. See Buffon and Daubenton, *Histoire naturelle,* 4:113–41.

minerals."[25] In light of this definition, the rigid separation between history and description in the *Histoire naturelle* must have appeared incongruous to Enlightenment readers. In fact, the distinction was blurred in the body of the quadruped volumes and disappeared entirely with Daubenton's withdrawl from the project in 1767. As a result, critical studies of the *Histoire naturelle* have tended to distort or ignore the history-description divide, despite ample attention to the notion of history in Buffon's proto-evolutionary thought.[26] In one of the most comprehensive studies on Buffon, Roger reversed the order in which history and description were actually presented, and implied that Daubenton's descriptions were incorporated into Buffon's histories.[27] Among literary critics, on the other hand, Daubenton's descriptive articles have been forgotten, and it is instead Buffon who has been said to incarnate "the ideal of the classical describer."[28]

Moreover, despite the clear separation between Buffon's histories and Daubenton's descriptions, the methodological basis for this separation in the quadruped volumes was often ambiguous. For example, Daubenton referred, in his own description of the horse, to his collaborator's description of the same animal: "M. de Buffon, in his history of the horse, described this beautiful animal at rest and in movement" (4:295). Since Buffon had already fulfilled the tasks of the describer, "all that remains is to detail the different kinds of horses we use for different purposes, and to describe the horse as an individual, as much from the outside as from the inside, to compare it to other animals, and to distinguish its kind in relation

---

25. *Dictionnaire de l'Académie française,* 1st ed., 1694, ARTFL Dictionary Project, http://www.lib.uchicago.edu/efts/ARTFL/projects/dicos.

26. On the question of whether Buffon conceived of species as historically modifiable, see Phillip R. Sloan, "From Logical Universals to Historical Individuals: Buffon's Idea of Biological Species," in *Histoire du concept d'espèce dans les sciences de la vie,* ed. Jean-Louis Fischer and Jacques Roger (Paris: Fondation Singer-Polignac, 1987), 101–40; and Arthur O. Lovejoy, "Buffon and the Problem of Species," in *Forerunners of Darwin, 1745–1859,* ed. Bentley Glass, Owsei Temkin, and William L. Straus, Jr. (Baltimore: Johns Hopkins University Press, 1959), 84–113. On the notion of history in Buffon's work, see Amor Cherni, *Buffon: La nature et son histoire* (Paris: Presses Universitaires de France, 1998); and John H. Eddy Jr., "Buffon's *Histoire naturelle:* History? A Critique of Recent Interpretations," *Isis* 85 (1994): 644–61.

27. Roger misleadingly suggests that the quadruped articles are generally organized in the following order: identification of the animal, anatomical description, exterior description, physiological characteristics, nature and temperament, and finally geographical distribution. Roger, *Buffon,* 353–54.

28. Philippe Hamon, ed., *La description littéraire: Anthologie de textes théoriques et critiques* (Paris: Macula, 1991), 41.

to all others" (4:295). Here, Daubenton reversed the roles of historian and describer established by Buffon in his opening chapter: his description would help the reader distinguish the horse from other species (the function of history for Buffon) and would include the different uses of various horses (an aspect of history as defined by Buffon). At the same time, his remarks implied that there were two different kinds of description at work in the *Histoire naturelle:* Buffon's description of the horse in general, "in the state of beautiful nature" (dans l'état de la belle nature), and his own description of the horse as an individual. While the exact nature of this distinction was not clear, Daubenton relegated the representation of beauty ("ce bel animal," "la belle nature") to Buffon's histories, as if to suggest that Buffon's descriptions would be more aesthetically pleasing and his own more technical. A similar opposition can be seen in de Sève's illustrations, which offer both elegant portraits and detailed anatomical studies (see figures 1 and 2).

Buffon's remarks about the relationship between history and description were similarly ambiguous. On the one hand, he claimed that it was in the domain of description, not history, that modern naturalists had surpassed their ancient counterparts: "We have said that the true history and the exact description of each thing were the two sole objects to be initially undertaken in the study of natural history. The ancients successfully realized the former and are perhaps as much above the moderns in this first part as the moderns are above them in the second" (1:49). This remark suggested that Daubenton's descriptions were crucial to the success of the *Histoire naturelle,* and that the modernity of the work lay in the excellence of its anatomical descriptions.[29] On the other hand, Buffon recommended that elements proper to history be introduced into the descriptive articles, in order to avoid descriptive monotony: "In order not to fall into a too frequent repetition of the same order, in order to avoid a monotonous style, the form of descriptions and the progression of the histories must be varied, whenever it is judged necessary; similarly, to make the descriptions less dry, some facts, comparisons, and reflections on the uses of various parts must be integrated into them, so that, in a word, you can be read without

---

29. Buffon's remark could also be interpreted as an ironic jab at his distinguished rival, René-Antoine Ferchault de Réaumur, whom Buffon criticized for favoring detailed description at the expense of broad theories of nature.

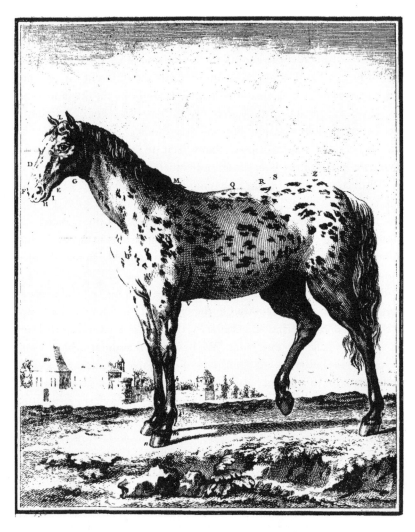

Figure 1. Engraving of a live horse by Jacques de Sève. From Buffon and Daubenton's *Histoire naturelle,* vol. 4, plate I (Paris: Imprimerie Royale, 1753). Courtesy of the Bibliothèque nationale de France.

boredom and without contention" (1:31). Buffon's suggestion that elements of history be incorporated into description raises the question of the relationship between style and methodology in the *Histoire naturelle.* Although the distinction between history and description served as a methodological

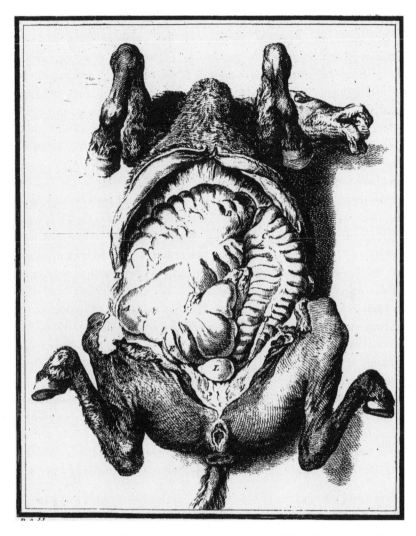

Figure 2. Engraving of a dead horse by Jacques de Sève. From Buffon and Daubenton's *Histoire naturelle,* vol. 4, plate X (Paris: Imprimerie Royale, 1753). Courtesy of the Bibliothèque nationale de France.

basis for the quadruped volumes, Buffon readily sacrificed the distinction in order to make his work more readable for nonspecialists.

Buffon displayed a similar concern for style and readability when he decided to cut Daubenton's descriptive articles from a new edition of the

Histoire naturelle in 1767. It has been speculated that Buffon's decision to sell an abridged version of the quadruped volumes to the publisher Charles-Joseph Panckoucke provoked Daubenton's angry withdrawl from the collaborative project (although the two men subsequently renewed their collegial relations). By some accounts, Buffon made this decision because he wanted to provide a more readable version of the already popular work.[30] Given the widespread praise for Daubenton's anatomical descriptions among the scientific community, Buffon's suppression of the descriptive articles appears to mark a clear move toward attracting a wider audience of nonspecialist readers.

At the same time, there were also practical and methodological issues motivating the split between Buffon and Daubenton. In 1767, when Daubenton left the project, the last quadruped volume had just been published. The next volumes would cover birds, facilitated by the Cabinet du Roy's recent acquisition of René-Antoine Ferchault de Réaumur's extensive collection of bird specimens.[31] Like his predecessor Mathurin-Jacques Brisson, whose *Ornithologie* (1760) provided an extensive catalog of Réaumur's bird collection, Buffon had mainly bird skins and mounted specimens at his disposal. It was therefore not surprising that Daubenton's detailed studies of internal anatomy would not be a part of the *Histoire naturelle des oiseaux*.[32]

There were also several important differences between quadrupeds and birds that necessitated a change in the format of the *Histoire naturelle*. First, for the 182 species described in the twelve quadruped volumes, there were roughly 2,000 species of birds to be described. Second, whereas form was the primary basis for distinguishing among quadrupeds, color was

---

30. On Buffon's motivations for cutting Daubenton's descriptive articles, see Yves Laissus, "*L'Histoire naturelle,*" in *Buffon, 1788–1988,* an exhibition catalog (Paris: Imprimerie Nationale, 1988), 85; Otis E. Fellows and Stephen Milliken, *Buffon* (New York: Twayne, 1972), 58; Roger, *Buffon,* 298; and Daniel Mornet, *Les sciences de la nature en France au XVIIIe siècle* (1911; repr., New York: Lenox Hill-Burt Franklin, 1971), 128. Mornet is alone in suggesting that Buffon may have cut the descriptive articles for fear of being eclipsed by Daubenton's superior reputation in scientific circles.

31. For a detailed discussion of Réaumur's collection, and for a comparison of Mathurin-Jacques Brisson's *Ornithologie* with Buffon's *Histoire naturelle des oiseaux,* see Paul Lawrence Farber, *Discovering Birds: The Emergence of Ornithology as a Scientific Discipline, 1760–1850* (1982; repr., Baltimore: Johns Hopkins University Press, 1997), 7–26.

32. Farber, *Discovering Birds,* 13.

essential for making distinctions among birds. According to Buffon, this difference represented a problem for the naturalist, because of the great difficulty of describing subtle differences in feather color:

> One of the principal [difficulties] is to provide, through discourse, an idea of the colors, for unfortunately the most apparent differences between birds are found in their colors more than in their shapes; for quadruped animals, a good drawing rendered by a black-and-white engraving is sufficient for the distinct knowledge of each animal, because, the colors of quadrupeds being small in number and relatively uniform, they can easily be named and indicated in words; but this would be impossible, or at least would suppose an immense number of words, and very boring ones, in the description of bird colors; there are not even terms in any language to express the nuances, shades, tones, and mixtures; and colors are nonetheless essential character-istics here, and often it is only by their means that a bird can be recognized and distinguished from others.[33]

In the study of birds, as E. C. Spary notes, "Language alone did not pro-vide a perfect match for the terms of the visual code"; unwieldy and tire-some verbal descriptions would thus have to be replaced by hand-colored engravings.[34]

In comparing the representation of quadrupeds and birds, Buffon made no mention of Daubenton's descriptions, implying instead that de Sève's black-and-white engravings had served the needs of visual representation in the quadruped volumes. Presumably Buffon did not wish to alert pro-spective buyers of the newly abridged editions of the *Histoire naturelle des quadrupèdes* to the fact that they would be missing something. Neverthe-less, for those familiar with Daubenton's measurement-based descriptions, Buffon's discussion of the third difference between quadrupeds and birds was a subtle reminder of Daubenton's absence. Unlike quadrupeds, most birds could be represented to scale in the luxurious folio edition of the *His-toire naturelle des oiseaux*. For larger birds, slight adjustments in scale were

33. Georges-Louis Leclerc de Buffon, *Histoire naturelle des oiseaux* (Paris: Imprimerie Roy-ale, 1770), 1:v–vi.

34. E. C. Spary, "Codes of Passion: Natural History Specimens as a Polite Language in Late 18th-Century France," in *Wissenschaft als kulturelle Praxis, 1759–1900,* ed. Hans Erich Bödeker, Peter Hanns Reill, and Jürgen Schlumbohm (Göttingen: Vandenhoeck und Ruprecht, 1999), 115–16.

communicated to the reader without recourse to description, by means of a scale system: "The largest birds have been reduced according to a scale indicated below the illustration: this scale is throughout a twelfth of the length of the bird, measured from the tip of the beak to the end of the tail.... We considered this small gesture to our readers necessary to give, at a glance, an idea of the size of the reduced objects, and so that they could be compared exactly with those that are represented in their natural size."[35] By integrating this scale system into the color plates, Buffon found a convenient way to serve one of the functions previously fulfilled by Daubenton's measurement-based descriptions. While this system could not possibly replace the detailed anatomical comparisons established by Daubenton, it could give readers a general impression of the relative sizes of various birds.

In addition to these stylistic and practical issues, there was also a deeper philosophical divergence that may have brought Buffon and Daubenton's partnership to an end. According to Paul Lawrence Farber, by the 1760s, Buffon had developed an understanding of natural species as historically modifiable, such that "animal form [could] be fully understood only with reference to the history of species."[36] Daubenton, on the contrary, remained attached to a static conception of species, in keeping with his goal of defining the essential characteristics of quadrupeds through comparative anatomy. Thus, argues Farber, the two men parted ways not only because of Buffon's stylistic priorities or because of the switch from quadrupeds to birds, but above all because "the entire worth of Daubenton's work [became] considerably devalued by Buffon's new position."[37] By the same token, Buffon's development of a dynamic understanding of species made the separation of history and description untenable, for if natural beings were historically modifiable, their form (part of description) might be partially determined by their environment (part of history).

Thus in his introduction to the *Histoire naturelle des oiseaux*, Buffon undercut the structure of the original quadruped volumes by claiming that history and description should never be presented separately: "How much

35. Buffon, *Oiseaux*, 1:ix.
36. Paul Lawrence Farber, "Buffon and Daubenton: Divergent Traditions within the *Histoire naturelle*," *Isis* 66 (1975): 73.
37. Farber, "Buffon and Daubenton," 72.

more do these difficulties increase when it comes to providing the description and history! These two parts, so much more essential than nomenclature, and which should never be separated in natural history, are very difficult to unite here, and what is more each one has specific difficulties that we have felt most strongly by the desire we had to overcome them."[38] In this passage, the ambiguities and tensions surrounding the history-description divide are most apparent. On the one hand, Buffon claimed that history and description should never be separated in natural history, as they had been in the earlier quadruped volumes. On the other hand, he underscored the difficulty of combining description and history, thereby suggesting that the traditional definition of *histoire* as a form of description was no longer operative.

Buffon scholarship has emphasized the important historical dimension in his natural philosophy, even before he wrote his historical account, *Les époques de la nature* (1778), of the earth's modifications over time. John Lyon and Phillip Sloan have given Buffon a central role in the "fundamental shift in consciousness" epitomized by "Kant's distinction in 1775 between the mere description of nature (*Naturbeschreibung*), and a genuine historical understanding of nature in its temporal development (*Naturgeschichte*)."[39] While the history-description divide in the quadruped volumes appeared initially to represent a distinction between two kinds of description, the ambiguities and renegotiations to which this divide was subjected over the course of Buffon's career were closely related to the emergence of *Naturgeschichte* in his work. Buffon's claim that history and description should never be separated in his *Histoire naturelle des oiseaux* was motivated by various factors, but central among them was his growing awareness that the form of natural beings was inseparable from their environment, their habits, and their evolution over time. One might ask, then, whether Buffon developed his own approach to description, in opposition to that of Daubenton and in response to his growing concern with historical modifications in nature. Although Buffon elaborated his concept of literary style relatively early in his career, his unpublished essay *De l'art d'écrire* suggests that his understanding of the art of writing was closely tied to the tensions

38. Buffon, *Oiseaux,* 1:v.
39. Lyon and Sloan, *Natural History,* 2.

and ambiguities surrounding the history-description divide in the *Histoire naturelle.*

Deathly Description

Daubenton's "De la description des animaux" was published in 1753, in the fourth volume of the *Histoire naturelle.* The same year, Buffon pronounced his *Discours sur le style* at his induction into the Académie française.[40] His reception speech may have been based in part on *De l'art d'écrire,* which he is thought to have written prior to his nomination to the Academy, although it has also been speculated that this unpublished essay was written much later in his life.[41] In *De l'art d'écrire,* Buffon focused almost exclusively on description, exploring the question of whether words could effectively paint: "Is it possible, one may ask, to trace a drawing with sentences and to present colors with words?"[42] In answering this question, Buffon touched on several issues raised in Daubenton's "De la description des animaux," such as the successive nature of language, the problem of detail, and the representation of animals at rest and in movement. Yet Buffon parted ways with his collaborator and formulated an implicit critique of Daubenton's descriptive method when he opposed two approaches to visual writing, *peindre* and *décrire.* Painting, as defined in *De l'art d'écrire,* shares many features with Buffon's theory of natural style in the *Discours sur le style,* while description is characterized as a deadening form of writing for the writer, the reader, and the objects described.[43]

---

40. The speech was subsequently published in 1777 in a supplementary volume of the *Histoire naturelle.*

41. On the likelihood that Buffon used *De l'art d'écrire* in preparing his reception speech to the Académie française, see Georges-Louis Leclerc de Buffon, *Oeuvres philosophiques,* ed. Jean Piveteau (Paris: Presses Universitaires de France, 1954), 491.

42. Buffon, *De l'art d'écrire,* in *Discours,* 39. Subsequent references to *De l'art d'écrire* and to the *Discours sur le style* appear parenthetically in the main text.

43. This association between description and death anticipates the Marxist critic Georg Lukács's vociferous condemnation of Gustave Flaubert and Émile Zola for their excessive use of description. For Lukács, description acts as a kind of fossilization, slowing down the dynamic of narrative and undercutting its potential to prompt the reader to action. The excesses of realist and naturalist description trap characters and readers alike, depriving them of life, movement, and will—qualities that can be reinstated only by the vital power of narrative. Georg Lukács, "Narrate

The first limitation of description, Buffon observed in *De l'art d'écrire,* was its exclusive focus on visual properties: "To describe well, it is sufficient to see coldly; but to paint requires all the senses. Seeing, hearing, touching, smelling, these are the many attributes the writer must sense and render in lively strokes" (39). This emphasis on the complex sensitivity required of the writer reflects the sensationist orientation of the *Histoire naturelle,* according to which knowledge is acquired through empirical observation. Yet contrary to Foucault's characterization of natural history in the classical episteme, Buffon did not accord an exclusive privilege to sight at the expense of the other senses.[44] In fact, in the *Histoire naturelle* he gave precedence to touch in the acquisition of knowledge, arguing that this sense corrects the inevitable errors of the others: "It is by touch alone that we can acquire complete and real knowledge, it is this sense that rectifies all the others, the effects of which would be nothing but illusions and would produce only errors in our minds, if touch did not teach us to make judgments" (3:363). Man's superior intelligence could thus be explained as a function of his highly developed sense of touch, which far surpassed that of other species. Sight, on the other hand, was one of man's weaker senses and was furthermore subject to multiple errors and illusions. In keeping with his position on the Molyneux problem, which asked whether a blind man recovering his sight would be able to distinguish between a cube and a sphere merely by looking at them, Buffon claimed that if man did not correct his erroneous visual perceptions with tactile information, he would see objects upside down and double. This meant that even the act of perceiving visual information was a complex process combining several kinds of sensory data.[45]

Thus as a purely visual form of writing, description reduced and distorted the data of empirical observation, cutting the reader off from the sensory combinations experienced in nature. The superiority of painting, in contrast, lay in its capacity for synesthesia, the simultaneous blending and stimulation of multiple senses. The painting writer brought the reader

---

or Describe?" in *Writer and Critic and Other Essays,* ed. and trans. Arthur Kahn (London: Merlin Press, 1970), 110–48.

44. See Foucault, *Mots et choses,* 137–76; and Buffon and Daubenton, *Histoire naturelle,* 3:305–70.

45. On the Molyneux problem, see Jessica Riskin, *Science in the Age of Sensibility: The Sentimental Empiricists of the French Enlightenment* (Chicago: University of Chicago Press, 2002), 19–68.

closer to the experience of firsthand observation, by incorporating a full range of sensory information into his text. In doing so, he infused his text and his reader with the vibrancy of the natural world.[46] Buffon's emphasis on sensorial complexity demonstrates the extent to which his theory of writing was informed by his perspective as a naturalist. Like Daubenton, he changed the terms of the *ut pictura poesis* debate, giving the writer a natural advantage over the painter in the transmission of sensorial data.

The second limitation of description concerned the preservation of form. Like Daubenton, Diderot, and Lessing, Buffon identified description's successive presentation of various parts and details as a stumbling block for the writer. Instead of focusing on distortion, however, he highlighted the deadening effect of this successive presentation: "Description presents all the parts of an object successively and coldly; the more detailed it is, the less effect it has. Painting, on the contrary, first capturing only the most striking traits, preserves the imprint of the object and gives it life" (39). Buffon was not far here from Daubenton's theory of the first brushstroke: the writer must begin by presenting a rapid overview of his subject's most distinctive traits. This would allow him to avoid the deadening effect of excessive detail, to preserve the vitality of his subject, and to rival the unity and simultaneity of pictorial representation.

In addition to beginning with a quick, overall sketch, the writer must use the resources of color to transform the disjointed pieces of description into an organic whole: "He must combine the subtlety of colors with the vigor of the paintbrush, lending them nuance, condensing or blending them, forming in the end a living whole, of which a description can present only dead and detached parts" (39). Here, Buffon suggested that the successive nature of language need not necessarily dissect a living being into separate parts, stripping it of coherence and life. Color participated both in the preservation of form and in the sensuality of writing, enlivening the writer, his reader, and his subject.

On a certain level, Buffon's conception of the art of writing thus appeared to deny the fundamental incompatibility between successive verbal

---

46. Buffon refers to the writer and the reader using the masculine pronoun *il* throughout his essay, in keeping with the gender of the terms *écrivain* and *lecteur* in French. In summarizing and analyzing his essay in English, I have respected this usage despite the problem of sexist language that it may pose for some readers.

language and simultaneous visual forms posited in Lessing's *Laocoön*. Like Lessing, Buffon condemned description precisely because it broke its object down into parts that could be presented only successively. At the same time, he upheld the temporal progression of language as the mark of the writer's superiority over the painter: "At the same level of genius, the writer has over the painter the advantage of having time at his disposal and making one scene follow another, whereas the painter can only present the action of a moment; he can thus produce only a sudden astonishment, an instant of admiration, which fades as soon as the object disappears" (40). Because he had the advantage of developing his representation over time, the writer, and not the painter, could "engrave" the objects of representation onto the reader's memory: "The great writer can not only produce this initial effect of admiration but also enliven, enflame, his reader with the representation of several actions that will all have warmth, and that by their union and rays will be engraved in his memory, and will subsist independently of the object" (40). Through this process, the warmth and energy proper to "painting" were communicated to the reader such that life was not only represented but also propagated by the work itself. The originality of Buffon's claim lay not in its emphasis on action, but in the notion that the temporal progression of writing made it more suited to the visual representation of nature than painting itself.

In keeping with Daubenton's opposition between portraiture and history painting, Buffon also stipulated that the writer must depict nature both at rest and in movement: "All the objects nature offers us, and in particular all living beings, make up the many subjects of which the writer must compose not only the portrait at rest, but also the moving painting, in which all the forms will be developed, all the traits of the portrait will appear animated, and will in their ensemble present all the external characteristics of the object" (40). The striking resemblance between this passage and Daubenton's "De la description des animaux" suggests either that Buffon contributed to his collaborator's methodological chapter, or that he was influenced by it. In either case, Buffon's preference for "moving paintings" stood in opposition to Daubenton's claim, in "De la description des animaux," that portraiture required superior genius as compared to history painting: "Only great masters succeed in making simple portraits, such as are needed to accompany the description of animals viewed at rest. But the subtlety of these portraits naturally rendered is not apparent to most connoisseurs, because they haven't spent enough time observing the character of the physiognomy of animals in nature" (4:125). Although Daubenton incorporated temporal progression into the art of description to mirror the progressive stages of empirical observation, his preference for portraiture limited him to a fairly static conception of description. In *De l'art d'écrire,* on the contrary, Buffon replaced static description with a conception of painterly writing that was endowed with the dynamic qualities of a living, moving being.

Like Daubenton, Buffon changed the terms of the eighteenth-century debate on the relationship between poetry and painting. In particular, he championed prose over poetry as a superior vehicle for visual representation, claiming that verse curtailed the writer's ability to paint: "Poetry has been compared to painting in all ages; but no one has ever thought that prose could paint better than poetry. Meter and rhyme constrain the freedom of the brush; for a syllable too few or too many, words that create images are rejected with regret by the poet and used to advantage by the prose writer. Style, which is but the order and movement one gives to one's thoughts, is necessarily constrained by an arbitrary formula, or interrupted by pauses that diminish its rapidity and alter its uniformity" (41).[47] Buffon's claim that verse detracted from the visual power of writing by introducing arbitrary formulas into the writing process paralleled his critique of the arbitrary definitions of nomenclature. To the extent that it imposed no artificial constraints on the writer, prose was more permeable to the qualities of nature. It allowed the writer to develop a natural style, which reflected the actual progression of his thoughts and perceptions rather than arbitrary formal rules.

Buffon's theory of writing as painting was also innovative in the sensorial awakening it sought to provoke in the reader. If description was death, for Buffon, it was because it deadened the reader's senses, cutting him off

---

47. A similar account of Buffon's attitude toward verse is given by Hérault de Séchelles in his "Visite à Buffon," written in 1785 after a visit to Buffon in Montbard: "[Buffon] is intransigent about style, and above all about poetry, which he doesn't like. He claims that it is impossible in our language to write four lines of verse in a row without making a mistake, without offending either the appropriate usage of words or the accuracy of ideas. He recommended to me never to write verse: 'I would have made poetry just like another,' he told me; 'but I quickly abandoned this genre, where reason only wears chains. It already has enough of them as it is, without imposing even more on it.'" Buffon, *Discours,* 68–69.

from the colors, smells, sights, sounds, and tastes of life itself. Painterly writing, on the other hand, created an impression of sensorial contact with the world, simultaneously engaging all six of the reader's senses. The sixth sense, for Buffon, was sexual pleasure, an organic sense that consisted in an explosive fusion of the other five. In a passage from the *Histoire naturelle* that paralleled Étienne Bonnot de Condillac's allegory of the statue, Buffon recounted the first man's awakening to nature and to sensorial perception.[48] From his original discovery of sight, the man went on to experience the pleasures of hearing, smelling, touching, and tasting. Only when these five senses had been acquired did he encounter a "second half of [him]self," and with this second half, a sixth, life-creating sense: "I felt her become animated under my touch, I saw her take thought from my eyes, while hers made a new source of life flow in my veins; I would have liked to give her my entire being; this strong desire fulfilled [or ended: acheva] my existence; I felt the birth of a sixth sense."[49] Buffon's characterization of sexual pleasure as a sixth sense was consistent with his sensationist theory of writing: just as the sixth sense led to the creation of life, the sensorial fusion of painterly writing enlivened the reader, allowing the writer to move beyond the simple representation of life into its creation.

Regardless of when it was written, *De l'art d'écrire* is an important text because it provides the missing link between Buffon's practice of natural history and his modern theory of literary style. In the *Discours sur le style,* Buffon defined style as "the order and movement one gives to one's thoughts" (19). Unlike scientific discoveries, which entered the collective domain of human knowledge and were eventually surpassed, a writer's style was properly his own and would not lose value over time. This was Buffon's meaning when he formulated his famous but ambiguous phrase "Le style est l'homme même" (Style is man himself). At the same time, a writer's style had to mirror nature itself, "without art and without any other ornamentation than that of nature" (17). Literary style was thus doubly individual, representing the fusion of the writer's individual perspective with the individual form of his subject. In this sense, Buffon's theory of literary style resembled Daubenton's theory of descriptive composition, "l'expression de la

---

48. See Étienne Bonnot de Condillac, *Traité des sensations* (Paris: Fayard, 1984).
49. Buffon and Daubenton, *Histoire naturelle,* 3:370.

chose." Despite Buffon's critique of his collaborator's descriptive method, he was evidently influenced by his theoretical reflections.[50]

Unlike *De l'art d'écrire,* the *Discours sur le style* did not explicitly address the problem of description. It did, however, bear the mark of Buffon's preoccupation with that problem, inasmuch as it elaborated a highly visual conception of literary style. Like the painter, the writer had to begin with a preliminary sketch of his subject, tracing its broad outlines before filling in secondary ideas:

> But before seeking the order in which one will present one's thoughts, another more general and more fixed order must be established, in which only first views and principal ideas should play a part: it is in marking their place in this initial outline that a subject will be circumscribed and that one will determine its breadth; it is in constantly reminding oneself of these first lineaments that one will determine the appropriate intervals separating the principal ideas, and that secondary and intermediate ideas will come into being to fill those intervals. (20)

Buffon's account of the various stages in the writing process downplayed the successive nature of language (one word, one sentence, one paragraph after another) and instead favored a model inherited from painting. In keeping with Daubenton's principle that a description should follow the various stages of observation, Buffon suggested that the composition of a written work proceeded by adding various layers onto an initial outline.

Yet Buffon combined this painterly metaphor with language and metaphors borrowed from the field of natural history. The written text must aspire not only to the unity of pictorial representation but also to the organic unity of living beings:

> Why are the works of Nature so perfect? It is because every work is a whole, and because Nature labors according to an eternal plan from which she never diverges; she prepares in silence the seeds of her productions; she sketches in a single act the primitive form of every living being: she develops it, she perfects it through a continual movement and within an established

---

50. It is also possible that Buffon contributed to Daubenton's "De la description des animaux," and that the theory of descriptive composition outlined therein is his own.

timeframe. The work astonishes; but it is the divine imprint whose features it bears that should strike us. (23)

This account of the perfection of nature suggests that Nature herself acted as a painter, first sketching a primitive form and then gradually perfecting her work of art. As Roger has shown, Buffon's theory of generation changed several times over the course of the *Histoire naturelle*. In 1753, however, when he pronounced the *Discours sur le style,* he seems to have believed that the overall structure of a living being was formed first, and that this initial form was only gradually complexified.[51] Thus the organic metaphors in Buffon's *Discours sur le style* mark the influence of his natural philosophy on his concept of literary style.

* * *

Description was at the heart of Buffon's project, not only because it occupied roughly half of the quadruped volumes, but also because it posed stylistic and methodological problems that impacted the shape and evolution of the *Histoire naturelle*. These problems were also instrumental in the development of Buffon's theory of literary style in *De l'art d'écrire* and the *Discours sur le style*. Although Daubenton's anatomical articles may be lacking in literary merit, his theory of description in the *Encyclopédie* and in "De la description des animaux" had important implications for subsequent descriptive projects of the Enlightenment. In particular, Daubenton pinpointed the representational challenges posed by the ideal of complete description. His two opposing descriptive methods, description as measurement versus description as painting, prompted him to reflect in an original way on the issues of descriptive length, detail, and coherence. Although Buffon cut his collaborator's "deadly" descriptions from the *Histoire naturelle* in 1767, Daubenton was the first to expose the representational challenges posed by the Enlightenment project of compiling an encyclopedic description of nature. On a certain level, Buffon's theory of natural style was an attempt to close the representational rift created by Daubenton's complex theory of description.

---

51. Jacques Roger, *Les sciences de la vie dans la pensée française du XVIIIe siècle* (Paris: Armand Colin, 1963).

2

BERNARDIN DE SAINT-PIERRE'S
STRAWBERRY PLANT

Jacques-Henri Bernardin de Saint-Pierre is best known today as the
author of *Paul et Virginie* (1788), a pastoral novel set in the exotic context of
the Île-de-France (present-day Mauritius) and replete with purple prose,
gushing sentimentalism, and dark undertones regarding the treatment of
African slaves in the French colonies. With this work alone, Saint-Pierre
might well have earned his reputation as one of the first great describers in
modern French literature.[1] The novel is stuffed with concrete (yet florid)
descriptions of the island's flora and fauna, based largely on Saint-Pierre's
travelogue, the *Voyage à l'Île de France* (1773).[2] What is often forgotten,

---

1. Although he is generally referred to today as Bernardin de Saint-Pierre or simply Bernardin, I have followed Colas Duflo in using Saint-Pierre's surname. See Colas Duflo, "Le hussard et
l'inscription," in *Études de la nature*, by Bernardin de Saint-Pierre, 7. For Daniel Mornet, "it is indeed Bernardin de Saint-Pierre who was the first to paint with definitive success the picturesque
beauty of the exterior world." Mornet, *Sentiment de la nature*, 435.
2. On the relationship between the descriptions in the *Voyage à l'Ile de France* and *Paul et Virginie*, see the introduction and notes in Paul Trahard and Édouard Guitton, eds., *Paul et Virginie,*

however, is that *Paul et Virginie* was originally published as the last chapter in a fragmented, encyclopedic work of natural history, the *Études de la nature* (1784–88).[3] With this work, Saint-Pierre intended not only to invent a new language for description but also to set a new course for the study of nature. Yet whereas his practice of description appeared modern and worthy of imitation to romantics such as François-René de Chateaubriand, his scientific theories and ambitions quickly appeared obsolete.[4] Hence Saint-Pierre's literary practice of description was divorced from its scientific context, just as *Paul et Virginie* was extracted (by Saint-Pierre himself) from its place in the *Études de la nature,* to be published as a freestanding novel from 1789 forward.

In order to recapture the coherence of Saint-Pierre's descriptive project, in its scientific and poetic dimensions, we must address its relationship to the Buffonian model of a general history of nature. Saint-Pierre himself explicitly framed the *Études de la nature* against the backdrop of this model, characterizing his work both as the ruins of a great painting of nature lost beyond repair and as a roll of preparatory sketches for a painting of nature not yet completed: "Descriptions, conjectures, perceptions, views, objections, doubts, and even my ignorance, I gathered it all together; and I called these ruins *Études,* like a painter the studies of a great painting he was unable to complete [un grand tableau, auquel il n'a

---

by Bernardin de Saint-Pierre, 2nd ed. (1964; Paris: Bordas, 1989); and Janine Baudry, "Un aspect mauricien de l'oeuvre de Bernardin de Saint-Pierre: La flore locale," *Revue d'histoire littéraire de la France* 5 (1989): 782–90.

3. Jean Fabre sees the inclusion of *Paul et Virginie* in the *Études de la nature* as a logical and meaningful aesthetic choice on Saint-Pierre's part: "This association was not entirely arbitrary....*Paul et Virginie* was indeed, in a certain way, this 'Painting of Nature' that the artist finally sensed he had brought to its point of perfection, a studio and competition piece, a master work, destined to crown the 'studies', understood in the technical sense of the term." Jean Fabre, "Paul et Virginie pastorale," in *Lumières et romantisme: Énergie et nostalgie de Rousseau à Mickiewicz,* 2nd ed. (1963; Paris: Klincksieck, 1980), 234.

4. For Jacques Horrent, Saint-Pierre's prose "constitutes the transition between the purely intellectual classical prose of the 18th century and the poetic prose of Chateaubriand." Jacques Horrent, "Le réalisme descriptif dans la tempête de *Paul et Virginie,"* *Cahiers d'analyse textuelle* 11 (1969): 25–26. Chateaubriand himself admired Saint-Pierre, praising his "talent for painting scenes of solitude." François-René de Chateaubriand, *Génie du christianisme,* ed. Pierre Reboul (Paris: Garnier-Flammarion, 1966), 1:322. On Saint-Pierre's influence on Chateaubriand, see Tanguy Logé, "Chateaubriand et Bernardin de Saint-Pierre," *Revue d'histoire littéraire de la France* 5 (1989): 879–90.

pu mettre la dernière main]."[5] As ruins, the *Études de la nature* looks back with nostalgia to the Buffonian model of a general history of nature. But as a collection of sketches, it lays the groundwork for a new approach to natural history, centering on the naturalist's sensitive perception of harmonic relationships in nature. Saint-Pierre's epistemology was based in sensation (and sentiment) rather than cognition; borrowing from a long philosophical tradition that viewed sensation as the basis for self-awareness, he reformulated Descartes' cogito as follows: "I sense [or feel], therefore I exist" (Je sens; donc j'existe) (3:109).[6] As a result, he made no distinction between the naturalist's knowledge of nature and his sensitive appreciation of nature's beauty. This aesthetic appreciation was in turn reflected in the naturalist's descriptions, which were to communicate both knowledge and pleasure to the reader by expressing the natural harmonies perceived by the naturalist. Thus, as Colas Duflo observes in the first modern edition of the *Études de la nature,* Saint-Pierre's "philosophy of nature founds an aesthetic, which articulates itself in its entirety in the painting of nature as he practices it."[7] Description was, for Saint-Pierre, the site of both scientific understanding and aesthetic appreciation. It was also, to the extent that it focused on harmonic relationships rather than isolated objects, fundamentally and intrinsically incomplete. With the fragments of his ruined painting, Saint-Pierre expressed both his emulation of Buffon and his break with the descriptive method that had made a general history of nature appear feasible.

In fact, Saint-Pierre resembled Buffon in several respects. Both men gained fame with multivolume works of natural history. Both were intendants to the same natural history garden, although by the time Saint-Pierre's brief six-month tenure ended in 1793, the garden was no longer called the Jardin du Roi, the French Republic having been declared and

---

5. Jacques-Henri Bernardin de Saint-Pierre, *Études de la nature* (Paris: Imprimerie de Crapelet, 1804), 1:139. Subsequent references appear parenthetically in the main text. The first modern edition of the *Études de la nature,* edited by Colas Duflo, was published in 2007, but for reasons of accessibility I have chosen to refer to the 1804 edition on which Duflo's edition is based.

6. Daniel Heller-Roazen traces this philosophical tradition, from Aristotle to the twentieth century, in *The Inner Touch: Archaeology of a Sensation* (New York: Zone Books, 2007). See in particular the chapter "Perception Everywhere," 163–78, for a discussion of how Descartes interrupts and obscures this tradition.

7. Duflo, "Hussard," 18.

the former king executed.[8] As writers, Buffon and Saint-Pierre shared a talent for visually evocative prose, and both were upheld as models for descriptive writing throughout the nineteenth century. But the differences between Saint-Pierre and Buffon are no less striking than their similarities. Whereas Buffon had come to represent the institution of natural history across Europe by the time of his death in 1788, Saint-Pierre was a marginal figure, an adventurer whose travels took him across Europe and as far as Russia, Martinique, Malta, and the Île-de-France. While Buffon observed animals primarily in his own menagerie, on fairgrounds, and in natural history cabinets in his native Montbard and in Paris, Saint-Pierre discovered his passion for botany in the distant Île-de-France (and later botanized with Jean-Jacques Rousseau on the outskirts of Paris). And although both Buffon and Saint-Pierre have been remembered as great describers, they hold very different places in the history of literary description: whereas Buffon is said to incarnate "the ideal of the classical describer," Saint-Pierre is more often associated with romantic and modern literary description.[9] The most marked difference between Buffon and Saint-Pierre, however, lies in their starkly divergent appraisals of the scope of natural history: whereas for Buffon, "a single part of natural history, like the history of insects, or the history of plants, is sufficient to occupy several men," for Saint-Pierre, "the complete history of the strawberry plant would be sufficient to occupy all the naturalists in the world."[10] In order to understand why Saint-Pierre was so radically skeptical about the naturalist's ability to describe even a single plant, we must take a closer look at the theory and practice of description elaborated in the *Études de la nature*.

Sketching amid the Ruins

The *Études de la nature* is composed of fourteen studies running anywhere from six to two hundred pages. The great variation in length among the

---

8. On the transformations of the Jardin du Roi during the Revolution, see E. C. Spary, *Utopia's Garden: French Natural History from Old Regime to Revolution* (Chicago: University of Chicago Press, 2000).

9. Hamon, *Description littéraire,* 41. For other examples of this view, see note 4 above.

10. Buffon and Daubenton, *Histoire naturelle,* 1:4, Bernardin de Saint-Pierre, *Études,* 1:113.

studies reflects the flexibility of the experimental literary form adopted by Saint-Pierre. Just as a painter's sketch may be highly elaborated or consist of a few simple lines, Saint-Pierre's studies vary greatly in their length and completeness. The first study, entitled "Immensité de la nature; plan de mon ouvrage" (Immensity of Nature; Outline of My Work), mirrors Buffon's opening chapter in the *Histoire naturelle,* outlining a vast and ambitious project rooted in the observation and description of nature. Yet whereas Buffon used the impersonal and collective pronouns *on* (one) and *nous* (we) and a forward-looking present tense, Saint-Pierre adopts the first-person pronoun *I* and the past tense in characterizing his project: "I formed, a few years ago, the project of writing a general history of nature, in imitation of Aristotle, Pliny, the chancellor Bacon, and several famous moderns" (1:103). Buffon was undoubtedly the most important of these modern naturalists, and Saint-Pierre's failure to cite his eminent predecessor betrays a certain "anxiety of influence."[11]

Like Buffon, Saint-Pierre devotes his opening study to the immensity of nature, and to the difficulty of achieving a complete description of it. Yet unlike Buffon, who embraced this challenge despite its difficulty, Saint-Pierre quickly rejects his initial ambitions, characterizing them as the product of a childish delusion: "I planned to begin my work when I had finished observing, and when I had gathered all the materials for the history of nature; but I was like a child who had dug a hole in the sand, with a seashell, to contain all the water in the ocean" (1:104). The absurd disparity between a small hole in the sand, carved out with a seashell by a child, and the infinite expanse of the ocean reflects Saint-Pierre's perception of the gap between his project and the Buffonian model. That gap dictates his title, his personal tone, and the metaphor of ruins that traverses the *Études de la nature.* Still, the Buffonian model casts a long shadow over the *Études de la nature,* as Saint-Pierre continues to insist throughout the work on its partial and fragmentary nature and even incorporates an outline of his abandoned project into his opening chapter.

It is difficult to give a sense of the overall structure of the *Études de la nature,* given Saint-Pierre's unsystematic approach to natural history and the metaphor of ruins that governs the shape of his work. He acknowledges

---

11. I borrow the phrase from Harold Bloom, *The Anxiety of Influence: A Theory of Poetry* (Oxford: Oxford University Press, 1973).

this disorder but promises to preserve some level of coherence with the following outline:

> In the midst of this disorder it was nonetheless necessary to adopt an order, without which the confusion in the material would have added still further to insufficiency of the author. I followed the simplest one. First I respond to objections against providence; next I examine the existence of a few senti-ments that are common to all men, and that are sufficient to recognize in all of nature's works the laws of its wisdom and goodness. Then I apply these laws to the globe, to plants, to animals, and to man. (1:139)

This outline does help clarify Saint-Pierre's purpose in undertaking the *Études de la nature:* he intended to transform the study of nature by refut-ing materialist arguments against divine providence, by identifying sen-sation and sentiment, rather than reason, as the proper basis for the study of nature, and by illustrating the divine laws of nature, as revealed to man through sentiment. Yet the outline does not reflect the actual structure of the *Études de la nature* in its final, "ruined" form. Saint-Pierre nevertheless spends some sixty pages giving a detailed overview of this phantom out-line, without informing his unwitting readers until after the fact that he no longer intends to follow it. In his overview, Saint-Pierre presents a work in five sections: in the first, he intends to combat materialist and mechanistic theories of nature, and in the remaining four, he intends to illustrate these laws with examples from the globe, plants, animals, and man.[12]

In fact, Saint-Pierre ultimately only covered plants in his illustration of natural laws, abandoning three of the five sections he originally projected. Yet only after his lengthy overview, which contains multiple digressions pertaining to sections not included in the actual *Études de la nature,* does he reveal his change in plan:

> Such is the vast outline that I intended to fill. I had collected for this pur-pose more materials than I needed; but several obstacles prevented me from bringing them together in their entirety. I will perhaps attend to this at a

---

12. On the coherence of Saint-Pierre's observation-based conception of natural harmonies in the *Études de la nature* and his more poetic conception of harmonies in the *Harmonies de la na-ture,* see Basil Guy, "Bernardin de Saint-Pierre and the Idea of 'Harmony,'" *Stanford French Re-view* 2 (1978): 209–22.

more favorable time. In the meantime, I have excerpted what was sufficient to give an idea of the harmonies of nature. Although my efforts are
reduced here to simple studies, I have nonetheless preserved enough order
for my general outline to be discerned. It is in this manner that a peristyle,
some half-ruined arcades, rows of columns, some simple planes of wall, still
present to travelers, on an island in Greece, the image of an ancient temple, despite the ravages of time and of the barbarians who have knocked it
down. (1:205–6)

The double metaphor of ruins and sketches, or studies, in this passage
reflects a persistent ambiguity as to whether Saint-Pierre considered the
Études de la nature the remains of a lost ideal (a testament to the past), or a
collection of sketches for a new painting of nature that might one day be
completed (a project for the future). In his opening remarks, he characterized his original project as a delusion, thereby suggesting that the ruined
state of the *Études de la nature* was inevitable. Here, he adopts a slightly
more optimistic and forward-looking tone: although the metaphor of architectural ruins again suggests that a complete painting of nature (or the
belief in its possibility) can never be recovered, Saint-Pierre nonetheless
insists that he has gathered enough materials to complete his project at
some future date. It is in this light that Saint-Pierre's inclusion of his original outline in his opening study can be understood: this phantom outline
serves, on the one hand, to preserve a memory of his abandoned project
(like the ruined temple) and, on the other hand, to make room, in the form
of digressions, for leftover material that might one day be incorporated
into a new painting.

Indeed, Saint-Pierre suggests elsewhere that despite the apparently personal nature of his work, he hopes that future naturalists may one day
complete the great painting projected in the *Études de la nature:* "I request
much indulgence. I am endeavoring to forge a new quarry. I don't flatter
myself to have penetrated very far into it. But the imperfect materials
I have drawn from it could one day allow men more capable and fortunate
than I to erect a temple to nature more worthy of her. Reader, remember
that I promised nothing but the frontispiece and the ruins" (2:149). Here,
Saint-Pierre uses the architectural metaphor to characterize the actual
structure of the *Études de la nature:* while the frontispiece corresponds to
the outline (and more generally to the new approach to nature elaborated

in the *Études de la nature*), the ruins correspond to the sole chapter illustrating natural harmonies in plants. The notion that other naturalists might one day complete the painting reflects the persistence of the Buffonian model, in which the description of nature was a collective and cumulative project. At the same time, in the remainder of his first study, Saint-Pierre elaborates an approach to description so radically different from the Buffonian method that "the life of a man of genius would hardly suffice for the history of a few insects" (1:122).

From Clay Pot to Globe

Saint-Pierre's first study is thus marked by a methodological tension: on the one hand, it outlines a general history of nature in the Buffonian tradition, while on the other hand, it elaborates an approach to description that makes any such project unfeasible. In explaining why he was forced to abandon his original project, Saint-Pierre characterizes this tension as the contrast between the infinite expanse of nature and his own limited perspective: "Nature is infinitely vast, and I am a very limited man [La nature est infiniment étendue, et je suis un homme très-borné]. Not only its general history, but even that of the smallest plant, is well beyond my abilities. Here is the occasion when I became convinced of it" (1:104). The anecdote that follows, in which Saint-Pierre recounts his experience of describing a strawberry plant, reveals just how much his conception of description diverged from that of Buffon. In Buffon's view, the naturalist could gradually progress in the immense task of describing nature by compiling successive descriptions of individual objects. For Saint-Pierre, in contrast, the mere task of describing a single plant involved a dizzying contemplation of the infinite network of natural harmonies connecting that plant to all of nature.

Saint-Pierre begins his anecdote by recounting how he was distracted from his work on the harmonies of the globe when he noticed some pretty flies on his strawberry plant:

> One summer day, while I was working on putting in order a few observations on the harmonies of the globe, I noticed on a strawberry plant that happened to be on my windowsill some tiny flies that were so pretty I was

tempted to describe them. The next day, I saw some more of another kind, which I also described. I observed, over a period of three weeks, thirty-seven different kinds; but in the end, there came so many different varieties and such a great number of them that I dropped this study [je laissai là cette étude], although very amusing, because I lacked spare time, and to tell the truth, expression [je manquois de loisir, et, pour dire la vérité, d'expression]. (1:104–5)

This passage establishes an important tension between the temptation to describe and Saint-Pierre's scientific pursuits: in order to describe the flies, he abandons his attempt to organize his observations on the harmonies of the globe, which was in fact one of the originally projected sections that was dropped from the *Études de la nature*. By situating this anecdote at a time when he still believed in his general history of nature, Saint-Pierre underlines the illusory nature of his original ambitions. How could he possibly have hoped to describe the entire globe if even the tiniest plant drew him into three weeks of describing? Hence Saint-Pierre's abandonment of his miniature study ("je laissai là cette étude") mirrors and justifies his abandonment of his general history of nature.

Yet Saint-Pierre also claims to lack the expressive ability necessary to describe the flies in his strawberry plant. Throughout the *Études de la nature,* and especially in his eleventh study on plant harmonies, he insists on the lack of any adequate descriptive language in the field of botany. Thus his purpose in the strawberry plant anecdote is not only to illustrate the necessarily fragmented state of any description of nature but also to found a new descriptive language. The following charming description of the flies in Saint-Pierre's strawberry plant is a good example of this attempt:

The flies I had observed were all distinct from one another, in their colors, their shapes, and their bearing [leurs allures]. There were golden ones, silver ones, bronze ones, tigered ones, striped ones, blue ones, green ones, dark ones, shimmering ones. Some had heads rounded like a turban; others, elongated like the point of a nail. On some the heads looked dark like a dot of black velvet; on others they sparkled like a ruby. There was no less variety in their wings. Some were long and brilliant, like blades of mother-of-pearl; others short and wide, resembling the weave of the finest gauze.... Some of the flies flew by whirling like butterflies; others rose in the air, setting

themselves against the wind, with a mechanism not unlike that of paper
kites, which I believe ascend by forming with the direction of the wind an
angle of twenty-two degrees and a half. (1:105–6)

This global and impressionistic (yet remarkably precise) description of the
flies marked a distinct departure from the standard eighteenth-century
practice of entomological description, whose high level of detail prompted
Buffon to remark: "A fly should take up no more space in the naturalist's
head than it takes up in nature."[13] Freed from the constraints of descriptive completeness, Saint-Pierre is able to focus on striking details, such as
the turban-shaped head of one fly or the kite-like flying mechanism of another. Having rejected his initial method of describing each variety individually and in turn, he is able to highlight strong contrasts in color, shape,
and bearing among the various flies. Also striking is his picturesque use of
analogies to familiar objects, a technique that allows him to give a sense for
the overall shape, color, texture, and motion of each fly with only one or
two words. Most of the analogies communicate more than one quality at
a time: the ruby its color, sparkle, and hard texture; the blades of mother-
of-pearl their iridescence and brittle fragility; the kite its delicate structure
and ascending movement.

Saint-Pierre's description also marked a departure from tradition in its
abandonment of any systematic framework for organizing descriptive material. It did not belong to a catalog of insect life, because Saint-Pierre was
not specifically concerned with entomology elsewhere in the *Études de la
nature.* Nor could such a description be used to complete the entomological catalogs of other naturalists, since Saint-Pierre did not even identify the
flies he was describing. Like so many other descriptions in the *Études de la
nature,* this one stood as a free-floating fragment, a testament to the beauty
of nature and to the pleasures of observation and description.

At the same time, Saint-Pierre's global description of the flies was consistent with his critique of naturalists working in the tradition of Réaumur
and Daubenton, who wrote isolated descriptions of individual insects and
quadrupeds divorced from their natural context. For Saint-Pierre, such
descriptions ran counter to the true object of natural history, because they

---

13. Buffon and Daubenton, *Histoire naturelle,* 4:92.

ignored and even distorted the harmonic relationships that connect animals and plants to their natural surroundings:

> Naturalists have mutilated the most beautiful part of natural history, by relating, as almost all of them do, isolated descriptions of animals and plants, without saying anything about the season or place where they find them. They have stripped them of all their beauty by this negligence; for there is not a single animal or plant for which the point of harmony [le point harmonique] is not attached to a specific site, to a specific hour of the day or night, to the sunrise or sunset, to the phases of the moon and even to the storms, even without considering the other contrasts and affinities [convenances] resulting from these. (2:258)

Saint-Pierre's insistence on context in natural history description goes to the very heart of his natural philosophy. As Duflo has noted, Saint-Pierre's epistemology was a "philosophy of relationships," leading to "a discourse in which one can read ecological perspectives before their time."[14] This philosophy was consistent with the broader current of vitalism that grew up in opposition to Cartesian and Newtonian mechanism in the second half of the eighteenth century. As Reill has shown, it is in the late Enlightenment that "we encounter natural philosophers vitalizing the world with living forces such as elective affinities, vital principles, sympathies, and formative drives."[15] Like Saint-Pierre, the vitalists paid close attention to "relation, *rapport, Verwandschaft,* cooperation of forces, and reciprocal interaction."[16] For Saint-Pierre, the theory of natural harmonies (or affinities) between an animal and its surroundings reflects both epistemological and aesthetic priorities: the naturalist must pay attention to natural harmonies not only because they provide a basis for understanding the workings of nature, but also because in them lies the true beauty of nature.

Yet when we see how expansive Saint-Pierre's conception of natural harmonies was, we begin to understand why he believed that the description of a single strawberry plant "would be sufficient to occupy all the naturalists in the world" (1:113). For even "in a clay pot, amid the fumes of Paris," the plant is home to slugs, butterflies, beetles, earthworms, wasps, bees,

---

14. Duflo, "Hussard," 8.
15. Reill, *Vitalizing Nature,* 7.
16. Ibid.

aphids, ants, and spiders. All of these insects would have to be included in a complete description of the plant, since "plants are the dwelling places of insects, and one cannot write the history of a city without speaking of its inhabitants" (1:106). If the strawberry plant were restored to its natural setting, "in the deep countryside, on the edge of the woods, or on the bank of a stream," the number of insects and animals frequenting it would be even greater and the circle of objects to be described even wider (1:107).

Yet Saint-Pierre's attention to natural relationships not only introduced a vertiginous expansion in the scope of natural history description. It also led him to consider the relationship between himself as a describer and the object of his description. This too reflected a broader trend among vitalist philosophers, for whom, as Reill explains, "the new conception of matter dissolved the strict distinction between observer and observed, since both were related within a much larger conjunction of living matter."[17] Saint-Pierre underlines this dissolution explicitly when he suddenly introduces the idea that the flies in his strawberry plant might be observing him: "Many were immobile, and were perhaps occupied, like myself, with observing" (1:106). The notion that the flies, like Saint-Pierre, have the capacity to observe nature, and that their perspective differs from that of the naturalist, changes the terms of natural history description. In Daubenton's descriptions, quadrupeds were treated as objects, to be manipulated, measured, and dissected, and there was no attempt to imagine what things might look like from their perspective. For Saint-Pierre, on the contrary, the strawberry plant cannot be described adequately without taking the flies' perspective into account: "It was not sufficient to observe [the plant] from my own level, so to speak, because in that case my science wouldn't have equaled that of the flies who occupied it" (1:107). What this means is that to describe from another perspective is to adopt a new science: in this case, the flies' sophisticated optical apparatus allows them to see in a manner that is simultaneously global and particular. Even using his microscope, Saint-Pierre cannot re-create their synthetic perspective: "My flies must have seen in a single glance, in my strawberry plant, a distribution and a collection of parts that I could only observe in my microscope separated from each other, and in succession" (1:108). Hence Saint-Pierre evokes the flies' perspective to criticize what Duflo terms "the excessive valorization,

---

17. Ibid.

since Descartes, of analysis, in favor of synthesis."[18] The "new science" of synthetic observation learned from the flies is consistent with the new approach to description elaborated in the *Études de la nature,* which involves both attention to natural context and disorienting shifts in perspective and scale.

Saint-Pierre offers an illustration of such shifts in perspective and scale when he incorporates a series of microscopic studies, both real and imagined, into his description of the strawberry plant:

> In studying the leaves of this plant, by means of a glass lens that magnified slightly, I found them to be divided into compartments bristling with hairs, separated by ducts, and strewn with glands. These compartments seemed to me like large carpets of greenery, their hairs like plants of a particular order, among which some were straight, others leaning, others forked, still others hollowed out into tubes, from the tips of which fell drops of liqueur; and their ducts, like their glands, seemed to me filled with a brilliant liquid. (1:108)

For Saint-Pierre, the shift in perspective and scale afforded by the magnifying glass opens up new levels of microcosm, with each leaf appearing to hold an entire field of microscopic plants just waiting to be described. These miniature plants must in turn be inhabited by microscopic beings, "who graze on the leaves of plants, like animals in our prairies, who sleep in the shade of their imperceptible hairs, and who drink from their sun-shaped glands liqueurs of gold and silver" (1:109). Here, Saint-Pierre gives his description a virtual dimension, extending the reach of natural history description beyond what can actually be observed with a magnifying glass.

This virtual dimension becomes even more pronounced when Saint-Pierre muses about how the (imagined) microscopic beings might view the flowers in his strawberry plant: "Each part of the flowers must offer them spectacles of which we have no idea. The flowers' yellow anthers, suspended from white filaments, present them with a pair of golden joists balanced on columns more beautiful than ivory; the corolla, vaults of ruby and topaz of an incomparable height; the nectars, rivers of sugar; the other flowering parts, cups, urns, pavilions, domes, that the human arts of architecture and

---

18. Duflo, "Hussard," 10.

metalworking haven't yet imitated" (1:110). Transforming the flowers' tiny organs of fructification into vast architectural structures, Saint-Pierre brings to his description the same "power of disproportion" that Barthes attributed to the *Encyclopédie* plates. For Barthes, the didacticism of the plates produced "a kind of overwhelming surrealism."[19] For Saint-Pierre, too, what began as a description intended to teach his readers about nature ends with an evocation of surreal perspectives that can only be imagined by the describer. In this sense, Chateaubriand, who was characterized by André Breton as a "surrealist in exoticism," was a direct descendant of Saint-Pierre, as indeed he claimed to be.[20]

But Saint-Pierre's evocation of virtual perspectives also sets the stage for a broader critique of the scientific methodology of his time. The microscopic beings "must see fluids ascending rather than descending; beading up rather than leveling out; and rising in the air rather than falling. Their ignorance must be as marvelous as their science" (1:110). Here, we can see that Saint-Pierre's habitual exaltation of ignorance was in fact grounded in a critique of scientific rationalism. Who was the naturalist, with his limited powers of observation, to claim that his science was superior to the "marvelous ignorance" of the flies? To study nature from a global perspective, in terms of its relationships, was to make room for new perspectives that might well unsettle the basic principles of the physical sciences: "Thus, as man comes closer to the elements of nature, the principles of his science fade away [s'évanouissent]" (1:111).

As we have seen, Saint-Pierre used the microscope and the magnifying glass to observe, imagine, and describe increasingly smaller levels of microcosm, thereby dramatically expanding the scope of natural history description and giving it a virtual dimension. But the principle of natural harmonies also required him to take a bird's-eye view of nature, and to consider the macroscopic network of natural harmonies connecting his strawberry plant to the entire globe. To complete his description, he would have to study the tiny plant in relation to the sun, the wind, the seasons, and the geography of all the places across the globe where it could be found, "from

---

19. Roland Barthes, "Les planches de l'*Encyclopédie*," in *Le degré zéro de l'écriture, suivi de Nouveaux essais critiques* (Paris: Seuil, 1972), 105.

20. André Breton, *Manifeste du surréalisme,* in *Oeuvres complètes,* ed. Marguerite Bonnet, Bibliothèque de la Pléiade 346 (Paris: Gallimard, 1988), 1:329.

the mountains of Kashmir, all the way to Archangel, and from the *Félices* mountain range in Norway all the way to the Kamchatka" (1:112). This geographical expansion, which reflects Saint-Pierre's passion for travel and travel writing, gives the naturalist an occasion to consider how different environments may have introduced variations into the strawberry plant's structure. In fact, Saint-Pierre's theory of natural harmonies, fanciful as it may sound to modern ears, was rooted in his sense that the environment impacts the physical makeup of plants and animals.

In the end, Saint-Pierre can only "conclude" his description of the strawberry plant by evoking all that remains to be described: "If one then considers that all these kinds, varieties, analogies, affinities, have in each latitude necessary relationships with a whole host of animals, and that these relationships are entirely unknown to us, one will see that the complete history of the strawberry plant would be sufficient to occupy all the naturalists in the world" (1:113). Indeed, a complete description would have to include not only the multiple varieties strewn across the globe ("Doesn't every latitude have its own?"), but also any plant bearing an analogical relationship to the strawberry plant "by the outline of its leaves,...by the shape of its flowers in bloom, and by that of its fruit" (1:113). This last remark adds an important new dimension to Saint-Pierre's theory of natural harmonies, one no less essential to his descriptive method than the shifts in perspective occasioned by observing the flies. Any resemblance between two plants, whether in terms of shape, color, smell, taste, or texture, itself constitutes for Saint-Pierre a natural harmony. This means that when the naturalist describes a plant from the Île-de-France by comparing it with a different plant found in Europe, he is not only making it easier for his readers to imagine a foreign plant, but also revealing an affinity or harmony between two points on the globe. Hence the analogical method introduced in Saint-Pierre's eleventh study, on plant harmonies, further reinforces the deep connections between scientific understanding and evocative description.

The Language of Flower Petals

Saint-Pierre's eleventh study, entitled "Application de quelques loix générales de la nature aux plantes" (Application of a Few General Laws of Nature to Plants), has been praised as "one of the best composed and best written of the book."[21] It is undoubtedly the most descriptive of the four-teen studies, consisting of an illustration of natural harmonies through examples drawn from vegetable life. As the "ruined" remains of Saint-Pierre's original project, this study takes the place of four of the five originally projected sections, which were to include studies of the earth, animals, and man. Once again, Saint-Pierre explains his decision to limit himself to this "light sketch" (in fact, the study runs some two hundred pages) as a function of his personal limitations: "I outlined at the very beginning of this work the immensity of the study of nature. There I proposed new perspectives to give us an idea of the order she established in all of her realms; but held back by my own insufficiency, I could only promise myself to trace a light sketch [une esquisse légère] of the order that exists in the vegetable realm" (2:97). But Saint-Pierre's specific choice of botany was in fact significant in several respects. First, botany represents the most important aspect of nature not covered in the *Histoire naturelle,* despite Buffon's original intentions and Daubenton's extensive contributions to the botanical articles in the *Encyclopédie.*[22] All of the projected sections dropped from the *Études de la nature,* in contrast, received ample treatment in the *Histoire naturelle,* in Buffon's influential history of the earth, in his anthropological discussion of human reproduction and races, and in the quadruped volumes. Thus, although Saint-Pierre claimed to set a new course for the study of nature, it seems that he did not wish to set that course in areas already covered by his illustrious predecessor.

Second, Saint-Pierre's choice of botany underlined his allegiance to Rousseau, whose passion for amateur botanizing had attained mythic status by the time of his death in 1778, and whose *Rêveries du promeneur solitaire* would be published in 1782. The two men first met in 1771, when Saint-Pierre had just returned from his trip to the Île-de-France and was seeking to pursue his newfound passion for botany on French soil.[23] He

---

21. "Avertissement des éditeurs," in *Études de la nature, extraits, Paul et Virginie,* by Jacques-Henri Bernardin de Saint-Pierre (Paris: Mignot, n.d.), 7.

22. On Daubenton's botanical articles, see Jeff Loveland, "Louis-Jean-Marie Daubenton and the *Encyclopédie,*" *Studies on Voltaire and the Eighteenth Century* 2003:12 (Oxford: Voltaire Foundation, 2003), 173–219.

23. Saint-Pierre developed his passion for botany during his nearly two-year stay on the Île-de-France, under the guidance of the island's intendant who was also an expert botanist, although the relationship apparently came to an abrupt end when the intendant discovered that Saint-Pierre was passionate not only about botany but also about the intendant's wife. René Herval,

found a willing interlocutor in Rousseau, who was at the time preparing a sort of correspondence course in botany, the *Lettres sur la botanique* (1771–74). Rousseau's influence on Saint-Pierre had both philosophical and literary dimensions. From a philosophical perspective, both thinkers criticized the materialist ideology of their time and asserted the primacy of sensation and sentiment in the study of nature. As Daniel Heller-Roazen has shown, such an assertion in fact belonged to a long philosophical tradition dating back to Aristotle, which identified a realm of perception, and even self-perception, that was shared by animals and humans alike and that was distinct from rational cognition. According to Heller-Roazen, this tradition was interrupted and in a certain sense obscured by Descartes, whose "definition of cogitation could not but transform the nature of sensation as it had been traditionally understood."[24] It is thus that we find Saint-Pierre attacking Cartesian tradition for its mechanistic treatment of animals, and in the same breath citing Rousseau's philosophy of sensibility:

> Famous philosophers, untrue to the testimony of their reason and conscience, dared to speak of [animals] as simple machines. They attribute to animals blind instincts that dictate all their actions in a uniform manner, without passion, without will, without choice, and even without any sensitivity [sensibilité] whatsoever. I once indicated my astonishment at this to J. J. Rousseau; I told him that it was quite strange that men of genius should have defended such an extravagant thesis. He answered me most wisely: *It's that when man begins to reason, he ceases to sense* [or feel: sentir]. (1:123–24)

In light of Heller-Roazen's account of the role of sensation in self-consciousness, we may interpret this passage not as a superficial "sentimentalist" rejection of reason, but as a deep-seated (and, paradoxically, well-reasoned) philosophical opposition to Cartesianism, consistent with Saint-Pierre's revised cogito "Je sens, donc j'existe" (3:109). It was also a view that owed more to Buffon than one might expect, since he accorded perception and even feeling (*sentiment*) to animals in the absence of rational thought.[25]

"Saint-Pierre (Jacques Henri Bernardin de)," *Dictionnaire des lettres françaises,* ed. Georges Grente, *Le XVIIIe siècle,* ed. François Moureau (1960; repr., Paris: Fayard, 1995), 1201.

24. Heller-Roazen, *Inner Touch,* 165.
25. Ibid., 281.

From a literary perspective, Saint-Pierre inherited Rousseau's belief that a new descriptive language was needed for the study of botany. Rousseau explored the difficulties of botanical description in his *Lettres sur la botanique,* written for his correspondent Madeleine-Catherine Delessert, who wished to introduce her young daughter to the study of plants.[26] In responding to Delessert's initial request for a catalog of familiar plants, Rousseau notes in his first letter that her ignorance of botany will make it impossible for her to understand any descriptive catalog he might send her:

> You have asked me for a little catalog of the most well-known plants with marks by which to recognize them [avec des marques pour les reconnoitre]. There is some difficulty in that; it is to give you in writing these marks or characters [ces marques ou caractéres] in a manner that is clear and yet not too diffuse. This seems to me impossible without using the language of the thing [la langue de la chose], and the terms of that language form a vocabulary that you wouldn't be able to recognize, if it hasn't been previously explained to you. (1151)

The problem posed here has obvious implications beyond the amateur study of botany: Rousseau is asking in effect how to establish the foundations for a descriptive language without prior knowledge of nature. Overall, his musings on the problem suggest that our knowledge of language is inextricable from our knowledge of the world. If Rousseau begins by explaining the basic terms of botany, without pictures or plant samples, he fears that his lessons will be too abstract for his pupil to follow them: "I am afraid that up to this point we have treated [botany] in a manner that is too abstract; by not applying our ideas to clearly determined objects" (1191). Yet from afar (since this is a correspondence course), Rousseau cannot point his pupil to specific examples, since she does not yet have enough knowledge to identify the plants he might refer to in his letters.

In response to this apparently insoluble problem, Rousseau devises an ingenious solution. He instructs his pupil to pick two samples of each plant

---

26. Jean-Jacques Rousseau, *Lettres sur la botanique,* in *Oeuvres complètes,* vol. 4, ed. Bernard Gagnebin and Marcel Raymond, Bibliothèque de la Pléiade 208 (Paris: Gallimard, 1969), 1149–97. Subsequent references appear parenthetically in the main text.

she wishes to study: "a larger one to be kept, and a smaller one to be sent to me" (1195). Once she has collected about twelve pairs of this kind, she must assign a number to each pair and send the smaller samples to her teacher. He will then identify, name, and describe each plant and send his numbered descriptions back to her. Using the numbers, she will match each of Rousseau's descriptions with the corresponding sample preserved in her herbarium. Only then, when the sample plants have been definitively named and described, can she use her herbarium to identify the plants she encounters in nature. With this strategy, Rousseau effectively circumvents the problem of describing unfamiliar plants to his pupil. No longer will the study of botany demand of her "a tiresome concentration on an imaginary object," nor of himself "difficult descriptions that could have been replaced by a single glance" (1191). With both pupil and teacher secure in the knowledge that they are looking at the same plant, the two correspondents can begin to converse and understand each other with ease: "If each of us on our end can have the same thing before our eyes, we will understand each other perfectly when speaking of what we see" (1191). In other words, description will come into play only once a firm referential basis for descriptive language has been established.

Thus Rousseau's ingenious double herbarium uses things, rather than words, to establish the foundations for a descriptive language. Yet it does gesture toward the symbolic encoding of plants in the reduced size of the samples sent to the teacher. Rousseau takes this symbolic encoding one step further when he devises his "Caractères de botanique," a set of characters that is to serve as a kind of shorthand for botanical description (see figure 3).[27] Unlike the vocabulary of botany, which Roussesau found "too abstract" for his purposes, these characters imitate the visual structures of the plants they represent. They do not, however, allow the reader to see the plants in all of their detail. Like the small samples sent to Rousseau, they are useful only to experienced botanists already familiar with the plants in question. They can thus be subjected to the critique Daubenton levels against descriptive nomenclature in his *Encyclopédie* article "Botanique." Nomenclature can never replace complete description, Daubenton contends, because

---

27. On Rousseau's symbolic languages, see Alexandra Cook, "Rousseau and the Languages of Music and Botany," in *Musique et langage chez Rousseau,* ed. Claude Dauphin, Studies on Voltaire and the Eighteenth Century 2004:08 (Oxford: Voltaire Foundation, 2004), 75–87.

Caractères de Botanique — Racines

Planta, vegetabilia, regnum vegetabile	Radix
Planta in Specie vel individuo	Radicula
Botanica	Radicatus, radicans
Botanicus	Radicale
Arbor	Napiformis
Arborescens arboreus	fusiformis
Herba. herbosus Herbaceus	filiformis
Frutex	Difformis
Suffrutex	Simplex
Fruticans Fruticosus	Repens
Perennis	Fibra fibrilla
Biennis	Fibrosa us um
Annuus	Capillus
Lignum	Capillatus
Lignosus	Capillaris
Grandes familles	Tuber
Palma	Tuberosa us um
Filix	Tuberculus
Muscus	Tuberculatus
Lichen	Bulbus
Alga	Bulbosus
Fungus	Bulbillus
Lilium	Tunica
Liliaceus	Tunicatus
Gramen Gramineus	Præmorsus a um
	Radix ramosa
	ramificatio

Figure 3. Manuscript page of Jean-Jacques Rousseau's "Caractères de botanique." Reproduced with permission of the Bibliothèque publique et universitaire de Neuchâtel (Ms R 21, fo 46, recto verso).

it does not serve the needs of a person who encounters an unfamiliar plant for the first time:

> If he begins by informing himself of the name of the plant he will not gain any insight from it, because the name of a thing we are unfamiliar with cannot bring any ideas into our minds. It is therefore necessary that he observe the plant, that he study it, & that he form a distinct idea of it; he will achieve this by seeing it, & if he expounds it, if he describes everything he has seen, he will communicate to others the knowledge he has acquired. Then the name will serve as a sign to recall the idea of this plant to himself & to those who have read the description: but it is impossible that a name ever stand in the place of a description; this sign can recall the idea of a known thing [une chose connue], but it cannot give the idea of an unknown thing.[28]

Like Rousseau's botanical symbols, nomenclature is according to Daubenton a form of shorthand for complete descriptions. Yet no matter how much information botanists attempt to include in plant names, even incorporating "a little part of the description...that they call the phrase," nomenclature can only ever reinforce knowledge previously acquired through a combination of observation and description.[29]

Saint-Pierre discusses the botanical characters in his eleventh study, claiming that Rousseau himself was ultimately dissatisfied with them because they could provide only the most schematic of representations:

> J. J. Rousseau showed to me one day a sort of algebraic characters he had devised to express the colors and shapes of plants with great brevity. Some of them represented the shapes of flowers, others those of leaves, still others those of fruits. They were in the shape of a heart, a triangle, a lozenge, etc. He used just nine or ten of these signs to form the expression of a plant. However ingenious and efficient this method was, he told me that he had given up on it, because it presented him only with skeletons. This sentiment was appropriate in a man whose taste equaled his genius, and may give cause for thought to those who want to offer abbreviations of all things, especially of nature's works. (2:351)

---

28. Louis-Jean-Marie Daubenton, "Botanique," *Encyclopédie,* ARTFL, 2:341.
29. Ibid.

Like Rousseau, Saint-Pierre seeks "a manner that is clear and yet not too diffuse" to describe plants, and it is for this reason that he admires Rousseau's botanical characters. Nonetheless, in keeping with Daubenton's critique of nomenclature, he insists that such "abbreviations" can be useful only once a complete description has been written: "After all, these characters could not be rendered precisely if the qualities of each plant were not first determined exactly in words: otherwise, the language of botanists, which is criticized today for speaking only to the ear, would make itself understood only to the eyes" (2:352). This leaves Saint-Pierre facing the same question posed at the beginning of the *Lettres sur la botanique:* what can serve as the proper basis for a new descriptive language in botany?

In an implicit criticism of the Linnean tradition of botanical description, Saint-Pierre begins his eleventh study by asserting that botany lacks any adequate descriptive vocabulary to express the harmonies of plant life:

> We are still so new to the study of nature that our languages lack the terms to express the most common harmonies: this is so true that however exact the descriptions of plants made by the most capable botanists may be, it is impossible to recognize [those plants] in the countryside if one hasn't already seen them in nature, or at least in a herbarium. Those who consider themselves the most capable in botany have only to attempt to paint on paper a plant they have never seen, on the basis of an exact description by the greatest masters; they will see how much their copy differs from the original. (2:349)

The standard to which Saint-Pierre holds botanical description is specifically geared toward nonspecialist readers: on the basis of a description, the reader must be able not only to recognize a familiar plant but also to depict an unfamiliar plant accurately without ever having seen the original. This standard reflects both Saint-Pierre's distaste for the Linnean tradition and his personal experience of describing unfamiliar plants from the Île-de-France to his European readers.

Yet the descriptive method outlined in the eleventh study is not limited to the study of botany: "The little I will say about it can be used to express oneself not only in botany and in the other natural sciences, but in all the arts where we are lacking at each moment terms to render the nuances and shapes of objects" (2:352). The method essentially consists of describing unfamiliar objects by making analogies to familiar ones, with an emphasis on the shared sensations evoked by the two objects; it is, as Saint-Pierre expresses it, "to describe nature through images and common sensations" (2:359). On one level, this method clearly owes something to Saint-Pierre's contact with colonial culture during his stay on the Île-de-France, since European colonists frequently named exotic plants by analogy to European ones.[30] Saint-Pierre thus gives credit to several popular travel writers in outlining his method:

> It is with comparisons [rapprochemens] of this kind that the Englishman Dampier and the Father du Tertre have given us, to my taste, the most accurate impressions of the fruits and flowers that grow in the tropics, by linking them [les rapportant] to the flowers and fruits of our climates. Dampier, for example, to describe the banana, compares it, stripped of its thick, five-planed skin, to a fat sausage; its texture and color, to fresh butter in winter; its taste, to a mixture of apple and Bon Chrétien pear, which melts in the mouth like marmalade. When this traveler speaks to you of a good fruit from the Indies, he makes your mouth water. (2:357–58)

Saint-Pierre clearly acknowledges here that he has inherited his descriptive method from the travel literature that was his favorite reading. On another level, though, his analogical method reflects the epistemological transformations ushered in by the movement of vitalism. As Reill notes, "Analogical reasoning became the functional replacement for mathematical analysis. With it one could discover similar properties or tendencies between dissimilar things that approximated natural laws without dissolving the particular into the general."[31] Saint-Pierre's particular contribution to this broad trend was to make explicit its implications for descriptive writing: through analogy the describer could reveal hidden affinities and the underlying natural laws that motivated them. He could also convey a full, sensorial impression (making the reader's mouth water) in just a few words, thereby avoiding both the skeletal abbreviations of Rousseau's symbols and the piecemeal presentation of Daubenton's measurement tables.

For Saint-Pierre, one of the principal advantages of analogical description was that it conveyed information all at once ("tout d'un coup") rather

---

30. Baudry, "Un aspect mauricien," 783.
31. Reill, *Vitalizing Nature,* 8.

than breaking it down into a series of successively presented parts: "These comparisons [rapprochemens] are also very useful in that they present the whole [l'ensemble] of the unknown object, without which we cannot form a clear idea of it. It is one of the defects of botany that it presents us with the characters of plants only in succession; it doesn't assemble them; it decomposes them" (2:362). Echoing Buffon's *De l'art d'écrire,* this critique of botanical description targets not only Linnaeus but also the practice of anatomical description in the quadruped volumes of the *Histoire naturelle.* Indeed, Saint-Pierre's analogical method can be seen as a response to the methodological tensions surrounding description in the *Histoire naturelle.*[32]

Saint-Pierre also echoes Buffon when he underlines the difficulty of describing subtle nuances in color, a task no less essential in botany than in ornithology. Whereas Buffon addressed this difficulty by replacing verbal descriptions with color plates in the *Histoire naturelle des oiseaux,* Saint-Pierre instead deplores the inadequate verbal palettes of his fellow botanists: "They get by with vague and indefinite expressions, such as blackish, grey, ash colored, brown, which they express, if the truth be told, using Greek or Latin words. But these words often serve only to distort their images, by representing nothing at all" (2:355). In place of such obscure and imprecise terms, Saint-Pierre proposes that colors be described by analogy to familiar forms of vegetable life. This descriptive palette would have the advantage of being more evocative, precise, and accessible than the traditional vocabulary of learned botany: "Thus, instead of saying in Latin, a blackish yellow or an ashlike color, to determine some particular nuance of color in the arts or in nature, one would say a yellow the color of a dried walnut or a grey of the bark of a beech tree. These expressions would be all the more exact, that nature invariably uses these sorts of shades in plants as determining characteristics and as signs of maturity, vitality, or decline, and that our peasants recognize the various kinds of wood in our forests

---

32. The critique of Daubenton becomes more explicit when Saint-Pierre takes up the example of human portraiture, claiming that it is impossible to describe a man by cataloging his traits: "Try to describe a man feature by feature, limb by limb; no matter how exact you are, you will never make his portrait for me: but if you compare him to some well-known personage, if you tell me, for example, that he has the size and the neck of Don Quixote, the nose of Saint Charles Borromée, etc., you will paint him for me in four words. It is the whole of an object that ignorant people, that is to say, almost all men, first pay attention to in order to know something." Bernardin de Saint-Pierre, *Études,* 2:363.

by simply inspecting their bark" (2:355–56). Like the comparison between a banana and a fat sausage, Saint-Pierre's coloristic analogies have the advantage of using terms that are familiar to most readers, and that create a distinct impression quickly and efficiently: "If you tell me that [the bark of a tree] resembles that of an oak tree, I grasp the nuance all at once [tout d'un coup]" (2:362). Still, it must be acknowledged that analogies of this kind still depend on the reader's knowledge of nature. Whereas peasants may be receptive to an extremely broad palette of descriptive terms (since they can recognize a tree by looking at its bark), readers from a Parisian salon may understand far fewer terms or may have only a vague notion of their nuance. More generally, the success of the analogical method requires that describer and reader share some common knowledge of nature, without which the describer cannot relate foreign objects to familiar ones.

Saint-Pierre's extended discussion of color also makes it clear that he intends, in keeping with his use of painterly metaphors throughout the *Études de la nature,* to rival the painter with his new descriptive vocabulary. As things stand, he claims, neither verbal language nor painting can capture the multiple shades of white found in nature: "Although we have only a single term white to express the color white, nature presents many different varieties to us. Painting, on this point, is just as barren as language" (2:352). In support of this claim, Saint-Pierre offers the example of an unnamed Italian painter who, in an attempt to represent three figures clothed in different shades of white, found himself obliged to place a tree in the middle of his painting so that one figure was in full shade, the second in partial shade, and the third in bright sunlight: "This is indeed what painters do in such cases. They diversify their whites with shadows, with intermediate shades and reflections; but these whites are not pure and are always altered with yellow, blue, green, or grey" (2:353). Nature, in contrast, can "use several kinds [of white] without corrupting their purity, by marking them with dots [les pointillant], by making them grainy [les chagrinant], by striping them or polishing them, etc. . . . Thus the whites of the lily, the daisy, the narcissus, the anemone nemorosa, the hyacinth, are all different from one another" (2:353). By using the names of these flowers, the describer can express the nuances found in nature and thereby surpass the art of painting.

Nonetheless, we are still faced here with the problem of how to establish a firm referential basis for descriptive vocabulary without prior knowledge of nature. Saint-Pierre acknowledges this, noting that his readers may not be familiar with, or sensitive to, the subtle differences in color between a daisy, hyacinth, and lily. Thus, even as he suggests that flower petals be used as the basis for a new descriptive vocabulary, he ends up describing those same flower petals through analogies to other objects: "The white of the daisy has something of the shepherdess's wimple; that of the hyacinth takes after ivory; and that of the lily, semitransparent and crystalline, resembles porcelain paste. I believe therefore that we can link [rapporter] all the whites produced by nature or by the arts to those of our flower petals. We would thus have in plants a scale of nuances of the purest white" (2:353). This passage makes it clear that Saint-Pierre's analogical method is not immune to the referential instability of language. If porcelain must be described in terms of petals, and petals in terms of porcelain, there is no guarantee that either comparison will communicate fine coloristic distinctions to the reader. Nonetheless, what matters most to Saint-Pierre is that a relationship (or harmony) between two things has been established. It is significant, in this case, that the relationship is one between nature and the arts, rather than between two aspects of nature. Thus Saint-Pierre's musings on descriptive language in general, and coloristic vocabulary in particular, take him beyond the realm of purely natural harmonies and into the complex network of relations between nature and culture. This move reflects the broader evolution of the *Études de la nature* as a project, which included in the end not only *Paul et Virginie* but also studies on education and on the ills of society.

On one level, then, Saint-Pierre's descriptive project was an attempt to found a "natural" descriptive vocabulary and to sidestep the barriers imposed by technical and learned language. Subscribing to what Murray Krieger called "the illusion of the natural sign," Saint-Pierre dreamed of a dictionary made up not of words but of plants: "Thus not only botany but all the arts could find in plants an inexhaustible dictionary of constant colors, which would be in no way burdened by barbarous and technical composite terms, but which would constantly present new images" (2:339).[33] This utopian language reflects Saint-Pierre's preoccupation with referential stability, a preoccupation also in evidence in Rousseau's double

---

33. Murray Krieger, *Ekphrasis: The Illusion of the Natural Sign* (Baltimore: Johns Hopkins University Press, 1992).

herbarium and in his botanical characters. And indeed, Saint-Pierre held botanical description to a strict referential standard, maintaining that the reader should be able to make an accurate sketch of an unfamiliar plant on the basis of a description.

On another level, however, Saint-Pierre's project sought less to fix a descriptive vocabulary than to establish relationships, or analogies, between things that were different but ultimately related. These analogies could be between two objects (the banana and the sausage) or between two terms for the color white ("porcelain paste" and "lily petal"), but they ultimately resided in the "common sensations" evoked by language and things alike. Saint-Pierre thus granted description the ultimate power of establishing a harmonic relationship between nature and language. The describer was no longer a mere copyist of nature, whose representation was necessarily inferior to the original. Both a poet and a scientist, he was charged not only with revealing the underlying affinities that order nature, but also with tapping into the mysterious connections between words and things.

* * *

Even in his own time, critics were quick to praise Saint-Pierre's evocative descriptions while denigrating his scientific theories. One such critic, quoted by Saint-Pierre in his 1789 preface to *Paul et Virginie,* put it as follows: "His supreme talent for painting nature must suffice to his glory, and he can better than another dispense with the merit of explaining it well."[34] It cannot be denied that Saint-Pierre was an amateur scientist whose theories lagged behind the major scientific advancements of his time.[35] Nevertheless, we should take him seriously when he contends that the beauty of his descriptions is inextricable from the theory of natural harmonies that underpins them. To a critic who praised his style but dismissed the theory of natural harmonies, Saint-Pierre responds: "I therefore dare to believe that I do not owe the success of the physical truths I have shown to my

---

34. Saint-Pierre cites this unnamed critic in an additional preface added to *Paul et Virginie* in 1789. See "Avis sur cette édition," in *Paul et Virginie,* ed. Robert Mauzi (1966; repr., Paris: Flammarion, 1992), 208.

35. Colas Duflo notes that Saint-Pierre can be considered "very behind with respect to the science of his time," but interprets this in terms of his critique of reason and the "disenchantement" of modern science. Duflo, "Hussard," 9–10.

style, but rather the success of my style to those same truths. I owe this success not to my personal emotions, but to the general sentiment of nature [au sentiment général de la nature], which influences my readers as much as it does me. Whoever senses [or feels] nature well translates it, and whoever translates it explains it [Qui sent bien la nature la traduit, et qui la traduit l'explique]."[36] Saint-Pierre's claim that the merit of his descriptions does not spring from his personal emotions, but rather from a general sentiment of nature, deserves particular attention, given the traditional association between his descriptive aesthetic and that of the romantics. If Saint-Pierre can be linked to various figures of the early romantic period, it is not because he viewed description as a conduit for lyric self-expression. Rather, it is because of his ambitious attempt to move scientific understanding toward a synthetic view of nature that could be attained, albeit only in a fragmented form, through aesthetic appreciation. This was the Saint-Pierre admired by the German naturalist and explorer Alexander von Humboldt, for whom, as Reill conveys it, "True natural philosophy was founded upon aesthetic appreciation, not upon the assumption that the mind's operation provided the model for nature. Thus, though science began with analysis, it ended with a creative, though not absolute, synthesis, using the evocative power of poetics."[37] Saint-Pierre's fragmented encyclopedia can also be linked to Novalis's *Das Allgemeine Brouillon* (1798–99), generally known in English as *The Universal Brouillon,* but also translated as *Notes for a Romantic Encyclopedia.*[38] Like Novalis, Saint-Pierre could only ever provide a working draft or studies for the vast encyclopedic work he envisioned.

For Saint-Pierre, describing nature was not a means of describing the self. Rather, it was a means of participating in the general sentiment of nature that for him made scientific understanding inseparable from aesthetic appreciation. Hence Saint-Pierre enjoins the naturalist to view nature as a

36. Bernardin de Saint-Pierre, *Paul et Virginie,* 211.

37. Reill, *Vitalizing Nature,* 243. See also 241 and 254, where Reill argues against one-sided interpretations of Alexander von Humboldt as a romantic, choosing to qualify him instead as "the greatest and probably the last of the Enlightenment vitalists." Mary Louise Pratt notes that Saint-Pierre was one of von Humboldt's "idols." Mary Louise Pratt, *Imperial Eyes: Travel Writing and Transculturation* (New York: Routledge, 1992), 138.

38. Novalis, *Notes for a Romantic Encyclopedia: Das Allgemeine Brouillon,* ed. and trans. David W. Wood (Albany: State University of New York Press, 2007).

painter, and to attend to the feelings of aesthetic pleasure that signal underlying harmonies in nature: "It suffices for me to recommend that naturalists study nature as great painters do; that is to say, by bringing together
the harmonies of the three realms.... Here is a sure means of recognizing
them: each time a natural object presents you with a feeling of pleasure,
you can be certain that it is offering you some harmonic concert [quelque
concert harmonique]" (2:261). The reader, too, should attend to the feelings of aesthetic pleasure evoked by a description, for they signal the presence of natural harmonies perceived by the describer and communicated
to the reader. They also serve to establish the most important harmony revealed by Saint-Pierre's descriptions, that between language and nature. It
is for this reason, above all, that Saint-Pierre's stunning descriptions must
be read in conjunction with the scientific project that gave them their full
meaning.

PART II

ENCYCLOPEDIAS

3

Diderot's Word Machine

The description of artisanal machines and techniques was central to Denis Diderot and Jean d'Alembert's *Encyclopédie* (1751–72) from its inception. In his 1750 "Prospectus," Diderot characterized the articles on the mechanical arts as the most difficult and unprecedented part of the project: "Perhaps never before have there been so many difficulties joined together, and so little assistance to overcome them."[1] While the full nature of these difficulties will only become apparent by the end of this chapter, a few major points can already be outlined here. First, unlike the sciences and the liberal arts, the mechanical arts stood, according to Diderot, in a special relationship to written expression, because their practitioners were not writers and

---

1. Denis Diderot, "Prospectus," in *Oeuvres complètes,* ed. Herbert Dieckmann, Jacques Proust, and Jean Varloot, vol. 5, *Encyclopédie I,* ed. John Lough and Jacques Proust (Paris: Hermann, 1976), 99. This edition will be abbreviated as DPV in subsequent notes.

could not in most cases describe their crafts.[2] This meant that Diderot's general principle for the *Encyclopédie*—that experts should be called upon to write articles within their own fields of knowledge—was rarely respected for the mechanical arts. As the "Prospectus" makes clear, it was Diderot himself, in his capacity as principal editor, who was to compensate for the artisans' inability to translate their knowledge into writing. Thus, although he frequently downplayed his role as editor, Diderot emphasized the key philosophical role he played with respect to the artisans: "the function that Socrates gloried in, the difficult and delicate function of assisting the birth of minds [faire accoucher les esprits], *obstetrix animorum.*"[3] Yet in order to perform this act of midwifery, Diderot had first to acquire an empirical knowledge of the mechanical arts, becoming an apprentice to the artisans just as they learned the art of expression from him: "In several cases, it was thus necessary to procure the machines, to reconstruct them, to put one's hand to the work, to become an apprentice, so to speak, and to make inferior pieces of work in order to teach others how to make superior ones."[4] Hence the articles on the mechanical arts became the site of an encounter (and exchange) between two kinds of knowledge: Diderot's ability to describe things, and the artisans' ability to manufacture them.

Second, the mechanical arts stood in a special relationship to time. As Daniel Rosenberg has argued, "For Diderot, the question of how to construct an encyclopedia is crucially a question of how to construct an encyclopedia in (historical) time."[5] This question was particularly acute for the mechanical arts, because the rapid progress of technological (and linguistic) change in this domain threatened to make articles describing specific machines and techniques obsolete even before they had been printed. Diderot underscored this in one of his many poignant references to his "wasted" efforts on behalf of the *Encyclopédie:* "Imagine that a man consumes part of his life describing the [mechanical] arts; that, weary of this tiresome task, he lets himself be drawn into more amusing and less useful activities,

---

2. On "artisanal literacy," "artisanal epistemology," and embodied knowledge, see Pamela H. Smith, *The Body of the Artisan: Art and Experience in the Scientific Revolution* (Chicago: University of Chicago Press, 2004).

3. Diderot, "Prospectus," DPV, 100.

4. Ibid.

5. Daniel Rosenberg, "An Eighteenth-Century Time Machine: The *Encyclopedia* of Denis Diderot," *Historical Reflections/Réflexions historiques* 25, no. 2 (1999): 229.

and that his initial work remains hidden in his portfolio: within less than twenty years, in the place of new and curious things, striking in their singularity, interesting by virtue of their uses, the reigning taste, a momentary importance, he will find only incorrect notions, outdated maneuvers, machines either imperfect or abandoned."[6] Hence, in dealing with the mechanical arts, the encyclopedist was torn between the urgency of keeping pace with technological changes and the tiresome and labor-intensive effort of describing machines and techniques. More than any other pages in the *Encyclopédie*, the articles on the mechanical arts are threatened by what Rosenberg calls Diderot's "acute sense of time's presence and evanescence," both because technology evolves so rapidly and because writing technical descriptions takes so much time.[7]

Third, the articles on the mechanical arts stood in a special relationship to the plates that accompanied them. In her edition of Diderot's major *Encyclopédie* articles, Marie Leca-Tsiomis justifies the scarcity of articles on the mechanical arts by noting that "Diderot's articles in this domain are usually long and the plates are necessary to read them, even though [the plates] were originally published separately, and subsequently to the volumes of text."[8] This justification suggests a disjunction between our reading of the articles on the mechanical arts and that of Diderot's contemporaries: whereas we find the articles unreadable without the plates, subscribers to the *Encyclopédie* originally encountered them without the "assistance" of images. Of course, the problem of temporal delays was a broader phenomenon in an encyclopedia published over two decades, as Diderot acknowledged when he noted that the system of cross-references could be handled effectively only if he had the entire work at his disposal from the beginning.[9] Yet this problem was particularly acute for the articles on the mechanical arts: either they required supplementary images to be read at all or they managed to circumvent the need for images, in a way that might make the subsequent publication of the plates superfluous.

---

6. Denis Diderot, "Encyclopédie," in *Oeuvres complètes,* ed. Herbert Dieckmann, Jacques Proust, and Jean Varloot, vol. 7, *Encyclopédie III (Lettres D-L),* ed. John Lough and Jacques Proust (Paris: Hermann, 1976), 183. Subsequent references appear parenthetically in the main text.

7. Rosenberg, "Eighteenth-Century Time Machine," 233.

8. Denis Diderot, *Choix d'articles de l'"Encyclopédie,"* ed. Marie Leca-Tsiomis (Paris: Comité des travaux historiques et scientifiques, 2001), 40 n. 20.

9. Diderot, "Encyclopédie," DPV, 228.

Fourth, the articles on the mechanical arts stood in a special relationship to knowledge. On one level, they were the most concretely representational articles in the *Encyclopédie,* describing in painstaking detail the machines, tools, and techniques that went into artisanal production. They appeared, in other words, to offer readers concrete knowledge of things in the world. On another level, however, they hid that knowledge in a shroud of technical language and artisanal expertise. As Diderot acknowledged in his "Prospectus," it was difficult to acquire knowledge of the mechanical arts without working on actual machines.[10] This is not to say that the articles on the mechanical arts did not produce knowledge; but they seemed to produce it in a different way than the miniature model of the stocking machine that Diderot is said to have taken apart and rebuilt repeatedly in order to understand the workings of the actual machine.

David Bates has argued that encyclopedic order in the *Encyclopédie* (as exemplified by the metaphor of the *mappemonde*) is self-consciously arbitrary but serves the epistemological function of revealing truths that cannot be perceived in the messiness of empirical inquiry.[11] This argument has important implications for the epistemological status of description in the *Encyclopédie,* since Diderot compares the multiple possibilities for ordering human knowledge to the multiple perspectives from which a machine can be described. As Bates suggests with respect to cartographic order, changes in perspective and scale are crucial for getting a handle on aspects of experience that would otherwise escape the limited grasp of human knowledge. Thus, if Diderot's descriptions of machines do in fact reproduce the problem of ordering knowledge in miniature, they may offer alternative solutions to the problem of encyclopedic order from those proposed in more programmatic texts such as d'Alembert's "Discours préliminaire" or Diderot's "Encyclopédie."

The articles on the mechanical arts may also provide an occasion for exploring the relationship, and possible disjunction, between words and things in a way that is crucial to the *Encyclopédie* as a whole. Questioning

---

10. Diderot, "Prospectus," DPV, 100.

11. David W. Bates, "Cartographic Aberrations: Epistemology and Order in the Encyclopedic Map," in *Using the "Encyclopédie": Ways of Knowing, Ways of Reading,* ed. Daniel Brewer and Julie Candler Hayes, Studies on Voltaire and the Eighteenth Century 2002:5 (Oxford: Voltaire Foundation, 2002), 1–20.

Foucault's characterization of encyclopedic order as a "homogenous order...which reduces identity to 'relations' on one systematic 'table' of reality," Bates insists on the heuristic value of encyclopedic order, when understood as Diderot and d'Alembert themselves conceived of it, as "a tool for provoking knowledge, not fixing it in one place."[12] Although we generally think of encyclopedic description as fixing knowledge through concrete representation, Bates's interpretation encourages us to consider how description might instead function as a heuristic device, as a virtual perspective that reveals something about our relationship to objects, or about the relationship between words and objects, that we cannot perceive in our everyday experience of them.

Describing the Infinite Machine

In his article "Encyclopédie," Diderot draws an important analogy between encyclopedic order and description.[13] More specifically, he compares the multiple systems for ordering human knowledge to the multiple perspectives from which a complex machine can be described:

> In general, the description of a machine can be started from any given part. The bigger and more complicated the machine is, the more connections there will be between its parts, the less familiar we will be with those connections, the more different outlines of descriptions we will have. What will it be then if the machine is infinite in every sense; if it is a question of the real universe and the intelligible universe, or of a work that is like an imprint of both? The real or intelligible universe can be represented from an infinite number of points of view, and the number of possible systems of human knowledge is as great as the number of these points of view. (211)

In fact, there are not two but three terms in Diderot's analogy, all of which are central to the *Encyclopédie:* describing a complex machine, representing

12. Ibid., 4.

13. On the "Encyclopédie" article, see Christie V. McDonald, "The Utopia of the Text: Diderot's 'Encyclopédie,'" *The Eighteenth Century: Theory and Interpretation* 21, no. 2 (1980): 128–44; Wilda Anderson, "Encyclopedic Topologies," *Modern Language Notes* 101, no. 4 (1986): 912–29; and Bates, "Cartographic Aberrations."

nature in its entirety, and ordering human knowledge. All three activities pose the problem of order, since the machine, nature, and knowledge can all be represented from multiple points of view. The "part" from which one starts the description is necessarily arbitrary and reflects the limited nature of human perspectives. As Diderot argues here and elsewhere, the only view that escapes the arbitrariness of human perspectives is that of God. Bates has drawn out the implications of this passage for Diderot's view of encyclopedic order as an arbitrary but nonetheless epistemologically valuable device that allows us to perceive some of the "'imperceptible nuances' that interconnect reality."[14] But the passage also sheds light on the epistemological status of description in the *Encyclopédie,* for it suggests that Diderot views the description of a machine not primarily as a catalog of its parts, but rather as an attempt to uncover the imperceptible connections among those parts. In its focus on hidden connections, this conception of description runs counter to Foucault's account of description in the classical episteme as a representational "grid" that focuses solely on "lines, surfaces, forms, reliefs," rather than hidden depths or internal workings.[15]

Diderot's analogy between encyclopedic order and description also raises the question of whether description must in fact limit itself to a single perspective. A number of critical studies have emphasized the many complementary (and at times competing) encyclopedic orders at work in the *Encyclopédie,* from the alphabetic order to the three human faculties of memory, reason, and imagination to the system of cross-references that has the potential both to reveal unexpected connections and to undermine the stability of the other systems. Close attention has also been paid to the various metaphors Diderot and d'Alembert use to characterize encyclopedic order, from the tree of human knowledge to the labyrinth to the world map to the broad avenue.[16] If we take Diderot's analogy between encyclopedic order and description seriously, we must then envision an

---

14. Bates, "Cartographic Aberrations," 16.

15. Foucault, *Mots et choses,* 145.

16. See Bates, "Cartographic Aberrations"; and Claudia Moscovici, "Beyond the Particular and the Universal: D'Alembert's 'Discours préliminaire' to the *Encyclopédie,"* *Eighteenth-Century Studies* 33, no. 3 (2000): 383–400. For an earlier discussion of the labyrinth metaphor, see Pierre Saint-Amand, *Diderot: Le labyrinthe de la relation* (Paris: J. Vrin, 1984), 62–82. See also Robert Darnton's classic essay, "Philosophers Trim the Tree of Knowledge: The Epistemological Strategy of the *Encyclopédie,"* in *The Great Cat Massacre and Other Episodes in French Cultural History* (New York: Basic Books, 1984), 191–213.

approach to description that juxtaposes or combines different perspectives in order to reveal hidden connections. And, to pursue the analogy further, we would have to consider that these perspectives might not only complement each other, like building blocks leading to the construction of a single structure, but might also erase or reconfigure earlier perspectives, just as a cross-reference can sometimes nuance or undercut the straightforward "truths" presented in a given article. In this sense, Diderot's analogy between encyclopedic order and description has implications not only for how descriptions may be written, but also, and perhaps more fundamentally, for how they should be read.[17]

At the same time, both Bates and Claudia Moscovici have emphasized the extent to which encyclopedic order provides a "philosophical bird's eye view" of nature and knowledge.[18] The metaphor of the world map, or *mappemonde,* implies a change in perspective (for Bates a "virtual perspective") that removes the philosopher from the labyrinth of empiricism and allows him to perceive connections that remain imperceptible from a closer vantage point. Yet this bird's-eye view is only epistemologically valuable when it is combined with the empirical specificity of more local perspectives within the labyrinth. Hence Moscovici, countering the characterization of d'Alembert's work as epistemologically closed, interprets d'Alembert's epistemology as an innovative combination of universalism and particularism.[19] Once again, these interpretations raise the question of what might constitute a bird's-eye perspective in description, and how it might be combined with more local, messy, and empirical perspectives. This question recalls the methodological tension between broad theories of nature and detailed empirical studies of nature in Buffon's work, which Reill associates with a broader "creative tension" in Enlightenment thought.[20]

The final aspect of Diderot's analogy between encyclopedic order and description that merits emphasis is the presence of man in the *Encyclopédie.* In his "Encyclopédie" article, Diderot stresses that man must serve as an animating presence within the *Encyclopédie:* "Above all, there

---

17. This interpretation is in line with the connection between ways of knowing and reading drawn in Daniel Brewer and Julie Candler Hayes's collection of essays, *Using the "Encyclopédie."*

18. Moscovici, "Beyond the Particular," 392.

19. Ibid., 387 n. 11.

20. Reill, *Vitalizing Nature,* 238–39.

is a consideration that must not be lost from view; it is that if we banish man or the thinking and contemplative being from the surface of the earth, this pathetic and sublime spectacle of nature is no longer anything but a desolate and mute scene. The universe falls quiet; silence and night take hold of it. Everything is transformed into a vast solitude where unobserved phenomena occur in an obscure and subdued manner" (212). Once again, to the extent that the description of a complicated machine serves as a microcosm for the *Encyclopédie* as a whole, this passage suggests that the describer must emerge as an animating presence within his descriptions. The figure of the describer would then be charged not just with a representational task but with a broader philosophical role of bringing together the various perspectives, from within the labyrinth and from on high, that reveal hidden dimensions of the objects described.

The Lover's Hundred Portraits

Diderot's analogy between encyclopedic order and the description of a machine underscores the epistemological significance of description in his eyes. But this was not the only time he evoked description to characterize the epistemological challenges of the *Encyclopédie*. In his long digression on language in the article "Encyclopédie," he evokes the fundamental indeterminacy of description to explain why it is so difficult to establish a stable basis for linguistic meaning. The specific linguistic question he is addressing is complex: can a precise description of the organs that function in the production of speech be used to represent (and thereby fix) the pronunciation of words? The anecdote he uses to address this question, however, is relatively straightforward: an Italian or Spanish lover wanted to acquire a portrait of his beloved but could not show her to any painter. So he wrote an extended and in his eyes perfectly accurate description of her charms and sent his description to a hundred painters. "The painters work," Diderot concludes, "and after a while our lover receives a hundred portraits, all of which rigorously resemble his description, and none of which resemble each other, or his mistress" (204). On the most basic level, this anecdote is significant because it suggests that description is fundamentally indeterminate: it is not only that one description can inspire a hundred different portraits, but also that none of these descriptions resembles the original.

Whether or not this anecdote reflects Diderot's actual view of description, it casts doubt on any straightforwardly representational view of description. As characterized here, description cannot give us any true knowledge of the objects it represents, and cannot even serve as a basis for recognizing those objects, as the Aristotelian concept of *mimesis* requires.

Yet, significantly, Diderot does not infer from this anecdote that description is a useless enterprise. Instead, he concludes that precise descriptions of the organs used in the production of speech can give us an approximate idea of how words are pronounced, especially when combined with a consideration of other structuring principles, such as the euphony of ancient languages: "One cannot, however, infer from this that these descriptions are entirely useless, because they will only ever convey an approximate pronunciation, or that euphony, the law to which an ancient language owes its harmony, does not have a continual impact of which the effect tends at least as much to bring us closer to it as to distance us from it" (204). This conclusion, which does not appear entirely consistent with the radical indeterminacy of description in Diderot's anecdote, is symptomatic of a broader tension at work in his treatment of language: on the one hand, in keeping with the view expressed in d'Alembert's article "Dictionnaire," Diderot acknowledges that the success of the encyclopedic project hinges on fixing linguistic meaning. On the other hand, he is aware that any attempt to fix language is subject to some level of corruption. It is significant that description should figure so centrally in his elaboration of this problem, since this suggests that description participates in the attempt to stabilize language and also contributes to linguistic change over time, just like the *Encyclopédie* itself.

The "Encyclopédie" article also engages more broadly with the question of how linguistic change mirrors and parallels the progress of knowledge. According to Diderot, "The vocabulary [of a people] is a relatively accurate record of the complete knowledge of that people" (189). Characterizing his own philosophical age as a time of rapid linguistic expansion, he notes that even women and children now manipulate the technical languages of painting, sculpture, architecture, and belles-lettres with ease. Soon, he predicts, the vocabulary of natural history, anatomy, chemistry, and experimental physics will have become equally familiar, to such an extent that language will be entirely transformed: "What will become of this? Language, even popular language, will show a new face; it will expand as our ears become accustomed to words, through the fortunate uses [applications heureuses] we will make of them" (185). Yet Diderot neglects to establish a clear causal relationship between linguistic changes and the progress of knowledge. We do not know whether the "applications heureuses" he refers to here are fortunate because they are based in true knowledge, or simply because they are linguistically pleasing to the ear.

This ambiguity leaves room for two very different ways description might function. As a representational practice, it might actually expand our knowledge of things, while as a linguistic practice it might simply expand our vocabulary by using unfamiliar words in harmonious or pleasing ways. Echoing Buffon and Daubenton, Diderot asserts that empirical knowledge must serve as a basis for description: "Things can only be well defined or described by those who have made a long study of them" (177). But he also allows for a more diffuse linguistic expansion that enlightens even those who do not fully understand the new words that are entering popular language under the influence of specialized forms of discourse. For example, he notes that men of letters will incorporate vestiges of debates and innovations in the arts without following them directly, and vice versa:

> These [vestiges] are like the reflections of a general light that falls on artists and men of letters, and of which they conserve a glimmer. I know that the abuse they sometimes make of expressions whose force is unknown to them reveals that they were not well informed about the philosophy of their time; but the good mind that gathers these expressions, that seizes upon a metaphor here, a new term there, elsewhere a word relating to a phenomenon, an observation, a system, perceives the state of reigning opinions, the general movement minds were beginning to take from them, and the nuance they were carrying over onto the common language. (191–92)

What this means is that a literary writer's use of a particular (technical) term does not necessarily require the full technical knowledge that lies behind it. In subsequent generations, philosophers (or good minds) will be able to perceive the general progress of knowledge, as a shared cultural phenomenon, by analyzing the coloration that literary language has taken. Hence Diderot seems to gesture toward a possible disjuncture between descriptive language and encyclopedic knowledge, in a way that is more symptomatic of the nineteenth-century realist and naturalist novels than of the Enlightenment practice of description. As Hamon has shown, the encyclopedic lists (of types of fabric in a department store, for example) found in Émile Zola's novels make demands on readers' lexical sophistication, without necessarily engaging their concrete knowledge of things in the world.[21] Such descriptions create an impression of encyclopedic knowledge, just as apparently trivial details create what Roland Barthes called a "reality effect" in the realist novel.[22] Clearly, we are in a different epistemological register in the *Encyclopédie*. Nonetheless, Diderot's "Encyclopédie" article exhibits signs of a growing tension between poetics and epistemology. This tension becomes even more evident in his famous description of the stocking machine, which stretched the encyclopedic ideal of popularization to its limit.

From Stocking Machine to Word Machine

Diderot's article on the stocking machine, "Bas," was first published in the second volume of the *Encyclopédie* in 1752. It is one of his most well-known articles, not only because of its remarkable complexity, but also because it is the only *Encyclopédie* article for which we have a manuscript in Diderot's hand. As Jacques Proust has established, this manuscript was in fact a description based on a set of drawings Diderot borrowed from the king's library in 1748 that represented a late seventeenth-century version of the stocking machine.[23] Diderot supplemented his knowledge of the machine by acquiring a report written by an artisan, Barrat, and by studying modern versions of the machine in workshops.[24] In other words, his knowledge

---

21. Hamon, *Du descriptif,* 52–60.

22. Roland Barthes, "L'effet de réel," in *Littérature et réalité,* ed. Gérard Genette and Tzvetan Todorov (Paris: Seuil, 1982), 81–90.

23. The manuscript version of the article, which Diderot subsequently revised for publication in the *Encyclopédie,* is reprinted in Denis Diderot, *Oeuvres complètes,* ed. Herbert Dieckmann, Jacques Proust, and Jean Varloot, vol. 6, *Encyclopédie II (Lettres B–C),* ed. John Lough and Jacques Proust (Paris: Hermann, 1976), 27–126. On this manuscript, see Herbert Dieckmann, "L'*Encyclopédie* et le fonds Vandeul," *Revue d'histoire littéraire de la France* 51, no. 3 (1951): 320–21, 323–26; and Jacques Proust, "La documentation technique de Diderot dans l'*Encyclopédie,*" *Revue d'histoire littéraire de la France* 57, no. 3 (1957): 346–48.

24. For an account, in part speculative, of the genesis of the "Bas" article, see Jacques Proust, "De l'*Encyclopédie* au *Neveu de Rameau:* L'objet et le texte," in *Recherches nouvelles sur quelques écrivains des Lumières,* ed. Jacques Proust (Geneva: Droz, 1972), 276–91.

of the machine was culled from a variety of sources: from images, from texts, from discussions with artisans, and from firsthand experience.

A famous anecdote about Diderot's fascination for the stocking machine suggests that there may have been still another source for his knowledge: according to his literary executor, Jacques-André Naigeon, Diderot had a miniature model of the machine constructed, and amused himself by taking it apart and putting it back together again, piece by piece.[25] This anecdote indicates one way we might understand Diderot's purpose in the "Bas" article: he was attempting, through his description of the machine, to give his reader an experience analogous to the actual process of disassembling and reassembling the machine, for it was only through a detailed description of the machine's parts that one could understand how it functioned. As Diderot himself put it, "One would promise oneself in vain any knowledge of the entire machine, without entering into the detail and the description of these parts."[26] The challenge of writing such a description (or of creating a miniature model of the machine) becomes evident when one considers that it was composed of some 2,500 parts. And the challenge was compounded by the fact that neither text nor image could represent all of the parts working together simultaneously; as Diderot observed, "The connections between the parts would require that one say and show at the very same time; which is not possible, either in the text [le discours], where things necessarily follow one another, or in the plates, where the parts cover one another" (2:98).

Diderot's view that the successive nature of language made it difficult, if not impossible, to achieve the simultaneity of visual representation was widely shared in the eighteenth century. Lessing, notably, founded the *Laocoön,* his essay on the limits of painting and poetry, on this very idea. What was more unusual, however, was Diderot's insistence on the limitations of the plates for representing the hidden workings of the machine.

---

25. Naigeon recounts this anecdote in his *Mémoires historiques.* See Jacques Proust, *Diderot et l'"Encyclopédie"* (Paris: Armand Colin, 1962), 194.

26. Denis Diderot, "Bas, s.m. (*Bonneterie, & autres marchands, comme Peaussier* &c.)," in *Encyclopédie,* ARTFL, 2:98. Although I have quoted Diderot's other writings for the *Encyclopédie* from the DPV critical edition of his complete works, I am quoting the "Bas" article from ARTFL, because the DPV edition provides Diderot's earlier manuscript version rather than the definitive version published in the *Encyclopédie.* Subsequent references appear parenthetically in the main text.

When Lessing wrote that "bodies with their visible properties are the true subjects of painting," he was not concerned with what might be hidden under the visible surface of the bodies represented on a canvas.[27] Diderot, in contrast, had to find a way to reveal all the hidden parts of the machine while at the same time representing them as a working whole.[28]

Diderot's solution was to break the machine down into a series of assemblages, each of which was composed of a more manageable number of parts. Then, he led his reader through a step-by-step reconstruction of the entire machine. He characterizes this method as follows: "To overcome these obstacles, we found it necessary to follow in this case a kind of analysis [une espece d'analyse] that consists of distributing the entire machine in several particular assemblages, representing below each assemblage the parts that cannot be perceived distinctly within it, to assemble successively these assemblages with each other, & thus to form little by little the entire machine" (2:98) (see figure 4). As Jacques Proust has shown, this method was not entirely Diderot's invention: it was at least in part inspired by the set of drawings he used to compose his original description in the manuscript version of the article.[29] Still, it was an innovation from the point of view of descriptive practice. What Diderot refers to as "une espece d'analyse" is in fact a complex dialectic of analysis and synthesis: whereas each section of the article treats an individual assemblage, breaking it down into its constituent parts, the article as a whole, read in conjunction with the plates, gradually reassembles these assemblages to form a working whole. The plates also combine analysis and synthesis in order to get around the problem of hidden parts: because each assemblage contains far fewer parts than the entire machine, hidden parts can be represented underneath various assemblages, thereby allowing the reader to visualize them and imagine their orientation within the machine. The complex process of grasping individual assemblages and then imagining how they fit together illustrates one way that description might combine multiple perspectives into a coherent

27. Lessing, *Laocoön*, 78.

28. According to Jacques Proust, it was in working on the "Bas" article, "well before going as an art critic to visit the salon painting exhibitions, several years even before the writing of the *Lettre sur les sourds et les muets,* that Diderot began thinking seriously about the relations between *pictura* and *poesis.*" Proust, "De l'*Encyclopédie* au *Neveu,*" 285.

29. Ibid., 279.

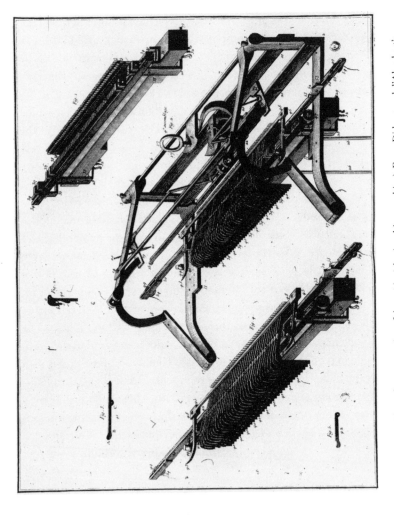

Figure 4. Plate of a cross-section of the *métier à bas* (stocking machine). From Diderot and d'Alembert's *Encyclopédie, Recueil de planches*, vol. 2A (Paris: Briasson, 1763). Courtesy of the Bibliothèque nationale de France.

whole, in keeping with Bates's interpretation of virtual perspectives in the article "Encyclopédie."

Thus, on one level, there is clearly an ideal of descriptive transparency at work in the "Bas" article. Diderot remarks that his method will allow the reader to achieve "without obscurity or fatigue the knowledge of a quite complicated whole" (2:98). The exclusion of obscurity from the reading process may seem surprising given the immense complexity of the machine and Diderot's own admission that neither image nor text can represent its workings in their entirety. How can the reader acquire a perfect knowledge of the machine if it cannot be represented without some level of obscurity? One answer might be that the obscurity proper to each representational framework dissipates when the reader engages in a dynamic back-and-forth between text and image. Yet this reading protocol has an important corollary: it means that the only place where the entire workings of the machine can be fully represented is in the reader's mind. Diderot suggests as much when, after describing the first assemblage, he warns his reader not to proceed further before gaining an intimate familiarity with the parts he has just described: "Here is the first assemblage; I warn [the reader] that before moving on to the second one, it is necessary to be very familiar with this one; otherwise, the parts multiplying and the poorly understood assemblages assembling together will form confusing masses of which nothing will be understood" (2:100). This warning serves to qualify Diderot's earlier claim that there would be no obscurity in the reading process; in fact, complete confusion can be avoided only if the reader internalizes all the parts and mechanisms of the machine at each stage of the description.

Diderot's insistence on the difficulties involved in grappling with these multiple assemblages reflects the epistemological complexity of the "Bas" article. This complexity has been neglected in interpretations of the *Encyclopédie* plates that insist on the ways in which the plates facilitate the viewer's appropriation of objects. In an influential article, Barthes interpreted the plates in terms of the *Encyclopédie*'s "acquisitive knowledge" (savoir d'appropriation), which he viewed as symptomatic of bourgeois culture and the alliance between knowledge and power in the encyclopedic project: "Formally (this is very perceptible in the plates), property depends essentially on a certain breaking down of things: to appropriate for oneself is to fragment the world, to divide it into finite objects, subjected to man in proportion to their discontinuity: for one cannot separate without eventually naming and classifying, and from then forward, property is born."[30] For Daniel Brewer, similarly, the innovative cross-section drawing used in many of the plates "suggests a way of representing, viewing, and understanding objects that disassembles them, slices through them like the surgeon's scalpel and the viewer's gaze in the anatomy plates, and reassembles them, not as they look, but rather according to an understanding of how they function and produce." This visual representation of objects, which Brewer links to the *Encyclopédie*'s broader ordering of knowledge, serves to "[construct] a world that can be controlled and made to work."[31] The plates can thus be seen as symptomatic of the Enlightenment belief in a world that can be "grasped, ordered, and ultimately mastered by the rational mind."[32]

Yet such interpretations downplay the epistemological complexity of the process of moving back and forth between plates and descriptions, which for Diderot was essential to interpreting the plates. In their emphasis on the viewer's appropriation of objects, both Barthes and Brewer privilege the (ideal) end result of that process, rather than the (real) process of grappling with different assemblages and trying to understand how they work and fit together. The "Bas" article suggests that Diderot considered that process far more important, from an epistemological point of view, than the reader's ultimate possession of the machine, if indeed complete mental reconstruction were even possible.

Interpretations of the *Encyclopédie* plates have also emphasized their idealizing strain, their tendency to efface the actual conditions of artisanal labor; as Proust explains, "They don't 'tell' the misery and exploitation, the fatigue, the pain, the violence, the fear, the herds of men, women, and children crowded into uncomfortable, dark, smoky workshops and factories."[33] In the "Bas" article, this idealizing strain takes on an epistemological dimension. As Barthes has noted, the idealization of the stocking

---

30. Barthes, "Planches de l'*Encyclopédie*," 93.

31. Daniel Brewer, "1751: Ordering Knowledge," in *A New History of French Literature*, ed. Denis Hollier (Cambridge, Mass.: Harvard University Press, 1989), 452. See also id., *The Discourse of Enlightenment in Eighteenth-Century France: Diderot and the Art of Philosophizing* (Cambridge: Cambridge University Press, 1993), 13–55.

32. Brewer, "1751: Ordering Knowledge," 449.

33. Jacques Proust, *Marges d'une utopie: Pour une lecture critique des planches de l'"Encyclopédie"* (Cognac, Fr.: Le temps qu'il fait, 1985), n.p.; and Barthes, "Planches de l'*Encyclopédie*," 104.

machine allows Diderot to represent it as a perfect manifestation of human reasoning: "It can be seen as a single and unique chain of reasoning, of which the fabrication of the machine is the conclusion; thus there reigns between its parts such a great interdependence that to remove a single one, or to alter the form of those one judges the least important, is to do damage to the entire mechanism" (2:98).[34] When viewed as an expression of human reason, the machine becomes perfectly transparent, with even its most hidden parts contributing logically toward the ultimate goal of making a stocking. In order to underscore the analogy between the machine and the human mind, Diderot claims that the machine is not the product of a long evolutionary history, but the brilliant creation of a single mind: "It came out of the hands of its inventor almost in the state we see it today; and as this circumstance should add greatly to [our] admiration, I preferred the machine as it was formerly to the machine as we have it, taking care simply to indicate their slight differences as they present themselves" (2:98). With this creation story, which resembles the divine creation of man in Genesis, Diderot erases the obscurity of historical modifications, the intervention of multiple human minds, and the messy process of experimentation generally associated with technological progress.

That Diderot chooses to describe the original stocking-making machine, with only occasional digressions addressing modern improvements, may seem surprising in the context of an encyclopedia devoted to recording the latest advances of human knowledge. As Proust has shown, this anomaly was due at least in part to the fact that Diderot was initially working with a set of drawings of an outdated seventeenth-century model of the machine.[35] But as a result, there was an uneasy coexistence between two different machines in the "Bas" article, the first associated with the ideal abstraction of human reason, and the second associated with the messy process of historical evolution:

> The differences between the old machine and the new are very slight; they do in truth add something to the perfection of the machine; but they add still more to the honor of the inventor: for one will notice that if this machine

34. For an analysis of this passage with respect to the plates, see Barthes, "Planches de *l'Encyclopédie*," 99–100.

35. Proust, "De *l'Encyclopédie* au *Neveu*," 290.

had to be built by beings infallible in their measurements, and operated by beings infallible in their movements, it would have been necessary to leave it as it was. The changes that were made were simply to make room for the convenience of trial and error [la commodité de tâtonner], and to achieve in practice the geometrical precision that the machine had in the mind of its inventor. (2:104–5)

This passage is full of ambiguities: first, Diderot admits that the modifications made to the original stocking-making machine have further perfected it. Then, he claims that the modifications can be considered improvements only to the extent that they accommodate the imperfect beings who must build and operate the machine. One then wonders whether the original stocking-making machine was ever actually built. Are we to assume that its inventor was an infallible being with the ability to obtain perfect measurements? Or, as the end of the passage suggests, did the original stocking-making machine only ever exist, in its perfect form, in the mind of its inventor? In fact, there are two very different machines in the "Bas" article: the first is an ideal, geometrical creation of the inventor's mind, while the second is the end result of a messy process of experimentation and modification (we are reminded here of the two circles in d'Alembert's article on geometrical description in the *Encyclopédie*). One exists only in the human mind, while the other is physically incarnated in the world. It is significant that the machine used by real people is associated with obscurity (through the expression "la commodité de tâtonner"), whereas the ideal machine is associated with the pure light of human reason. Although the *Encyclopédie* is generally interested in the evolution of the mechanical arts and the practical knowledge of artisans, Diderot prefers the original or ideal machine precisely because its logic is not obscured by the vicissitudes of actual practice.

Thus in their emphasis on idealization, interpretations of the *Encyclopédie* plates tell only half the story. They do not account for the coexistence of real and ideal machines in Diderot's "Bas" article, or for the friction between them. It is true that Diderot's reader is invited to emulate the "ideal" light of human reason found in the original inventor's mind. But that same reader is explicitly encouraged to emulate a different kind of mental activity, involving not reason but memory and imagination. This becomes clear when Diderot tells an anecdote about the commercial history of the stocking-making machine. Citing a dictionary of commerce, he tells the story of how a French inventor, frustrated by the elaborate system of privileges in France, took his invention to England and set up shop there. The English jealously guarded the valuable invention, forbidding the transport of machines, models, or illustrations from the island under penalty of death. Thus when a French citizen subsequently undertook to restore the machine to his nation, he, like Diderot's reader, had to memorize all its parts and mechanisms in order to reconstruct the machine from memory upon arrival in France. Explicitly connecting this mental effort to that of his readers, Diderot concludes: "A Frenchman had enriched them with this gift, a Frenchman returned it to his homeland, through an effort of memory and imagination that will only be fully conceived by the end of this article" (2:99). After reading the "Bas" article, Diderot's readers should thus be able to understand not only the machine itself but also the tremendous mental effort required to restore it to French soil.

In this sense, the function of Diderot's "Bas" article is not purely didactic. In addition to understanding the machine, readers are invited to understand and admire the faculties of the human mind used in its invention, transmission, and preservation; as Proust remarks, "To describe the parts of a machine and to analyze its functioning is at the same time, and inextricably, to enter into the intimate mechanisms of the mind that invented it and, in an indirect manner, to explore the paths by which the human mind constitutes its knowledge in general."[36] While the original act of inventing the machine reflects the transparent and perfect logic of human reason, the subsequent act of restoring the machine to French soil reflects the equally important faculties of memory and imagination. It should be noted here that the three mental faculties referred to in the "Bas" article—reason, memory, and imagination—are the three primary branches on the tree of knowledge represented graphically in the *Encyclopédie,* and discussed by d'Alembert in his "Discours préliminaire." This suggests that the reader of the "Bas" article is being invited to admire not only the inventor's mind but also the human mind more generally.

Yet the *Encyclopédie* was both a monument to human knowledge and a testament to its immense fragility. In his "Avertissement" to the eighth

---

36. Ibid., 293.

volume of the *Encyclopédie,* published in 1766, Diderot evokes the possibility of a catastrophic revolution that might one day destroy human civi-
lizations and usher in a new age of obscurity. In such circumstances, the
Encyclopédie would serve as a bulwark against the complete destruction
of human knowledge: "If a revolution of which the germ is perhaps being
formed in some canton unknown to the world, or is being brooded secretly
[se couve secrètement] in the very center of policed countries, breaks out
in time, topples cities, disperses peoples once again, and brings back ignorance and obscurity, if a single complete copy of this work is conserved,
all will not be lost."[37] This apocalyptic vision, with its biblical overtones,
represents the *Encyclopédie* as a modern equivalent of Noah's ark, carrying
in its multiple volumes the basis for a new civilization. It underlines the
extent to which the *Encyclopédie* was deeply engaged not only with transmitting knowledge but also with protecting it from the destructive forces
that are constantly preying on all forms of human civilization.

In the same "Avertissement," Diderot emphasizes the collaborative nature of the *Encyclopédie* and represents the efforts of the encyclopedists as
a collective struggle to preserve the fabric of human society: "Would we
dare to mutter of our troubles and regret our years of work if we could
flatter ourselves with having weakened this spirit of volatility [esprit de
vertige] so contrary to the repose of societies, and with having induced our
fellow men [nos semblables] to love each other, to tolerate each other, and
lastly to recognize the superiority of universal morality over all particular moralities that inspire hatred and trouble and that break or weaken
the general, common bond?" (8:ii). It is perhaps through this notion of a
collective struggle that we can best understand the central role Diderot
ascribes to his reader in the "Bas" article. By emulating the citizen who
restored the stocking-making machine to his nation, Diderot's reader not
only gains an understanding of the machine but also participates in the
collective encyclopedic enterprise of preserving knowledge and assuring
its transmission to future generations and across revolutionary ruptures.
Realistically, Diderot could hardly have expected that his reader would, in
the event of a catastrophic revolution, be able to reconstruct the stocking-
making machine from memory. As Proust has noted, the very idea that

---

37. Denis Diderot, "Avertissement des éditeurs," *Encyclopédie,* ARTFL, 8:ii.

the machine could be reconstructed from memory, even by an experienced artisan, is highly unlikely.[38] Diderot could, however, have believed that the experience of struggling to understand how a complicated machine works by reading and looking at pictures would cultivate in his reader a deep appreciation for the human efforts that went into inventing, transmitting, and preserving the machine. After the inventor, the first object of such admiration must be Diderot himself, who sought to understand the machine by looking at drawings, reading descriptions, and visiting workshops.

There is, then, an underlying sense of urgency in Diderot's "Bas" article. By moving too quickly and succumbing to confusion, the reader not only puts his or her personal knowledge at risk but also jeopardizes the ideal of a civilization based on the transmission and preservation of knowledge. Yet roughly halfway through his long article, Diderot suggests that his reader may be the weak link in the chain along which knowledge is transmitted. Entertaining the very real possibility that his reader may understand nothing at all after reading descriptions of the first four assemblages, he gives two possible explanations for this potential incomprehension: "We can thus move on now to the fifth assemblage and consider ourselves persuaded that it will rather be due to the reader's inattentiveness, or to the composition of the machine, than to our fault, if we haven't been understood up to this point" (2:103). Although Diderot denies that his own article may be responsible for his reader's potential confusion, he hesitates between attributing it to the reader's inattentiveness or to the complexity of the machine itself.

This hesitation reflects a broader tension at work in the *Encyclopédie* between the goal of popularization and an awareness of the increasing specialization of fields of knowledge. In the "Avertissement" to the eighth volume of the *Encyclopédie,* Diderot emphasizes the encyclopedic ideal of popularization: "May general instruction advance with such a rapid step that twenty years from now there will be in a thousand of our pages hardly a single line that is not popular!" (8:ii). But, in his article "Encyclopédie," he grants that no single man can know and understand everything: "I do not by any means believe that it is granted to a single man to know everything that can be known;…to understand everything that is intelligible" (175).

---

38. Proust, "De l'*Encyclopédie* au *Neveu*," 277.

The stocking-making machine, "one of the most complicated and consequential machines we have," stretches the ideal of popularization to its limits and forces Diderot to confront the potential uselessness of his text for his reader; it is in this sense that Proust has referred to the "failure of the 'Bas' article."[39]

Thus when Diderot grants in the middle of his article that the stocking machine may be too complicated for his reader to understand, he is reflecting not only on the difficulty of describing a machine but also on the limits of human knowledge more generally. It is significant that this moment of aporia occurs in the middle of the article. If the reader has simply been inattentive, the solution is clearly to go back and review the first four sections more carefully, in keeping with Diderot's earlier warnings. But if the reader's confusion is instead a factor of the machine itself, it becomes unclear what reading protocol should be followed. Should he or she simply stop reading and abandon any attempt to gain knowledge of the machine? Or is there something other than knowledge of the machine to be gained from reading further? As I have suggested, even an unfruitful mental effort may serve to increase the reader's admiration for the inventor, for Diderot himself, and by extension for the entire enterprise of the *Encyclopédie*.

But Diderot's acknowledgment of the reader's potential incomprehension also highlights the potential for a disjuncture between words and things in the "Bas" article. In fact, the article is as much about naming the multiple parts of the machine as it is about explaining how they work. In some cases, terms such as *arrêtant, petit coup,* and *noix du rouloir* are highly technical and probably unfamiliar to most readers, and Diderot is obliged to give definitions for them. In other cases, anthropomorphic terms such as *oreille* (ear), *gueule* (mouth or muzzle), *bras* (arm), *gorge* (bosom), and *ventre* (belly) facilitate recognition but also transform the reader's perception of the machine by drawing connections to the human body. Thus Diderot refers to his second assemblage as *"the frame of the machine,* its skeleton, its body, its crude parts" (*la cage du métier,* sa carcasse, son corps, ses parties grossieres), only to explain that the third is commonly called "the soul of the machine" (l'âme du métier) (2:101). The fourth, in turn, is described as the reunion of body and soul.

---

39. Diderot, "Bas," *Encyclopédie,* ARTFL, 2:98; and Proust, "De l'*Encyclopédie* au *Neveu,*" 302.

In marked contrast to these highly accessible metaphoric terms are terms that highlight the obscurity and instability of language. We learn, for example, that the *platine à plomb* must not be confused with the *plomb à platine,* and that the *barre fondue* (melted bar) can also be called the *barre fendue* (cleft bar). The latter example is particularly striking because it introduces a troubling ambiguity regarding the origins of technical language. On the one hand, Diderot explains each term as an accurate description of some aspect of the part in question: "melted bar [barre fondue], because the lower part of its frame is molded and filled with pewter; cleft bar [barre fendue], because of the openings or clefts that the little squares of copper with which it is covered leave between each other" (2:101). On the other hand, the subtle vowel shift from *fondue* to *fendue* suggests that this is an instance of linguistic corruption. Just as the machine underwent various physical modifications over time, the words used to describe its parts were gradually transformed. Indeed, the imperfect people who were incapable of obtaining perfect measurements could easily have mistaken *fondue* for *fendue.* Or Diderot himself might have been unsure about which was the proper term (the limits of his technical knowledge are in evidence in the manuscript version of the article when he leaves some items in his list of the machine's parts blank).[40] What is remarkable about the example of the ambiguity between the *barre fondue* and the *barre fendue* is that it seems to signal both the transparency and the obscurity of descriptive language. Like the two machines, ideal and real, described in the "Bas" article, these two terms establish a tension between an ideal language in which words offer a transparent reflection of the things they describe, and a real language in which linguistic obscurity and instability block the transmission of knowledge and reveal the materiality of language.

Hence the "Bas" article underscores the extent to which description can be more than an occasion to put images before the reader's eyes, in keeping with its traditional definition in classical rhetoric. By acknowledging that his reader might not grasp the machine itself, Diderot makes room for an encounter with language that does not depend on its transparency or intelligibility. Instead of discovering the machine itself, the reader discovers the

---

40. See Diderot, "Bas," DPV, 33–34, 38–40.

manner in which objects have the potential to reveal language to us in new and unexpected ways.

* * *

The stocking machine stretched the encyclopedic ideal of popularization to its limits, by virtue of its complexity and the high level of technical detail involved in its description. This is underscored by the *Encyclopédie méthodique,* in which in the article "Manufactures" characterizes the stocking machine as too complicated to be described: "It is a very ingeniously contrived machine, made of polished iron; it is not possible to describe its construction here, because of the number and variety of its component parts, and even a person who sees it will find a real difficulty in understanding how it works."[41] As we have seen, Diderot acknowledged this difficulty in his description of the machine. But just as he did not infer from his anecdote about the lover's hundred portraits that description was a useless enterprise, he did not abandon his description of the stocking machine. This was because for him, the epistemological value of description did not lie solely in making objects intelligible to his readers. Description also served as a microcosm for the epistemological challenges of the encyclopedic project, and as an occasion for an exchange between linguistic and artisanal expertise.

The "Bas" article was also an occasion for a confrontation between language and objects. Clearly, Diderot expected his reader to gain some knowledge of the stocking machine. But he also acknowledged that his reader might be unable (or unwilling) to engage in a mental reconstruction of the machine. In a similar way, in his *Salons,* Diderot alluded frequently to the difficulty of constructing mental images on the basis of descriptions.[42] Yet in both cases the reader's potential recalcitrance did not invalidate the epistemological value of Diderot's descriptions: on the contrary, it was the struggle to envision and understand the machine, without ever having seen it, that gave the reader a heightened awareness both of the machine's complexity, and of the words used to describe it. Hence Diderot's

---

41. Quoted in Paul Mantoux, *The Industrial Revolution in the Eighteenth Century: An Outline of the Beginnings of the Modern Factory System in England,* trans. Marjorie Vernon (1928; repr., New York: Routledge, 2006), 191 n. 4.

42. See, for example, Diderot, *Salon de 1767,* 621–22.

reader came to appreciate the two kinds of knowledge at play in the "Bas" article: the artisan's knowledge of the stocking machine, and the writer's knowledge of language. However much concrete knowledge the "Bas" article communicated, it was also an epistemologically and linguistically disorienting experience that forced the reader to confront a strange bunch of words that did not coalesce into any coherent picture. We may catch glimpses of the stocking machine in reading the "Bas" article, especially when assisted by the plates. But we also catch glimpses of a highly specialized language, which remains largely incomprehensible even as it casts its diffuse light over us.

4

DELILLE'S LITTLE ENCYCLOPEDIA

In his portrait of Jacques Delille, one of the most eminent poets and translators in Enlightenment France, the romantic critic Charles Augustin Sainte-Beuve characterized the descriptive genre practiced and theorized by Delille as a failed poetic project.[1] Despite the overwhelming popularity of descriptive poetry in the eighteenth century, this critical judgment has persisted into our own time: no scholarly or popular editions of French descriptive poems are currently available, and only a few of the original editions are accessible through the Bibliothèque nationale de France's digital library. In his introduction to an anthology of French eighteenth-century poetry, which includes only a few, brief excerpts of descriptive poetry, Michel Delon asks: "Must we then join the critics [of descriptive poetry] in speaking of a failure? It is rather that poetic emotion is for us no longer found in these hundreds, in these thousands of alexandrines, but in the gap

---

1. Charles Augustin Sainte-Beuve, "Delille," in *Portraits littéraires,* ed. Gérald Antoine (Paris: Robert Laffont, 1993), 392–93.

between a project and its realization, in the paradox of a properly poetic impulse that manages to express itself in prefaces and notes but that falls apart as soon as it attempts to take form."[2] Like Delon, Sainte-Beuve was struck by the voluminous prose notes that have made descriptive poetry both unwieldy and unreadable for subsequent generations. These notes, as he put it, "formed a little encyclopedia around the poem, giving you a smattering of universal instruction."[3] Sainte-Beuve was particularly caustic with respect to the apparent inconsistency between this prosaic little encyclopedia around the poem, and the poets' use of elaborate circumlocutions to avoid naming things directly in their verse. In his view, Delille's poetry was little more than "a series of circumlocutions accompanied by indispensable notes."[4]

Hence descriptive poetry has come to epitomize what Gustave Lanson once called the "poetry without poetry" of the French eighteenth century, by virtue of its attempt to give poetic form to Enlightenment encyclopedism.[5] Instead of offering a truly poetic encyclopedia, it simply weighed down its verse with encyclopedic fragments, thereby achieving neither true instruction nor the beauty of poetic form. On the other side of the coin, the structuralist critic Michael Riffaterre attempted to restore descriptive poetry's status as poetry by claiming that it was not in fact about the world at all: "The descriptive genre, more than any other literary form, appeared necessarily to open out onto reality. This is not the case: all forms of mimesis do nothing

---

2. Michel Delon, introduction to *Anthologie de la poésie française du XVIIIe siècle* (Paris: Gallimard, 1997), 20.

3. Sainte-Beuve, "Delille," 413.

4. Ibid., 397. Delon refers to the "acrobatic syntax" required to make room for these circumlocutions. Delon, *Anthologie,* 17.

5. Gustave Lanson, *Histoire de la littérature française,* 18th ed. (1895; Paris: Hachette, 1924), 641. Delon notes, however, that despite Lanson's initially categorical rejection of French eighteenth-century poetry, he was one of the first to propose a reevaluation of the period's poetic production. Delon, *Anthologie,* 8; and Lanson, *Histoire,* 639–44. In addition to Delon's *Anthologie,* attempts to reevaluate eighteenth-century French poetry include Jean Roudaut, *Poètes et grammairiens du XVIIIe siècle, anthologie* (Paris: Gallimard, 1971); id., "Les exercices poétiques au XVIIIe siècle," *Critique* 181 (1962): 533–47; id., "La poésie du XVIIIe siècle lue au XXe siècle depuis 1950, réponses à un questionnaire," *Oeuvres et critiques* 7, no. 1 (1982): 139–150; Édouard Guitton, *Jacques Delille (1738–1813) et le poème de la nature en France de 1750 à 1820* (Paris: Klincksieck, 1974); id., "La poésie en 1778," *Dix-huitième siècle* 11 (1979): 75–86; Sylvain Menant, *La chute d'Icare: La crise de la poésie française (1700–1750)* (Geneva: Droz, 1981); and Jean Roudaut, ed., "Poetry and Poetics," in *Transactions of the Fifth International Congress on the Enlightenment,* vol. 4, Studies on Voltaire and the Eighteenth Century 193 (Oxford: Voltaire Foundation, 1980), 1571–1658.

more than create an *illusion* of reality."[6] What Riffaterre and Sainte-Beuve share is an implicit rejection of poetic encyclopedism: the function of poetry, it would seem, is not to give us knowledge of the world.

Yet when descriptive poetry is situated within the broader context of Enlightenment efforts to describe the world, its poetic project appears in another light. If descriptive poetry has been deemed unreadable from the romantics forward, it is because it has too often been read through the lens of either classical or romantic poetics: from a classical perspective, descriptive poetry is found lacking because, as the Enlightenment critic Marmontel suggested in his article "Descriptif," it abandons the "reasonable" principles (and proportions) of classical poetics by dint of its encyclopedic ambitions. From a romantic perspective, it is found lacking because it eschews lyric self-expression and remains too exclusively focused on the encyclopedic, prosaic description of nature. If, however, descriptive poetry is read through the lens of the encyclopedic projects it emulated, the contours of its poetic project come into clearer focus, and it appears as a rich site of epistemological experimentation and linguistic transformation. It also appears as a modern poetic project inasmuch as it created a space for the emergence of the describer, even as its practitioners eschewed lyric self-expression.

Poetics of a Modern Genre

The invention of descriptive poetry is generally credited to the Scottish poet James Thomson, whose poem *The Seasons* was first published in 1730. When it was translated into French in 1759, Thomson's poem sparked a vogue for descriptive poetry in France that would not die down until the first decades of the nineteenth century.[7] Yet, unlike the French poets, Thomson did not provide a programmatic poetics for the genre that came to be associated with his name. It was Jean-François de Saint-Lambert and Jacques Delille who offered an extended theoretical reflection on the poetics of the genre, and who linked it explicitly to the encyclopedic aspirations

---

6. Riffaterre, "Système," 30.

7. For a comprehensive account of Thomson's influence in France, see Margaret Cameron, *L'influence des "Saisons" de Thomson sur la poésie descriptive en France (1759–1810)* (Paris: Honoré Champion, 1927).

of their time. Saint-Lambert, who published his own poem *Les saisons* in 1769, was a regular contributor to the *Encyclopédie* and frequented the philosophical circles around the Baron d'Holbach, Madame Necker, and Madame d'Épinay. A protégé of Voltaire (despite their competition for the scientific thinker Emilie du Châtelet's attentions) and a member of the Académie française, he was an ardent champion of the philosophical cause. Although many, including Diderot, privately criticized *Les saisons* for its cold and monotonous style and excessive use of epithets, the poem's preface was widely praised and was seen as a poetic platform worthy of a philosophical age.[8]

One of the most striking things about Saint-Lambert's preface is the way he refuses to bind the descriptive genre to any guiding rules or principles, while at the same time offering a series of reflections that constitutes a programmatic poetics of the genre. As he remarks, "This new genre has its poetics which is not very extensive; it undoubtedly has its rules and principles; I don't claim to give them here, but may I be permitted to offer a few reflections."[9] Saint-Lambert's awkward refusal to acknowledge that he was in fact formulating the poetics of the descriptive genre underscores the precarious position of the descriptive poets. On the one hand, to the extent that they wished to claim a generic status for descriptive poetry, they needed a programmatic statement of the genre's poetics (in the tradition of Aristotle's *Poetics* for tragedy). On the other hand, to the extent that they wished to invent a modern poetic genre, sufficiently flexible and expansive to accommodate their encyclopedic ambitions, they could not allow the genre to be limited by any rule or principle more restrictive than the broad principle of describing nature. Indeed, the very idea of a modern poetic genre suggested that the classical framework within which poetry had traditionally been understood was no longer sufficient. Thus the descriptive genre participated in the broader dismantling of the classical hierarchy of poetic genres in the late eighteenth century.[10]

---

8. See the article on Saint-Lambert in the *Biographie universelle, ancienne et moderne,* ed. M. M. Michaud, 2nd ed. (Paris: Louis Vivès, [1880]), 37:348–53.

9. Jean-François de Saint-Lambert, *Les saisons,* in *Oeuvres de Saint-Lambert* (Clermont, Fr.: Pierre Landriot, 1814), 1:17.

10. See Guitton, "Poésie," 75–86. According to Guitton, poetic genres were more rigidly classified in the eighteenth century than ever before, but this very rigidity signaled the discomfort of theorists of poetry in the face of a changing poetic landscape. Thus Saint-Lambert's claim to generic novelty was met with criticism, despite the popularity of the poem itself.

Saint-Lambert underlines the modernity of the descriptive genre, presenting his poem as a departure from all that had previously been thought possible in French poetry: "I present for the public's judgment a work of a genre not yet attempted by the French. Several men of letters and of taste felt that the details of nature and country life could not be rendered in French verse; but I had given little thought to the matter when I began my poem; I was young, and what these enlightened men judged impossible did not even seem difficult to me."[11] From the outset, Saint-Lambert distinguishes French descriptive poetry from its English and German counterparts, suggesting that the genre might have eluded the French without his intervention. In this way, he manages to situate himself as an innovator rather than an imitator, even as he gives credit to the English and German poets for having invented a poetic genre with no ancient antecedents: "Rural poetry [La Poésie champêtre] has been enriched in this century by a genre that was unknown to the ancients.... The English & the Germans created the genre of descriptive poetry; the ancients loved & sang the countryside; we admire & sing nature."[12] Given that he does not claim to have invented descriptive poetry, Saint-Lambert's status as an innovator depends upon the particularity of the French case. Unlike Thomson, who "sang nature to a people who know and love her," he claims to sing nature "to a nation who ignores her or sees her with indifference."[13] The French insensitivity to nature has important implications for the practice of the genre: whereas the English poet can count on his readers having already seen and appreciated the beauties he describes, the French poet describes scenes and objects that are unfamiliar to his readers. Hence Saint-Lambert characterizes his poetic project as an attempt to make his readers fall in

---

11. Saint-Lambert, *Saisons,* 1:5.

12. Ibid., 1:14. Some modern critics have characterized descriptive poetry as a subset of the ancient genre of didactic poetry. See Ruth Helen Webb and Philip Weller, "Descriptive Poetry," in *The New Princeton Encyclopedia of Poetry and Poetics,* ed. Alex Preminger and T. V. F. Brogan (Princeton: Princeton University Press, 1993), 283–88. Others, notably Riffaterre, have suggested on the contrary that didactic poetry is a subset of the descriptive genre. Riffaterre, "Système," 15. One way of avoiding such confusion is to pay closer attention to the way eighteenth-century poets understood and categorized the two genres: what seems important here is that they viewed descriptive poetry as a modern poetic genre with no ancient antecedents, but also acknowledged the influence of didactic poetry on their project.

13. Saint-Lambert, *Saisons,* 1:27.

love with a woman they have never seen: "The English poet speaks to lovers of their mistress; he is sure to please them. I want to inspire love for a beautiful woman who has never been seen, and I show her portrait."[14] Thus not only must the French poet describe scenes and objects his readers have never seen, but his description must also be sufficiently compelling to instill in them a lasting passion for nature.

In 1769, the same year that Saint-Lambert published *Les saisons,* Jacques Delille published a translation of Vergil's *Georgics,* with a lengthy preface on the georgic genre and on the benefits it could bring to the impoverished French poetic idiom.[15] Both the preface and the translation earned Delille lasting fame, allowing him to trade in an obscure professorial post for election to the Académie française five years later. Much later in his career, in the preface to his own *L'homme des champs, ou Les géorgiques françaises* (1800), Delille returned to his reflections on the georgic genre and explicitly linked them to his lifelong practice of descriptive poetry.

Like Saint-Lambert, Delille associated descriptive poetry with a poetic sensibility that was rare in French letters. For him, this sensibility marked a departure from the human passions that are the focus of classical tragedy. In response to critics who claim that descriptive poetry is lacking in sentiment, Delille elaborates on the nature of this sensibility in his preface to *L'homme des champs:*

> There are besides two species of sensibility. The one makes us feel for the sorrow of our equals, and derives its source from the ties of blood, friendship, or love, and describes the pleasure or pain of those great passions that constitute the happiness or misery of mankind. This is the only species of sensibility that some writers will acknowledge. There is, however, another, far more scarce and not less to be valued. It is that kind of sensibility which, like life, expands itself over every part of a work; that gives an interest to objects that are the most foreign to man; that makes him participate in the destiny, happiness, and death of an animal, or even of a plant; that gives an interest to places that he had inhabited, or where he had been educated, and

---

14. Ibid., 1:31.

15. Michel Delon characterizes this preface as "one of the century's most beautiful reflections on poetry." Delon, *Anthologie,* 18.

that have been witnesses of our pains or pleasures; and to the melancholy aspect of ruins.[16]

The first sensibility, associated with tragedy, appears far more passive than the second: rather than transforming the objects it represents, it merely taps into preexisting human passions. The second, associated with descriptive poetry, transforms readers' perceptions of the world around them, creating interest where it did not previously exist and enlivening things foreign to man. It is a rare and disinterested sensibility, "not only appertaining to the tenderness of social affections, but to a superabundance of sentiment that expands itself overall, animates all, and interests itself for all."[17] Delille's emphasis on sentiment is significant, in light of the misunderstanding that surrounds descriptive poetry to this day; for even critics attempting to recuperate descriptive poetry have characterized it as a poetry of reflection, in opposition to the romantic poetry of sentiment.[18] For Delille, on the contrary, descriptive poetry allows its readers to participate in a diffuse sentiment that extends far beyond social relations, and that lives and propagates itself in all of nature. By becoming aware of this sentiment, readers come to understand their place in the larger universe, in a way not unrelated to Saint-Pierre's notion of natural harmonies.[19]

Like Saint-Lambert, Delille thus sees it as his role to transform French readers' relationship to nature from one of indifference to one of active involvement. Yet in order to do so, he must first draw his readers in by

---

16. I quote this passage from a contemporary English translation of the preface and poem: John Maunde, *Rural Philosopher; or, French Georgics: A Didactic Poem, Translated from the Original of the Abbé Delille; Entitled "L'homme des champs"* (London: G. Kearsley, 1801), xviii–xix. It should be noted that Delille refers to this poem as a descriptive poem, not as a didactic poem. On this distinction, see note 12 above. For the original, see Jacques Delille, preface to *L'homme des champs, ou Les géorgiques françaises* (Paris: Levrault, Schoell et Cie, 1804), 20–21.

17. Maunde, *Rural Philosopher,* xix. For the original, see Delille, *Homme des champs,* 21–22.

18. According to Delon, Lanson paved the way for a reevaluation of French eighteenth-century poetry, despite his initial condemnation, by acknowledging that there could be "a poetry of the mind just as there is a poetry of sentiment." Delon, *Anthologie,* 8; and Lanson, *Histoire,* 639–44. It was along similar lines that Jean Roudaut proposed his own reevaluation of eighteenth-century French poetry in his anthology, *Poètes et grammairiens du XVIIIe siècle.*

19. In this sense, Roudaut's general characterization of poetry is particularly apt when it comes to the descriptive genre: "For poetry, in the sense we understand it today, as a means of inventing a place for man in the cosmos, of saying his relation to the world, of affirming his solidarity with all creation, the invisible and the hidden, could never disappear." Roudaut, *Poètes et grammairiens,* 10.

manipulating the formal devices of poetry. The descriptive poet, he claims, must cultivate stylistic perfection and compositional innovation to compensate for the lack of human drama in his subject: "There the reader finds neither action that may excite lively curiosity, nor passions that may forcibly agitate his mind. This interest then must find a substitute in the most accurate details, and the perfection of the most pure and brilliant style."[20] In a marked departure from Aristotle's *Poetics,* Delille gives priority to style over the representation of human action. Yet his emphasis on style cannot be reduced to an empty formalism. Indeed, it is through the mastery of formal elements that descriptive poetry achieves its transformative effect: initially drawn in by style, readers gradually come to perceive the interest of the scene or objects described. Through the manipulation of language, the readers' capacity for attention is thus expanded to include objects they would previously have ignored. Thus Delille's emphasis on *la difficulté vaincue,* or conquered difficulty, for which he has often been mocked, reflects his deeply held belief that poetic language can transform our perceptions of the world.[21]

Yet Delille also expands significantly on Saint-Lambert's claim for the specificity of French descriptive poetry, offering an analysis of the restrictions imposed on French poetic language by classicism. For him, descriptive poetry is not only a means of cultivating readers' sensitivity to nature; it is also, and perhaps more importantly, a means of expanding and diversifying a poetic idiom that has been impoverished by its almost exclusive focus on tragedy and comedy: "It is well known that the style of tragedy is that of noble conversation, and the style of comedy that of familiar conversation. Our language, trapped until now between these two genres, has remained timid and poor and will never gain richness or vitality as long as, imprisoned on the stage, it does not dare to take on all subjects suited to great and beautiful poetry."[22] Hence Delille seeks not

---

20. Maunde, *Rural Philosopher,* xiii-xiv. For the original, see Delille, *Homme des champs,* 13–14.

21. See Delille, *Géorgiques,* xl, where this concept is discussed: "Another charm of poetry, and of all the other arts, is conquered difficulty [la difficulté vaincue]. One of the things that strikes us the most in a painting, in a statue, in a poem, is that one is able to give such flexibility to marble, that a colored canvas creates the illusion of sight, that verse, despite the constraints of meter, achieves the same liberty as ordinary language."

22. Delille, *Géorgiques,* xvi.

only to cultivate sensitivity to nature in his readers but also to free poetic language from its imprisonment on the French stage. His project thus obliges him to confront the question of how the poet can reveal or create poetic qualities in words previously deemed unpoetic. In this context, what Sainte-Beuve viewed as Delille's "accumulation of words and tiresome enumerations" appears less as a symptom of poetic failure than as a symptom of his bold attempt to stretch the classical poetic idiom to its breaking point.[23]

Delille's poetic project appears even more audacious when one considers the distinctly political overtones of his analysis of French poetic language. In the preface to his translation of the *Georgics,* Delille attributes the linguistic diversity of Vergil's poetry to the political autonomy enjoyed by the Roman people. In France, on the contrary, the stratification of society has led to a stratification of language, such that popular terms and expressions have been excluded from the "noble" realm of poetry:

> In our case, the barrier separating noblemen from the people has separated their language; prejudice has degraded words like men, and there are, so to speak, noble terms and plebeian terms [des termes roturiers]. A haughty scrupulousness has thus rejected a host of expressions and images. In becoming more decent, our language has been impoverished; and just as those in high places [les grands] have left the practice of the arts to the people, they have also left them the terms that paint their operations. Hence the necessity of using timid circumlocutions, of resorting to the slowness of periphrasis; of being long-winded, for fear of being lowly [d'être long, de peur d'être bas]; in such a way that the fate of our language quite resembles that of those ruined gentlemen, who condemn themselves to indigence for fear of losing rank and title [de peur de déroger].[24]

By referring specifically to the language of the mechanical arts, Delille links his poetic project to Diderot's effort in the *Encyclopédie* to bestow intellectual dignity on artisanal labor, and more broadly to the embourgeoisement of French culture. The political resonance of the passage was not lost

---

23. Sainte-Beuve, "Delille," 404–5 n. ****. Sainte-Beuve quotes this phrase from one of Delille's contemporaries but notes: "We would have little to say on the matter that was not already better said by [Delille's] contemporaries."

24. Delille, *Géorgiques,* xxviii.

on Victor Hugo, who borrowed the phrase "des termes roturiers," in a slightly modified form, in his dramatic manifesto of revolutionary poetics, "Réponse à un acte d'accusation," published in *Les contemplations* in 1856:

> Je fis souffler un vent révolutionnaire.
> Je mis un bonnet rouge au vieux dictionnaire.
> Plus de mot sénateur! Plus de mot roturier![25]

> [I made a revolutionary wind blow.
> I put a red cap on the old dictionary.
> No more senatorial words! No more plebeian words!]

Yet despite the political overtones of his poetic project, Delille has been remembered more for his timid circumlocutions than for his radical attempt to expand French poetic language. In part, his reputation as the epitome of Old Regime poetic conventions is due to the hostility with which he greeted the French Revolution: he remained a staunch royalist throughout the Revolution, and in response to Maximilien Robespierre's demand for a hymn to be performed at the Festival of the Supreme Being, he wrote a "Dithyrambe" that subtly expressed his resistance to revolutionary tyranny. After emigrating in 1795, he wrote a poem entitled *Le malheur et la pitié* (1803) that condemned revolutionary violence and called for the Restoration.[26] Indeed, Mercier may well have had Delille in mind when he defined "Hierarchy" in his dictionary of revolutionary neologisms, *La néologie* (1801), with the following quotation: "'There is in our language,' said a royalist, 'a hierarchy of style, because the words in it have been classed, like the subjects in a monarchy.'"[27] Yet although he himself was far more receptive to the Revolution than Delille, Mercier's manifesto in favor of revolutionary neologisms probably owed just as much to Delille

---

25. Victor Hugo, "Réponse à un acte d'accusation," in *Oeuvres poétiques,* ed. Pierre Albouy, Bibliothèque de la Pléiade 195 (Paris: Gallimard, 1967), 2:496.

26. See Guitton, *Jacques Delille,* 431–35, 468–77.

27. Louis Sébastien Mercier, "Hiérarchie," in *La néologie, ou Vocabulaire de mots nouveaux, à renouveler, ou pris dans des acceptations nouvelles* (Paris: Moussard-Maradan, 1801), 1:522. In his critical edition of *Les contemplations,* Pierre Albouy cites this passage and notes the influence of both Mercier and Delille on Hugo's conception of the liberation of poetic language. See Hugo, *Oeuvres poétiques,* 1348. On the important intertextual relationship between Mercier and Hugo, see Helen Temple Patterson, *Poetic Genesis: Sébastien Mercier into Victor Hugo,* Studies on Voltaire and the Eighteenth Century (Geneva: Institut et Musée Voltaire, 1960).

as Hugo's red bonnet on the old dictionary. For all three writers, social stratification was inscribed into the very fabric of the French language, and it was the role of the poet or prose writer to transform language to suit changing times.

Circumlocution: From Verse to Prose

In his political analysis of poetic language, Delille suggests that poets resort to "timid" circumlocutions in fear of defying poetic conventions. In a certain sense, he thus paved the way for his subsequent reputation as a servile, conventional Old Regime poet. Whereas Hugo has been credited with calling a pig a pig ("I called the pig by its name; why not?"), Delille has been mocked for taking two decades "to impose on poetic language a cow without an adjective, a completely naked cow."[28] In fact, the descriptive poets were well aware of the linguistic barriers facing them and could themselves be humorous about their use of circumlocution. In his *Harmonie imitative de la langue française, poème en quatre chants* (1785), Pierre-Antoine-Augustin de Piis asks an indiscreet pig to back away from his poem:

> Mais quel vil animal allonge son grouin?
> Ah! c'en est trop, recule, et vas grogner plus loin,
> Toi que doivent chasser, par un dégoût semblable,
> Les Français de leurs vers, et les Juifs de leur table.[29]

> [But what vile animal is advancing his snout?
> Ah! It's too much, move back, and go snort farther away.
> You that must chase, by a similar disgust,
> The French from their verse, and the Jews from their table.]

---

28. Hugo, "Réponse à un acte," 496; and Pierre Citron, "À propos des mots interdits," in *Delille est-il mort?* Collection Écrivains d'Auvergne (Clermont-Ferrand, Fr.: G. de Bussac, 1967), 222. In this caustic article about Delille's poetic language, Citron argues that Delille's paradoxical use of circumlocution was a sign of his increasing conventionalism once he was accepted into the Académie française in 1774. The heavy sarcasm in the article (with remarks such as "Delille is a Tartuffe—and he's got the face of one," and "Here, we are in the realm of true poetry: very far from Delille") suggests that Citron intended to answer the question "Is Delille dead?" in the affirmative. Citron, "Mots interdits," 222 and 225.

29. Pierre Antoine de Piis, *L'harmonie imitative de la langue française, poème en quatre chants* (Paris: Ph.-D. Pierres, 1785), 50. Subsequent references appear parenthetically in the main text.

De Piis's ostentatious avoidance of the word *cochon* is clearly ironic, given that it appears after a long enumeration of equally unpoetic animals, including the *boeuf* and the *boul-dogue*. Just as he does not hesitate to shock French sensibilities with such plebeian terms, de Piis playfully evokes, in a poem devoted to the harmony of the French language, sounds that are generally considered painful to the ear, such as the "painful pleasure" of fornicating cats (51).

Whether playful or earnest, the descriptive poets' use of circumlocution underlines the gap between their poetic project, which is based in concrete description, and the heritage of a classical poetic language more suited to the expression of metaphysical themes. As Jean Roudaut summarizes it, "The history of poetry in this century is a series of desperate attempts to allow a language forged for the expression of spiritual realities to attain perceptible reality."[30] Yet circumlocution could also have a more positive poetic function, serving to establish connections between verse and prose in a way that opened poetry out onto the world. A good example of this can be found in Delille's most ambitious poem, the title of which illustrates the continuity between poetry and science it sought to establish: *Les trois règnes de la nature, par Jacques Delille; avec des notes par M. Cuvier, de l'Institut, et autres savants* (1808) (The Three Realms of Nature, by Jacques Delille; with Notes by M. Cuvier, of the Institute, and Other Scholars [or Scientists]). In one of the "tiresome enumerations" attacked by Sainte-Beuve (a list of metals spanning several pages), Delille includes the obscure but potentially poetic terms for molybdenum and tungsten but resorts to circumlocutions, complete with prose notes, for the more pedestrian terms lead and platinum:

> Le fer cultivateur, et le bronze qui tonne,
> Et ce métal docile où l'onde s'emprisonne;
> L'étain, l'argent, et l'or qui brille sans rivaux;
> Et ce nouveau métal, le plus lourd des métaux,
> Que long-temps à nos yeux déroba la nature,

---

30. Roudaut, *Poètes et grammairiens*, 19. Delon concurs with the view that circumlocutions are a sign of the poets' laborious and unsuccessful attempt to use a poetic idiom wholly unsuited to the concrete objects they wanted to describe. Delon, *Anthologie*, 17. On the other hand, both Roudaut and Guitton have also explained the use of circumlocution by characterizing it as a form of description. Guitton, *Jacques Delille*, 178; and Roudaut, *Poètes et grammairens*, 18.

Et de nos arts féconds la richesse future;
Et le mercure enfin, qui, connu par son poids,
En globules roulants glisse et fuit sous nos doigts.[31]

[Cultivating iron, and resonating bronze,
And this docile metal that imprisons waves;
Steel, silver, and gold, which shines without rivals;
And this new metal, the heaviest of metals,
That nature long hid from our eyes,
And of our fertile arts the future riches;
And mercury finally, which, known by its weight,
In rolling drops slips and falls through our fingers.]

In these lines, the circumlocutions add a level of mystery to an otherwise concrete enumeration of objects, sparking the reader's curiosity and initiating a quest for knowledge. On a concrete level, they prompt the reader to refer to what Sainte-Beuve called "the little encyclopedia around the poem," the lengthy prose notes written by Georges Cuvier and other scholars. For example, the line "Et ce nouveau métal, le plus lourd des métaux" refers us to the following prose note:

Platinum: it has only been found so far in mines in Peru, in the form of grayish grains, mixed with black sand. Several metals are combined with it, and it took thirty years of research to learn how to remove them from it. It is mainly with arsenic that this can be done. Pure platinum is heavier than gold and just as resistant; its color approaches that of silver, and its hardness that of steel, of which it also shares the beautiful polish. In addition to these advantages, it is perfectly malleable and endures the hottest fire. All these qualities make platinum extremely precious for the flasks used in chemistry, for the mirrors of telescopes, and more generally for all instruments that require a fine polish and long use. M. Vauquelin just recently discovered several strands of platinum in some silver mines in Estramadure.[32]

This passage indeed appears as a fragment of encyclopedia; it could easily have been lifted from the *Encyclopédie* or from Buffon's *Histoire naturelle des minéraux* (1783–88). The note's most immediate function is to resolve

---

31. Jacques Delille, *Les trois règnes de la nature, par Jacques Delille; avec des notes par M. Cuvier, de l'Institut, et autres savants* (Paris: Frères Mame, 1808), 2:12.

32. Ibid., 2:44–45.

the enigma created by the circumlocution: the metal in question is platinum. But the note also explains and expands upon the information alluded to in the circumlocution, offering the reader specific information about why platinum long remained inaccessible to man, and what makes it valuable for arts such as astronomy and chemistry. In this way, circumlocution works to open poetic verse out onto the prose of the world, to link the beauty of poetic language to the mysteries of scientific discovery. In doing so, it transforms the term "platinum," giving it poetic qualities and paving the way for its entry into poetic language. At the same time, by prompting the reader to move back and forth between verse and prose, circumlocution introduces a new dynamic into the reading of poetry, analogous to the subversive and liberating system of cross-referencing in the *Encyclopédie*.[33]

Yet circumlocution can also be interpreted as a response to the descriptive poets' anxious sense that their poetry risked becoming nothing more than a prosaic inventory of the world's objects. Many Enlightenment writers, including Diderot, perceived the philosophical spirit of their age as antithetical to poetry. While Delille may not have shared this view, in the last canto of *Les trois règnes de la nature* he characterizes his age as a time of poetic disenchantment:

> Ils sont passés ces temps des rêves poétiques,
>
> . . . .
>
> Nos vergers sont sans dieux, nos forêts sans miracles;
> Au sang du beau chasseur adoré par Cypris,
> La rose ne doit plus son brillant coloris;
> L'eau ne répète plus le beau front de Narcisse,
> Ce long cyprès n'est plus le jeune Cyparisse,
> Ces pales peupliers les soeurs de Phaéton,
> Ce vieux tilleul Baucis, ce chêne Philémon:
> Tout est désenchanté; mais, sans tous ces prestiges,
> Les arbres ont leur vie, et les bois leurs prodiges.
> Je veux les célébrer; je dirai quels ressorts
> Des peuples végétaux organisent les corps.[34]

---

33. Delon has characterized the movement from verse to prose as follows: "The prose note underlines the contradiction between [the poets'] ambition and the means [at their disposal], between a dream and a linguistic and social reality. The prose commentary becomes necessary to the comprehension of verses that threaten not to suffice in themselves, verses that are discredited by virtue of their attempt to translate a modern form of knowledge." Delon, *Anthologie,* 18.

34. Delille, *Trois règnes,* 2:55–56.

[Those times of poetic dreams have passed,
. . . .
Our orchards are without gods, our forests without miracles;
To the blood of a beautiful hunter adored by Cypris,
The rose no longer owes its brilliant coloring;
Water no longer mirrors the beautiful forehead of Narcissus,
This tall cypress is no longer the young Cyparissus,
These pale poplars the sisters of Phaeton,
This old lime tree Baucis, this oak Philemon:
Everything is disenchanted; yet, without all the prestige,
Trees have their life, and the woods their marvels.
I want to celebrate them; I will say what workings
Organize the bodies of vegetable peoples.]

There is a mournful decrescendo in these lines, as the beauty of lost poetic dreams dwindles down into the more prosaic "saying" of the mechanical workings of the natural world. Unlike the metaphor-laden lines that describe a time when roses owed their color to the blood of a beautiful hunter, the last four lines are almost entirely lacking in metaphor and imagery. Trees are not inhabited; they simply have vegetable life; the woods are bereft of miracles, since the poet can explain their structures and mechanisms. Hence Delille poses the question of what makes a universe poetic, and how the modern poet can replace the magical transformations of Ovid's *Metamorphoses* with a new poetry of nature. While his explanations of nature might appear to participate in the disenchantment he describes, he seeks to recover a sense of enchantment through the dynamic exchange between circumlocution and scientific end matter, replacing the fables of bygone ages with the modern marvels of science.

Thus circumlocution and enumeration can be seen as two sides of the same coin: as the poem threatens to become nothing more than a list of objects, circumlocution serves to separate literal meaning from its poetic expression, to "say" the world without naming it directly. Circumlocution can be seen as an anxious poetic response to the closeness between poetry and encyclopedia during the period of disenchantment described by Delille. Without circumlocution, poetry risks becoming nothing more than a catalog and explanation of the world. What then does it offer that cannot already be found in Diderot and d'Alembert's *Encyclopédie*, or even in the prose notes that form "a little encyclopedia around the poem"? In a period when prose was increasingly being championed as more supple, expressive, and modern than verse, the descriptive poets could no longer count on versification being valued for its own sake.[35] They had to find ways to make their encyclopedic project properly and necessarily poetic, and circumlocution participated in that effort by initiating a quest from language to knowledge and back again.

Imitative Harmony: The Art of Painting with Sounds

The other characteristic formal device of descriptive poetry, imitative harmony, can be understood in a similar light. This technique, elegantly defined by Delille as the "art of painting with sounds," was for the descriptive poets a means of combining the encyclopedic and the poetic, by simultaneously capturing the sounds and visual aspects of things.[36] Imitative harmony was not simply an attempt to make the reader hear the sounds of the world through the formal devices of poetry, although this was part of it. Far more complex, it sought to stimulate visual impressions through the manipulation of sounds. It therefore represented the possibility for a virtual melding of text and image, analogous to the combination of prose descriptions and plates in the *Encyclopédie*.

In addition to emphasizing the importance of imitative harmony in his theoretical writings, Delille offers both illustrations and guiding precepts for aspiring poets in *L'homme des champs:*

> Quels qu'ils soient, aux objects conformez votre ton;
> Ainsi que par les mots, exprimez par le son.
>
> . . . .
>
> Que d'un pas lent et lourd le boeuf fende la plaine;
> Chaque syllabe pèse, et chaque mot se traîne.
> Mais si le daim léger bondit, vole et fend l'air,

---

35. See Menant, *Chute d'Icare,* especially the second chapter, entitled "Le débat," which treats the quarrels surrounding verse and prose during the first half of the eighteenth century. The most important period of debate concerning the value (or lack thereof) of verse followed the publication of Antoine Houdar de la Motte's *Discours sur la tragédie* (1730), which "relaunches...the indictment against verse and above all against rhyme, already frequently attacked in the preceding decades." Menant, *Chute d'Icare,* 53.

36. Delille, *Homme des champs,* 12.

> Le vers vole et le suit, aussi prompt que l'éclair.
> Ainsi de votre chant la marche cadencée
> Imite l'action et note la pensée.[37]
>
> [Still let your tone its several objects tell;
> For sound and sense together still should dwell.
> . . . .
> When the slow oxen labour o'er the plain,
> At every word should drag the weighty strain;
> When the fleet roebuck flies and cuts the air,
> The verse should follow like the lightning's glare.
> Thus let your song, that runs in measur'd note,
> Express each movement, and each thought denote.][38]

An example of imitative harmony can be found in Delille's description of the ox's slow and heavy passage across the plain. The difficulty of passing from the "f" of *boeuf* to the "f" of *fende* "paints" the laboriousness of the steer's plodding step, and the emphasis on the silent *e* of *fende* seems to break through the heaviness of the line, just as the animal's step breaks through the crusted earth. Moreover, the heaviness in the subjunctive *fende* contrasts with the lightness of the verb *fend* two lines later as the deer gracefully darts through the much lighter air. Similarly, imitative harmony itself is painted with the line "Chaque syllabe pèse, et chaque mot se traîne," as the repeated silent *e*'s create a slow, heavy rhythm, and the almost complete break at the hemistich after "pèse" sets up the more droning movement of "chaque mot se traîne."

With these illustrations of imitative harmony, Delille sought to dispel his contemporaries' belief that the French language did not naturally lend itself to harmonic effects. A similar motivation prompted de Piis to write his poem *L'harmonie imitative de la langue française*. Better known as a writer of songs and vaudevilles than as a descriptive poet, de Piis wrote for the Comédie-Italienne before the Revolution and founded several vaudeville theaters and published his *Chansons patriotiques* during the Revolution. His sole descriptive poem is something of an anomaly, both

---

37. Ibid., 142–43. In the "Advertisement" to his English translation of this poem, John Maunde rails against Delille's tendency to borrow liberally from his English models with literal translations, making the English translator's job equally frustrating and futile. Maunde, *Rural Philosopher,* vii–viii. These lines indeed appear to have been written in imitation of Alexander Pope.

38. Maunde, *Rural Philosopher,* 113–14.

in his own career and in the corpus of descriptive poetry, not least because of its humorous tone. Nonetheless, in one of its serious moments, it confirms Delille's definition of imitative harmony as the art of painting with sounds:

> Il est, n'en doutons pas, il est une Harmonie,
> Qui naît du choix des mots qu'enchaîne le Génie,
> Et, dans tous les sujets, par des accords divers,
> On peut à la musique égaler l'art des vers.
> On peut la surpasser, j'ose le dire encore;
> Volez, Alexandrins, qu'une image décore,
> En calculant vos sons, tristes ou gracieux,
> Vous peindrez à l'oreille aussi vîte qu'aux yeux.
>
> (3)

> [There is, have no doubt, there is a harmony,
> That is born of the choice of words enchained by genius,
> And, in all subjects, by diverse chords,
> One can to music make equal the art of verse.
> One can surpass it, I dare to say again;
> Fly, alexandrines that an image adorns,
> In calculating your sounds, sad or graceful,
> You will paint to the ear as quickly as to the eyes.]

In these lines, de Piis attributes two different functions to imitative harmony: it allows the descriptive poet to surpass both the painter and the musician, by painting for the eye and the ear simultaneously. But it also allows the poet to take on a far wider range of topics than was traditionally admitted in classical French poetry, thereby expanding poetic language and reinforcing the connections between poetry and encyclopedia.

In fact, de Piis's entire poem serves to illustrate the encyclopedic breadth of French poetic language. This can be seen most clearly when he imagines a group of exacting friends who demand that he use imitative harmony to re-create the sounds of machines, quadrupeds, and musical instruments:

> Ils voudront me contraindre, à saisir les effets,
> Du bruit de nos métiers, des cris du quadrupède,
> Et du son qu'en son sein chaque instrument possède.
> Eh! bien, je me dévoue à ces nombreux travaux.
>
> (37)

[They will want to force me to capture the effects,
Of the sounds of our machines, of the cries of quadrupeds,
And of the sound that in its breast each instrument possesses.
Well then! I devote myself to these numerous tasks.]

Not coincidentally, de Piis's friends challenge him with subjects drawn from the most important descriptive enterprises of the Enlightenment: artisanal machines and quadrupeds. By alluding to the *Encyclopédie* and the *Histoire naturelle,* de Piis suggests that poetry has an important role to play in the Enlightenment project of describing nature. His theory of imitative harmony can thus be seen not only as a means of expanding the reach of poetry, but also as a means of rivaling the contributions of those monumental works of descriptive prose.

Yet with de Piis's encyclopedic aspirations comes a risk: how far can poetry go in abandoning the structural principles of classical poetics without losing coherence? The disintegration of poetic design in de Piis's poem is exemplified by the title of his third canto, which reads: "Attempts to imitate the noise of machines, the sounds of musical instruments, and the echo and cries of animals" (37). It can also be seen in the unmotivated transitions between various sections of the poem. After describing the cacophony of a house under construction, for example, de Piis turns his attention to the intoxicating effects of wine, with the most artificial of transitions:

> Près de ces ouvriers voilà, pour mon malheur,
> Que le hazard dirige un perfide émouleur,
> Qui sur sa meule en feu, par un jeu qui l'amuse,
> Aiguise les outils de si près qu'il les use.
> Puisse-t-il, entre nous les repasser si bien
> Que pour nous étourdir il n'en reste plus rien!
> Si pour me ranimer je gagne mes Pénates,
> Oh! de quel bruit plus doux, cher Bacchus tu me flattes!
> (40–41)

[Near to these workers here, to my misfortune,
Chance directs a perfidious grinder,
Who on his fiery grindstone, in a game he finds fun,
Sharpens his tools so closely that he wears them down.
May he, between you and me, grind them so well

That to deafen us nothing more remains!
If to revive myself I reach my Penates,
Oh! with what a sweeter sound, dear Bacchus, you flatter me!]

This passage is symptomatic of the way de Piis handles transitions throughout the poem, both in its artificiality and in its use of silence to facilitate the
transition between different kinds of sounds: the deafening sounds of the
construction site fall silent when the grinder sharpens his tool down to
nothing, and this silence provides a pretext for moving on to the more
pleasant sound of champagne bubbling out of bottles. Other similar examples include de Piis stifling the sounds of Adam and Eve's sexual union by
transitioning abruptly to quadruped noises, and concluding his third canto
with an evocation of the indignant monkey falling silent when he realizes
he cannot speak (48, 51). The subsequent transition from champagne to
music takes these unmotivated transitions to an almost absurd level:

On est, quand on a bu, plus propre à la musique.
Et je peindrai les sons que ce bel art m'indique.

(42)

[One is, after drinking, more amenable to music.
And I will paint the sounds that this beautiful art indicates to me.]

Such unmotivated transitions highlight the lack of internal structure in de
Piis's poem: since his sole purpose is to illustrate the encyclopedic breadth
of French poetic language, he can take on any subject and arrange his various descriptions in any order he pleases. In fact, he even seems to revel in
this disintegration of poetic design, which frees him from the strictures
of classical poetry and brings his poem closer to the arbitrary alphabetical
order of the *Encyclopédie*.

De Piis's emulation of this arbitrary encyclopedic order is especially
apparent in his first canto, which explores the harmonic possibilities of
the French language in alphabetical order. Even more than Delille's list
of metals, this canto is indeed an accumulation of words, consisting in an
enumeration of harmonically expressive words with no apparent relation
between them except their first letter. Yet for de Piis, the alphabet itself
serves as a motivating and unifying poetic principle, since he attributes
semantic meaning to the sound and visual aspect of each letter. The objects

listed under the letter *C,* for example, all share the trait of being hollow, like the letter itself:

> Le *C* rival de l'*S,* avec une cédille,
> Sans elle, au lieu du *Q,* dans tous nos mots fourmille,
> De tous les objets creux il commence le nom;
> Une cave, une cuve, une chambre, un canon,
> Une corbeille, un coeur, un coffre, une carrière,
> Une caverne enfin le trouvent nécessaire;
> Par-tout, en demi-cercle, il court demi-courbé,
> Et le *K,* dans l'oubli, par son choc est tombé.[39]
>
> (12)

> [The *C,* rival of the *S,* with a cedilla,
> Without it, in place of the *Q,* in all our words swarms,
> Of all hollow objects it begins the name;
> A *cave* [basement], a *cuve* [vat], a chamber, a canon,
> A corbeille, a *coeur* [heart], a coffer, a *carrière* [quarry],
> A cavern, in conclusion, finds it necessary;
> Everywhere, in a semicircle, it runs half-bowed,
> And the *K,* into oblivion, by its shock has fallen.]

For de Piis, each letter of the alphabet has its own intrinsic imitative harmony. This harmony is both visual and musical: the hollowness of the letter as it appears on the page mirrors the hollowness of the objects beginning with *C:* a canon, a coffer, a cavern. At the same time, the harsh sound of *K* echoes the sound of things falling into those hollow objects. Letters interact with each other, on the page and in the reader's ear, just as objects do: hence the letter *K* has fallen into oblivion (into the hollowness of the letter *C*) with a resounding clunk. In this way, de Piis's poetic rendering of the alphabet foregrounds the materiality of language in both its visual and its aural dimensions. His first canto is an attempt to create a truly motivated descriptive language, quite possibly in order to counterbalance the inevitable disintegration of poetic design in his encyclopedic poetic enterprise. At the same time, his use of the alphabet illustrates the

---

39. This canto poses obvious translation difficulties, since both the first letter and the meaning of the words must be respected.

extent to which descriptive poetry lacks a center of gravity: each letter, like each descriptive fragment, can become a poem in its own right, containing within it infinite possibilities for poetic expansion. And just as the alphabetical order of the *Encyclopédie* gives readers the freedom to follow their own exploratory reading path, the empty center of de Piis's poem creates a dizzying freedom for both the poet and his reader, demonstrating the encyclopedic breadth of poetic language without even beginning to exhaust its possibilities.

The Describer amid the Fragments

The disintegration of poetic design is even more marked in Delille's poem *Les trois règnes de la nature,* which Sainte-Beuve sarcastically called "the crowning glory of the genre" (le bouquet du genre).[40] At the beginning of each canto, Delille provides an *argument,* or summary, ostensibly in order to give his readers a sense for the overall design of the canto. Yet rather than elucidating the logic of the poem, these summaries underscore the seemingly haphazard arrangement of the descriptive fragments that make up each canto. In fact, the various sections outlined do not even seen to belong to the same genre of poetry, or in some cases, to any genre of poetry at all. For example, Delille's summary of a canto devoted to water reads as follows:

> The various effects of water in the creations and scenes of nature.—Properties of water.—Painting of a flood.—Episode of Musidore surprised in the bath by her lover.—Streams, lakes, and rivers.—Mineral waters.—Usefulness of water in the mechanical arts.—Different combinations of water subjected to the action of fire.—Water reduced to ice.—View of the picturesque winter ice.—Description of hail.—Snow.—The deplorable death of a woodsman surprised far from his cabin, and buried in the snow.—The generous instinct of dogs, who bring lost travelers back to the Saint-Bernard hospice.[41]

This summary appears to encompass at least three representational registers: scientific discourse (the effects, properties, and uses of water), aesthetic

40. Sainte-Beuve, "Delille," 401.
41. Delille, *Trois règnes,* 1:190.

discourse (paintings and picturesque views), and narrative discourse (the episodes of Musidore and the lost woodsman). The register of other sections is more ambiguous: streams, lakes, and rivers are simply named, as if removed from any representational framework; the instinct of generous dogs has both narrative and scientific implications; the description of hail potentially encompasses all of these registers. It may present itself as a textual equivalent of the object itself, as a painting with claims to aesthetic beauty, as a scientific account of how hail is formed, or as the story of a hailstorm and its ravaging effect on a poor farmer's crops. Sandwiched as it is between sections that have distinct scientific, aesthetic, or narrative implications, the term "description" may potentially refer to any and all of these forms of discourse. In fact, when one turns to the poem itself, the section in question addresses the formation of hail, its devastating impact on shepherds and farmers, and its visual and aural properties.

Hence Delille uses the term "description" as an umbrella term for the multiple forms of discourse he integrates into his poem. In a striking reversal of classical poetic principles, he even incorporates narrative fragments into the broad category of description. Whereas classical theorists, including Marmontel in his article "Descriptif," insisted that description must be motivated by a dominant narrative framework, Delille instead uses narrative as a pretext for further description. A good example can be found in the anecdote "Episode of Musidore surprised in the bath by her lover" in a canto devoted to water and its properties. Musidore is a character who will never again appear in the poem, and the anecdote is justified solely by the occasion it provides to describe her bath. Like the transition from construction site to wine in de Piis's poem, Musidore's abrupt appearance in Delille's poem appears highly artificial. This and other narrative fragments appear to be motivated not primarily by the story they tell, but by the pretext they provide for illustrating the encyclopedic breadth of descriptive poetry.

Indeed, the incorporation of narrative fragments into descriptive poetry makes it a truly encyclopedic genre, encompassing not just the universe and its objects, but also all forms of poetic representation. Not content to simply incorporate fragments of encyclopedia and words previously deemed unpoetic, the descriptive poets sought to subordinate narration to description, by placing things, their descriptions and explanations of how they work, above plot structure. This reversal of classical principles was not without risks, for it threatened to make the genre infinitely digressive and gave readers multiple occasions to interrupt their reading. In the absence of a narrative thread or logical "argument," what would hold the readers' interest and guarantee their continued engagement with the poem?

As we have seen, it was precisely in these terms that Marmontel criticized descriptive poetry in his article "Descriptif," published in the *Encyclopédie méthodique* in 1782. Remaining loyal to the precepts of classical poetics, Marmontel stipulated that description could play an important role in the classical genres of epic, didactic poetry, and dramatic poetry, but that it could not, in and of itself, be constitutive of a poetic genre. Descriptive poetry would inevitably "fatigue" its readers, Marmontel argued, because it abandoned all structuring principles except the poet's intention to describe. Whereas in classical poetic genres, "description is connected to a story that introduces it, with an intention to instruct or to persuade, with an interest that serves as its motivation," the descriptive poet "describes to describe, and describes again after having described, passing from one object to another, with no other cause than the mobility of the gaze and of thought."[42] Yet with this critique, Marmontel implicitly acknowledged that the descriptive genre placed the poet at the center of his own act of creation. By the very flexibility of his project, the describer emerges amid the fragments as the sole motivating force and organizing principle for poetry.

* * *

One way of interpreting descriptive poetry would thus be to see it as paving the way for romantic poetry. As we have seen, many ingredients typically associated with romantic poetry surface in some form in the descriptive genre: the sensitivity to nature, the dismantling of the classical genre hierarchy, the political analysis of poetic language, the attempt to introduce "low" words into poetry, and above all, the central place of the poet as the source of poetic creation. Viewed in this light, Sainte-Beuve's bold statement that "it is permissible to assert, with complete certainty, that the victory of the new school is proved at the very least by the complete ruin of the old" appears to deny unjustly the important contribution the old school made to the new.[43] Yet a richer interpretation would be one that does justice to descriptive poetry as a poetic project in its own right. If, as

---

42. *Grammaire et littérature,* 1:592.
43. Sainte-Beuve, "Delille," 392–93.

Annie Becq has claimed, descriptive poetry appears as "one of the possible sites for the emergence of the modern notion of poetry," it is not because it paved the way for romantic poetry, but rather because it confronted the gap between poetic language and our knowledge of the world and sought to transform language, through circumlocution, prose notes, and imitative harmony, in order to fill that gap.[44] In a certain sense, descriptive poetry "failed" because its ambitions were too encyclopedic; like the cabinet of natural curiosities described in Delille's *L'homme des champs,* it strived to be "L'extrait de la nature et l'abrégé du monde" ("The world and nature, in abridgment shown.")[45] Limited only by the most flexible of poetics, the descriptive poets were drawn into describing larger and larger portions of the world. By virtue of their encyclopedic ambitions, they encountered both the limits of their own knowledge—hence Delille called upon Cuvier and others to write the prose notes for *Les trois règnes de la nature*—and the limits of the poetic language available to them. In their effort to "guide the Muse where earth's last confine lies," the descriptive poets found themselves stranded amid the fragments of a poetic encyclopedia, which had little to say about their personal emotions, but everything to say about their relationship to knowledge.[46]

---

44. Becq, "Réflexion sur la poétique," 237.
45. Delille, *Homme des champs,* 115; and Maunde, *Rural Philosopher,* 87.
46. Maunde, *Rural Philosopher,* 102.

Part III

Moral and Political Topographies

5

MERCIER'S UNFRAMED PARIS

More than any of the writers discussed thus far, Louis Sébastien Mercier incarnates the figure of the Enlightenment describer. As already noted, he explicitly identified himself as a *descripteur,* tracing the genesis of his twelve-volume description of Paris and its social mores, the *Tableau de Paris* (1781–88), to his childhood love for description.[1] His identity as a

---

1. Mercier, *Tableau de Paris,* 2:1497. All subsequent references appear parenthetically in the main text. Scholarship on Mercier has benefited incalculably from the critical edition of his most important works, under the direction of Jean-Claude Bonnet. In addition to the edition of the *Tableau de Paris* already cited, these include *Le nouveau Paris,* ed. Jean-Claude Bonnet (Paris: Mercure de France, 1994); *Mon bonnet de nuit, Du théâtre,* ed. Jean-Claude Bonnet (Paris: Mercure de France, 1999); and *Néologie,* ed. Jean-Claude Bonnet (Paris: Belin, 2009). See also Jean-Claude Bonnet, ed., *Le Paris de Louis Sébastien Mercier, Cartes et index* (Paris: Mercure de France, 1994); and id., ed., *Louis Sébastien Mercier (1740–1814): Un hérétique en littérature* (Paris: Mercure de France, 1995). For an excellent introduction to the *Tableau de Paris,* with attention to its neglected literary qualities, and for a translation of selected chapters, see Louis Sébastien Mercier, *Panorama of Paris: Selections from "Tableau de Paris,"* based on the translation by Helen Simpson, ed. and with a new preface and translations of additional articles by Jeremy D. Popkin (University Park: Pennsylvania State University Press, 1999). Unless otherwise noted, however, all translations are my own.

describer was inseparable from the metaphor of painting as writing that surfaced frequently in his work: in the *Tableau de Paris,* he noted: "I held nothing but the brush of the painter in this work"; and in his dictionary of revolutionary neologisms, *La néologie* (1801), he referred to his writing as *mots-couleurs* (word-colors).[2] Yet Mercier was not in fact as fond of the visual arts as this metaphor might suggest. During the revolutionary decade and until his death in 1814, he railed against the idiocy of painting before the Council of Five Hundred, as a member of the Institut, and in multiple newspaper articles. This bitter iconoclasm was in part a reaction against the propagandistic use of the visual arts by the Jacobins, and especially the deputy-painter Jacques-Louis David, during the most radical phase of the Revolution. As we will see in chapter 6, Mercier was imprisoned during the Terror for his support of the Girondins, and he held the Jacobins, and Robespierre in particular, whom he referred to as a *sanguinocrate* (bloodocrat), responsible for the worst excesses and failures of the Revolution.[3] Many of his attacks against painting thus appear to have been retrospectively directed against the radical imagery promulgated by David and other pro-Jacobin artists during the Terror.[4]

Yet Mercier's radical iconoclasm also had aesthetic origins, and can be traced to the innovative descriptive poetics he developed in the *Tableau de Paris.* As Jeremy Popkin notes, Mercier consciously chose to publish the *Tableau de Paris* without illustrations and maps and "was particularly unhappy with the 96 engravings inspired by his work that a German artist, Balthasar Anton Dunker, published in 1787."[5] Mercier's resistance to illustration was deeply engrained in his poetics of description. A best-selling work published over a period of eight years, the *Tableau de Paris* offered a global description of Paris that unfolded over time, in rhythm with the constant flux of the city and the multiple perspectives of its moving describer. Readers were invited to explore Paris as a shifting moral and physical topography, a site of continual transformation for which "it is hardly possible that the painting of this year resemble next year" (2:1309). Yet Mercier did

---

2. See Mercier, *Tableau de Paris,* 1:17; and id., *Néologie,* 1:xl-xli.

3. See the chapter "Sanguinocrate" in Mercier, *Nouveau Paris,* 457.

4. On the Revolution's radical imagery, see Lynn Hunt, *Politics, Culture, and Class in the French Revolution,* 20th anniv. ed. (1984; Berkeley and Los Angeles: University of California Press, 2004), 87–119.

5. Popkin, preface to *Panorama of Paris,* 19.

not seek only to represent change; he sought also to effect change through the precise and evocative description of social and political abuses. Thus, although he frequently referred to his work as a painting and himself as a painter, the *Tableau de Paris* founded an innovative conception of the *tableau* that was consistent with his critique of painting. Refusing the limitations of the pictorial frame, Mercier's painting of Paris was temporally and spatially expansive, transforming the Parisian topography into a history of the present and participating in the changes it documented.

Unbreakable Images

Mercier's iconclasm reached its paroxysm under the Directory, when he delivered a virulent speech attacking painting to the Council of Five Hundred, and reiterated his attacks in the debate that ensued in the *Journal de Paris*.[6] Yet his iconoclasm in fact predated the revolutionary decade: all of his major works, and notably the *Tableau de Paris,* are peppered with venomous condemnations of painting and painters.[7] Painting, the "idiot sister" of poetry, is "a childish production [un enfantillage] of the human mind, a continually impotent enterprise that is in most cases laughably intrepid," and painters are "the most useless men in the world, charging exorbitant prices for an art that in no way interests the happiness, tranquillity, or even the pleasures [les jouissances] of civil society; a cold and false art of which any true philosopher will sense the inanity."[8] Such extreme statements of

---

6. See the recorded proceedings of the Council of Five Hundred ("Conseil des Cinq Cents, séance du 28 frimaire," *Journal de Paris,* Nonidi 29 Frimaire l'an V—lundi 19 décembre 1796 vieux style) for Mercier's speech concerning the right of painters to be freed from patenting obligations. Mercier's extreme iconoclastic statements in this speech are frequently referred to in readers' letters and in Mercier's responses to them in subsequent issues of the *Journal de Paris* for 1797. For a selection of Mercier's newspaper articles on the topic, see the section "Musées" in "Musées, jardins et fêtes de Paris: Textes publiés dans la presse de 1797 à 1800," in Mercier, *Nouveau Paris,* 943–1009.

7. For a broad selection of Mercier's texts and articles on painting, see the section "Peintre/Peinture" in Louis Sébastien Mercier, *Dictionnaire d'un polygraphe: Textes de L. S. Mercier,* ed. Geneviève Bollème (Paris: Union Générale d'Éditions, 1978), 315–25. In the *Tableau de Paris,* see the chapters "Vente de tableaux," 2:829–35; "La harpe," 2:1290; "Fête de sainte Cécile," 2:1392–94; and "Muséum," 2:1520–21.

8. The first two comments appear in Mercier's speech before the Council of Five Hundred (see note 6), and the third appears in the chapter "Muséum," Mercier, *Tableau de Paris,* 2:1521.

iconoclasm may come as something of a surprise from an author who just as frequently referred to his words as colors, his pen as a paintbrush, and his works as paintings.

Yet both of the opposing poles of Mercier's authorial identity—iconoclast and painter—reflect the innovative approach to description he developed in the *Tableau de Paris* and pursued in a different form in his account of revolutionary Paris, *Le nouveau Paris*. Imagining a critic who cries "You are an iconoclast," Mercier responds: "No, for I won't call you an iconolater [iconolâtre]; the proof is that I want to give you images that are within you, that renew themselves continuously and that nothing can break."[9] The aesthetic model upheld here marks a departure from the traditional understanding of painting in three respects: the images are internal, they are constantly changing, and they form an unbreakable whole. Referring on several occasions to this model as *la peinture intérieure,* or inner painting, Mercier links it explicitly to the descriptive practice of his time, and to Buffon in particular:

> You want to represent for me earthly objects with earthly things; blind ones! The image will no longer be within you as it truly is; it will from then on be outside of you, cold, petty, inanimate, and it will no longer be anything but a cut-up and bizarre image [une image coupée et fantasque]. Read these beautiful pages from Buffon, and sense for once that it is only in written words that the supreme imitation of the horse, the donkey, the lion, the cat, and the hummingbird lies; and close your eyes to see better; all of nature is within you; painting makes ridiculous frames.[10]

True painting, according to Mercier, can only be realized in written form, since writing neither frames its images arbitrarily nor removes them from the inner sanctum of readers' minds. Buffon's descriptions thus exist in continuity with the internal, global perceptions of nature that all readers see when they close their eyes. Painting, in contrast, reduces and exteriorizes those images, enclosing them in frames that are "ridiculous," both because they are arbitrary and because they are material.

In an article published in the *Journal de Paris* in 1797, Mercier specifically attacks the limitations of the pictorial frame: "There is in every kind

---

9. Mercier, "Musées," *Nouveau Paris,* 963.
10. Ibid., 965. For an extended discussion of *la peinture intérieure,* see 954.

of form something divine, and that seems to belong to no completely isolated form in the universe. Yet painting perpetually isolates the object, in-
cessantly cuts up the great frame of nature, and at times in a manner that is
narrow and ridiculous. It thus always destroys the form it seems to want to
make more beautiful."[11] Implicit in this critique is Mercier's aesthetic ideal
of a global form of representation, expansive enough to encompass the immense "frame of nature." So attached is Mercier to what Anthony Vidler
has called "the path of totalizing observation" that he deems anything less
than a total painting to be worthless.[12] As long as painting can represent
only one perspective on any given object or scene, it can have no place in
his aesthetic framework: "There is thus no true painting except one that
brings together the totality of objects, their harmonic relationships; and if
the imitation is not complete, it is worthless [nulle]. Painting thus marks
its absolute impotence at the very moment it can only offer a given side,
and even this surface is still either false or inaccurate."[13] Using a vocabulary
reminiscent of Saint-Pierre's language of natural harmonies, Mercier emphasizes the hidden relationships that tie objects together and give them
their true meaning. For both writers, the model of a consecutive catalog of
individual objects must be abandoned in favor of a global, impressionistic
description that acknowledges and reveals those relationships.

Mercier's critique of painting thus reflects the aesthetic model on which
the *Tableau de Paris* was based: in this twelve-volume description of Paris,
he seeks to provide a single representation of the city, within which multiple objects and scenes are to be perceived and understood in relation to
each other. This model informs his title: *Tableau de Paris* in the singular,
rather than the more predictable *Tableaux de Paris* in the plural (as the
work is often mistakenly called). This title suggests that the work must
be read not as a series of portraits or sketches of various aspects of Paris
and Parisian life, but rather as a single object, viewed from many different angles and on many different occasions. Mercier indeed presents the
work in this way in his preface, when he writes: "Here it is, traced just as it
came out from under my pen, as my eyes and my understanding [entende-
ment] brought its parts together" (1:14). Although the work is spread out

---

11. Mercier, "Musées," *Nouveau Paris,* 955–56.
12. Anthony Vidler, "Mercier urbaniste: L'utopie du réel," in Bonnet, *Hérétique,* 237.
13. Mercier, "Musées," *Nouveau Paris,* 956.

over twelve volumes, published over a period of eight years, and is broken down into hundreds of chapters of a few pages each, readers are nonetheless invited to interpret it as a single painting, by using their eyes and minds to compose and recompose a coherent inner vision of Paris.

Mercier's innovative conception of the *tableau* marked a departure from the reigning aesthetic principles of his time: from Anthony Ashley Cooper, third earl of Shaftesbury, to Diderot and Lessing, eighteenth-century theorists emphasized the crucial aesthetic choice of the single moment represented in a painting.[14] As Michael Fried has shown, this emphasis was part of a broader preoccupation with creating the aesthetic conditions for the beholder's absorptive contemplation of art.[15] Even in his brilliant "Promenade Vernet," in which he transformed a series of Vernet landscapes into a meandering promenade traversing multiple landscapes, Diderot exhibited a particular preoccupation with pictorial framing and unity. Although it shares some obvious features with Mercier's conception of the *tableau,* the "Promenade Vernet" is punctuated by a series of distinct points of view (corresponding to individual paintings) that are strongly framed. In a similar way, Diderot insisted in his writings on theater that the theatrical *tableau* be a moment of arrested movement on the stage, and that this moment be carefully chosen and framed for its maximal dramatic impact.[16]

A similar preoccupation with framing can be seen in the *Encyclopédie* article "Tableau," which highlights the manner in which the actual frame serves to reinforce the unity of the painting it encloses: "The ingenuity of men has found several ways to make paintings more able to make a strong impression on us; . . . they enclose them in edges [des bordures] that cast a new shine on the colors, and that seem, by separating the paintings from surrounding objects, better to join together the parts of which they are composed, more or less as a window seems to bring together the various

---

14. The relevant works are Shaftesbury's *Characteristicks of Men, Manners, Opinions, Times* (1711) and especially *A Notion of the Historical Draught or Tablature of the Judgment of Hercules* (1713); Diderot's *Essais sur la peinture* (written in 1765); and Lessing's *Laocoön.* On the comparison between the limitations of the moment in painting, as opposed to poetry, see Wladyslaw Folkierski, *Entre le classicisme et le romantisme: Étude sur l'esthétique et les esthéticiens du XVIIIe siècle* (Paris: Honoré Champion, 1969), 171–89, 425–41, 529–57.

15. Michael Fried, *Absorption and Theatricality: Painting and Beholder in the Age of Diderot* (Chicago: University of Chicago Press, 1980).

16. See Pierre Frantz, *L'esthétique du tableau dans le théâtre du XVIIIe siècle* (Paris: Presses Universitaires de France, 1998).

objects one sees through its opening."[17] In keeping with the Albertian definition of a painting as a window opening out onto another world, the "Tableau" article represents the framing or isolation of objects not as a limitation of painting, but as one of its most important aesthetic resources.[18] By establishing a clear boundary between the world of representation and the real world, the frame unifies the various objects represented in the painting and focuses the beholder's attention on them. Besides the frame, the "Tableau" article also emphasizes the doctrine of three unities, generally associated with the French classical theater of the seventeenth century. In painting, as in theater, the article stipulates, "one must represent of a subject 1°. only what can have happened in a single moment; 2°. only what can easily be taken in with a single glance; 3°. only what is enclosed in the space that the painting seems to encompass."[19] These rules serve to reinforce the device of the pictorial frame, enclosing the objects represented within a single moment, point of view, and spatial configuration.

Mercier's conception of the *tableau*, in contrast, rejects both the "ridiculous frames" of painting and the restrictions imposed by the three unities. In the chapter "Tragédistes" (Tragedians) in the *Tableau de Paris,* he rejects the rule of the three unities as it had traditionally been applied in classical French tragedy: "What has the miserable rule of the three unities produced? Caricatures, to the extent that it opposes bringing together times, places, situation, men, and things. The action would be more real, more verisimilar, if our mind could follow, in conformity with the truth, the distance between places and times and see the separation between real events" (2:751). As Pierre Frantz has noted, Mercier's opposition to the three unities was central to his theory and practice of dramaturgy; like Diderot, he favored the modern genre of the *drame,* and wrote in his *Nouvel examen de la tragédie française:* "May the place change, and the time flow, rather than the truth falter."[20] But in the context of the *Tableau de Paris,* Mercier's critique of the three unities also had broader aesthetic implications for his practice of description. As a global description that unfolds over time,

---

17. Louis de Jaucourt, "Tableau (*Peinture*)," in *Encyclopédie,* ARTFL, 15:804.
18. On the opposition between the Albertian conception of painting, as exemplified by the Italian tradition of narrative painting, and the "art of describing," exemplified by seventeenth-century Dutch still-life painting, see Alpers, *Art of Describing.*
19. Louis de Jaucourt, "Tableau," in *Encyclopédie,* ARTFL, 15:804.
20. Cited in Frantz, *Esthétique du tableau,* 109.

offers multiple points of view, and reconfigures space in accord with the moving describer, the *Tableau de Paris* sought to create both a new form of *tableau* and a virtual model for a new form of theatrical representation.

A History of the Present

Far from limiting itself to a single moment, in keeping with the first of the three unities, the *Tableau de Paris* records the multiple transformations in Paris and Parisian life from 1781 to 1788, giving readers who peruse it from start to finish the remarkable impression that Paris is changing before their eyes. During this period of intense urban construction, as many old structures were being destroyed as new ones were being built: the insalubrious cemeteries were finally moved to the outskirts of the city; the hazardous houses on the bridges of the Seine were destroyed; the city gates of Saint-Antoine, Saint-Honoré, and La Conférence were demolished; the Palais was rebuilt after having burned down.[21] But Mercier is equally attentive to the more elusive and ephemeral transformations of fashion, colloquial speech, and everyday customs, to the change from *ventre et dos de puce* (belly and back of the flea) to *boue de Paris* (Paris mud) as the fashionable color of the season, and to expressions such as *essuyer les plâtres* (to wipe the plaster), whose origins he fears may be lost.[22] The rapidity of these various transformations lends a great urgency to his writing, as he seeks to keep pace with the changing face of Paris: "Let us hurry these chapters along, and catch up, if possible, with the physiognomy of the moment. Oh! How well Boileau put it: 'The moment when I speak is already far from me'" (1:411).

The plethora of articles on fashion in the *Tableau de Paris* is symptomatic of Mercier's broader attempt to capture a fleeting present. As Chantal Thomas has noted, Mercier in fact assiduously recopied descriptions from fashion magazines for the *Tableau de Paris*, despite his moral and economic

---

21. See the chapter "Il fait bon crier un peu," Mercier, *Tableau de Paris*, 2:1031–33, in which many of these changes are referred to.

22. See the chapters "Plâtres neufs" and "Parures," Mercier, *Tableau de Paris*, 1:923–24 and 1:395–99. According to Mercier, the expression "essuyer les plâtres" refers to the practice of allowing prostitutes to occupy new buildings in which the plaster is still wet and thus gives off dangerous fumes.

critique of the luxury industry.[23] His interest in fashion description is particularly apparent in the chapter "Parures" (Apparel), where he expresses regret that the ancients kept no record of their fashions for future generations:

> But after all, what did it cost them to give us the description of their coiffure, of its accessories, its variations, and its brilliant ensemble? Why didn't writers speak about the arrangement of hair? Why did they neglect to acquaint us with the admirable edifice, where it began, where it ended? Where did one place the topaz and the pearl? In what manner were the flowers interlaced, etc.? Who prevented them thus from painting the moving sphere of fashion [la sphère mouvante des modes]? ... (1:397)

With this series of unanswered questions, Mercier creates a description composed of blanks, touching on all the elements required to form an image of ancient coiffure, but leaving readers free to compose and recompose these elements in their imagination. This is the only description he can offer, not only because the ancients left no record of their fashions, but also because fashion itself, as inexhaustible as nature, simply cannot be described: "Oh! I myself feel it, in wanting to take up the pen here; it is impossible to paint this art, the most vast, the most inexhaustible, the most unfettered by common rules" (1:397). Nevertheless, like Saint-Pierre with his strawberry plant, Mercier immediately follows this assertion with a charming list of au courant head coverings:

> Indeed, if I wanted to depict a toque trimmed with two prodigious "attentions," a bonnet à la Gertrude, à la Henri IV, a bonnet with turnips, a bonnet with cherries, a bonnet *à la fanfan;* then speak of the artist's bonnet, of "pleated sentiments," of "slavery crushed"; try as I might to depict the diamond scratcher, the bejeweled comb, to tilt the physiognomy, to offer girdles in an unfamiliar style: I would only trace words; and Homer himself, with all his genius, chose to paint the shield of Achilles rather than the coiffure of Helen. (1:397)[24]

By claiming that even Homer, whose description of Achilles' shield was the unsurpassed model of *ekphrasis,* could not have described Helen's

---

23. Chantal Thomas, "'La sphère mouvante des modes,'" in Bonnet, *Hérétique,* 45.

24. I have consulted Helen Simpson's translation of this tricky (and lovely) passage but have not followed it on most points. See Mercier, *Panorama of Paris,* 63.

coiffure, Mercier underscores his attempt to surpass the ancients through his description of Parisian fashions. At the same time, he expresses his fear that any description of the "moving sphere of fashion" will inevitably be "cold and unintelligible" (1:398). As Thomas observes, Mercier's "love of fashion is perhaps above all a love of names," and his list (rather than description) of fashionable Parisian head coverings prefigures the lists copied from encyclopedias in Zola's naturalist novels.[25] What is particularly striking about Mercier's list, however, is that he chooses terms that are so historically specific (such as a hat representing the eradication of slavery) that subsequent generations are unlikely to associate them with a precise mental image (of a hat, in any case). In this way, Mercier conveys both the charm of a lost vocabulary and the ephemerality of fashion trends. Perfectly aware that the *sentiments repliés* (pleated sentiments) and the *cordelières d'un goût inconnu* (girdles in an unfamiliar style) will be unfamiliar to future readers, Mercier includes them in his *Tableau de Paris* not only for the linguistic pleasure they provide, but also to mark the passage of a fleeting present.

Thus when Mercier suggests that readers unfamiliar with any of the above-named bonnets go to the Opera to see the real thing—"Let us be quiet then, and send to the Opera the foreigner who is jealous to know the changes in our brilliant fashions: may he contemplate them on the heads of our women, and not in a cold and unintelligible description"—he is perfectly aware that this is a false solution (1:397–98). For he explicitly destines his work both to contemporary readers and to future generations ("I dare to believe that in one hundred years people will come back to my *Tableau*") and repeatedly expresses frustration at not knowing how previous generations lived, what their clothes looked like, and how their cities were organized (1:18). Hence the chapter "Parures" does not end with this refusal to describe but goes on to offer yet another evocative list of the fashionable colors, head coverings, hats, and skirts of the day. This time, however, Mercier conveys the rapid succession of fashion trends through the *form* of his description. After remarking that "the fashionable color, at the moment I am writing, is *dos et ventre de puce* [back and belly of the flea]," he immediately retracts that claim in a footnote, which reads: "*Boue de Paris* [mud of Paris] et *merde d'oie* [goose shit] have since prevailed. My

---

25. Thomas, "Sphère mouvante," 45.

book is half-antique. I wanted to speak of the *coiffure à l'hérisson* [hedge-hog coiffure]; the *coiffure à l'enfant* [child's coiffure] banished it. Feathers have become rare; they no longer float in a panache. Oh! how can one paint something that, by its extreme mobility, eludes the paintbrush?" (1:398). By using a footnote to revise his earlier description, Mercier inscribes the temporal relationship between *dos et ventre de puce* and *boue de Paris* into his description, illustrating the impossibility of fixing any stable image of Parisian fashions. Elaborating a form of description that underscores the historical contingency of his representation, he finds a way to paint the temporal essence of the "moving sphere of fashion" better than any cold or unintelligible description could do.

Description as an Agent of Change

In its attempt to capture a fleeting present, the *Tableau de Paris* is inha-bited by a sense of nostalgia for views of the city, cuts of dress, and every-day customs that Mercier knows will soon pass. It is destined to readers of future generations, for whom these minute details of Parisian life would otherwise remain elusive. Yet the *Tableau de Paris* takes on a new dimension when one considers that it is destined not only to future readers with no di-rect access to the scenes and objects described, but also to the contemporary inhabitants of Paris who live in their midst: "Many of its inhabitants are like foreigners in their own city: this book will perhaps teach them some-thing or will at least place under a sharper and more precise point of view scenes that as a result of seeing them often they no longer notice: for the ob-jects we see every day are not those we know the best" (1:14). By sharpening the perceptions of contemporary Parisians, Mercier hopes to open their eyes to social abuses and injustices they see every day but no longer notice. Thus inasmuch as it is intended for contemporary readers, the *Tableau* is written not in the hopes of *preserving* the objects described, but rather of *eradicating* them. In this sense, the urgency of Mercier's writing, reflected in the spon-taneous retractions, revisions, and digressions that characterize his style, is fueled not only by his desire to capture the "physiognomy of the moment," but also by his engagement with the social problems of his day (1:411). Not merely a history of the present written for future generations, the *Tableau de Paris* is also a work of social criticism written for Mercier's contemporaries.

The *Tableau de Paris* is thus bound to be "half-antique" by the time it is published for two very different reasons. On the one hand, as we have seen, the rapid changes in trends, customs, and language make it nearly impossible to paint "that which, by its extreme mobility, eludes the paintbrush" (1:398). On the other hand, if the *Tableau de Paris* is successful in its reformist aims, its description of particular social abuses may no longer be relevant for future generations.[26] Mercier himself remarks on this paradox, noting in his preface that several of the abuses described in the *Tableau de Paris* have already been reformed: "I put pressure on several abuses. Their reform is now being taken care of more than ever before. To denounce them is to prepare their ruin. Certain ones even fell while I was still holding the pen. I acknowledge it with pleasure; but the moment is still too recent for my words to be completely irrelevant" (1:16). This remark reveals the delicate situation of a work that is both eminently contemporary— even journalistic—and at the same time intended for future generations; for in justifying his description of recently fallen abuses by saying they are still recent, Mercier suggests that some of his descriptions will indeed be irrelevant for future generations. On a broader level, the double urgency of Mercier's writing in the *Tableau de Paris* reveals the paradox underpinning his entire descriptive approach: for him, the act of description is a means of both preservation and destruction, of painting and erasing.

The paradoxical status of a work both journalistic and literary, calling for change and seeking to preserve, is further reflected in Mercier's ambiguous attitude toward the reading habits of his contemporaries. In the chapter "Bouquiniste" (Bookseller), he observes with some dismay that Parisians are no longer willing to read long books and predicts a continued trend toward shorter and shorter forms of writing: "Hardly anyone in Paris reads works of more than two volumes.... Our good ancestors read novels in sixteen tomes, and these still weren't too long for their evenings.... As for us, soon we will only be reading on screens" (1:350). This reference to the practice of embroidering proverbs on fireplace screens can be understood as a metaphor for brief and ephemeral forms of written expression—like

---

26. For a brilliant analysis of this paradox in the context of Mercier's journalistic writings, see Shelly Charles, "L'écrivain journaliste," in Bonnet, *Hérétique,* 83–120. As Charles notes, "The writing of the present becomes, more than any other [writing], a writing for the future. This is not the least of the paradoxes of Mercier's aesthetic" (94).

the various forms of journalism that were rapidly expanding in the late eighteenth century—which are perhaps best suited to Mercier's calls for urgently needed reforms. As soon as the reform is realized, the screen or newspaper article becomes irrelevant and must be replaced with another. At the same time, Mercier's nostalgia for multivolume works reflects his wish that the *Tableau de Paris* be read and interpreted as a single work; for it is in part the voluminous nature of the work that allows Mercier to create a sense of temporal unfolding, and to underscore the contrast between the ephemeral nature of certain phenomena and the unfortunate staying power of others.

A prime example of this can be found in the two chapters Mercier devotes to the force-feeding of pigeons in the first and last volumes of the *Tableau de Paris:* "Quai de la Vallée" (the site of a fowl market on the banks of the Seine), and "L'engaveur subsiste encore" (The Force-Feeder Still Exists). In the first of these chapters, Mercier follows a standard procedure in the *Tableau de Paris,* "painting" a highly detailed picture of a distasteful and insalubrious practice, in the hopes of opening Parisian eyes to its dangers, and encouraging prompt reform. In this case, he describes the *engaveur*'s, or force-feeder's, practice of preparing his fowl for sale: "Can you imagine (will I dare to write it?) that all these pigeons who arrive, and who cannot be sold or consumed the same day, are force-fed by men who blow grain from their mouths down into the gullet. When they cut the birds' necks, they take this same half-digested grain, and the same mouth blows it again into the pigeons who won't be killed until the day after" (1:183). As is often the case when treating off-putting topics, Mercier signals his reluctance to shock the reader but appeals to the necessity of reform to justify the distasteful nature of his description: "I beg your pardon, reader, for having traced this disgusting painting, but I preferred to offend your delicacy for a moment, rather than to avoid giving you a useful recommendation" (1:183). In keeping with the goal expressed in the opening pages of the *Tableau de Paris,* Mercier hopes that the detail and focus of his distasteful portrait will reveal to Parisian eyes a practice that they see regularly but no longer perceive. The chapter "Quai de la Vallée" is thus one example in which the visual power of description serves not to preserve a record of a Parisian custom, but rather to hasten its disappearance.

By revisiting the same topic some 2,500 pages later, however, Mercier both reinforces and transforms his initial critique by giving it an important temporal dimension. Although his portrait of the force-feeder "made delicate imaginations shudder," Mercier observes with horror that over the years 1781 to 1788, pigeons have continued to be force-fed, and Parisians have continued to eat them.[27] Was the initial *tableau* not disgusting enough? Mercier adds another touch: "Will I add that the lip of this force-feeder, jabbed by the multiple pecks of the pigeons' beaks, becomes cancerous; it must be cut out; I have the attestation of the surgeon, which proves that this profession (still public at the moment I am writing [encore public au moment où j'écris]) is no less dangerous than disgusting" (2:1356). This sentence captures a tension that traverses the *Tableau de Paris,* between the possibility of rapid change and the staying power of oppressive and dangerous structures and practices. On the one hand, the parenthetical remark "encore public au moment où j'écris" signals the possibility that between the moments of writing and publication the practice may be abolished; on the other hand, Mercier's repetition of the word *encore* from the chapter title reinforces the reader's sense of the duration of the practice. In reminding us of the earlier chapter, the title "L'engaveur subsiste encore" heightens our awareness of the time that has passed between the two. By placing the two chapters about the force-feeder in the first and last volumes of the *Tableau de Paris,* Mercier makes this period of time, during which a barbarous and unsanitary practice has subsisted, coincide with his writing, and our reading, of the *Tableau de Paris.* What better way to drive home his point that "to write against abuses is thus not always to reform them"? (2:1356). Unlike the cemeteries being moved to the outskirts of the city (in response to which Mercier exclaims triumphantly: "The pen has at last decided the hammer"), the force-feeding of pigeons is one instance in which description has not erased its object from Parisian life (2:1032). As readers of the *Tableau de Paris,* we are reminded of other ongoing abuses, such as the dangerous lawlessness of coach drivers, maiming and killing pedestrians in their mad rush to the Opera, and the persistent lack of any legislation preventing them from doing so. Mercier's repeated references to these accidents, against the backdrop of a continually changing city, create an echoing effect throughout the *Tableau de Paris* and even into *Le nouveau Paris,* as if to say "It's happening, it's happening again, it's still happening..."[28]

---

27. Mercier, *Tableau de Paris,* 2:1356.
28. See, for example, Mercier, *Nouveau Paris,* 492.

In this way, Mercier resolutely refuses that his *tableau* be framed by one moment or even one period of time; as long as the force-feeders keep stuffing pigeons, and as long as cries of "Gare! Gare!" (Watch out! Watch out!) are the only protection afforded to pedestrians, his work as a describer must go on.[29]

A Kaleidoscope of Views

In addition to representing and hastening change with his description, Mercier incorporates multiple points of view into his *Tableau de Paris,* thereby rejecting the second of the three unities outlined in the *Encyclopédie* article "Tableau." Unlike the painter, criticized for presenting only one side of a given object, Mercier promises in his preface to paint Paris from several different angles: "I made neither an *inventory,* nor a *catalog;* I crayoned according to my views; I varied my *Tableau* as much as I could; I painted it from several angles [sous plusieurs faces]" (1:14). By emphasizing that the *Tableau de Paris* is neither an inventory nor a catalog, Mercier distinguishes his project from the tradition of topographical descriptions of city streets and monuments. He also underscores his departure from the Enlightenment tradition of compiling an exhaustive catalog of nature's objects (despite his emulation of Buffon). Although the form of the *Tableau de Paris,* with its short, titled chapters devoted to various aspects of Parisian life, seems to follow this tradition, these chapters can also be seen as a series of contrasting points of view on Paris, the basis for what Shelly Charles has called Mercier's "fractured aesthetic."[30]

A good example of the rapid shifts in point of view that characterize Mercier's aesthetic can be found in two successive chapters in the fourth volume of the *Tableau de Paris,* "Balcons" (Balconies) and "Faux cheveux" (False Hair). The first chapter presents a bird's-eye view of a Parisian traffic jam, from the vantage point of a balcony: "It is quite a curious spectacle to see, in complete tranquility, from the height of a balcony, the number and diversity of vehicles that stop and cross each other; the pedestrians who, resembling birds under the rifle of a hunter, slip through the wheels of all

---

29. See the chapter "Gare! Gare!" Mercier, *Tableau de Paris,* 1:107–9.
30. Charles, "Écrivain journaliste," 102.

these carts prepared to run them over. The one who steps over the gutter in fear of being spattered, and who, losing his balance, covers himself in mud from head to toe; the other, who pirouettes in the other direction, an unpowdered visage, and a parasol under his arm" (1:916). For this particular subject, Mercier chooses the balcony as the ideal vantage point from which to view the "moving painting of *vis-à-vis, berlines, désobligeantes, cabriolets,* and *carosses de remises*" in the Parisian streets: although Mercier is far enough away to observe the overall traffic pattern of these various vehicles, he is close enough to observe the behavior and demeanor of the pedestrians (1:917). Thus while the comparison of the scurrying pedestrians to birds startled by a hunter's shot reinforces the readers' sense that they are viewing the scene from afar, the choice of a few striking details to characterize the pedestrians' appearance ("unpowdered visage," "parasol under his arm") creates a contrasting sense of proximity and visual acuity.

By placing the chapter "Faux cheveux" immediately after "Balcons," however, Mercier creates an even greater sense of perspectival contrast when he zooms in on the elaborate coiffure of a beautiful woman. Unlike the blank description of the ancient woman's coiffure, this description gives an extremely precise and magnified view of the wigmaker's remarkable construction, as if viewed under a microscope: "Quite independently of the fake hair, there enters into this coiffure an enormous *pillow,* bulging with hair, a forest of hairpins seven to eight inches long, and of which the sharp points rest on the skin. A great quantity of powder and pomade, that include scents in their composition, and that soon contract a certain acridity, irritate the nerves. The imperceptible sweating of the head is stopped, and it cannot be so without the gravest danger" (1:919). Whereas the balcony was the most appropriate vantage point from which to describe the disorder of the Parisian streets, this close-up view of an elegant lady's head is necessary to uncover the secrets of the wigmaker's art, for as Mercier remarks in concluding this chapter, "Today the wig or the *tower* imitates natural [hair] to such an extent that one can be mistaken from near and from far" (1:921). Thus in order to transform readers' perceptions of this highly unnatural construction, Mercier must describe it from a vantage point far closer than those of everyday life, even uncomfortably close. Readers' perceptions are transformed not only with respect to the beauty of the wigmaker's creation—"the little pillow, essential foundation of the edifice, is sometimes only changed when the fabric is destroyed (will I dare to say it!) by the foul filth that inhabits this brilliant diadem"—but also with respect to the woman herself (1:920). The image of the "beautiful woman" presented in the opening sentence is gradually deconstructed under the insistent and uncomfortably close gaze of the describer, as she calms "the intensity of those itches by putting the scratcher [grattoir] into use. The blood is carried impetuously to the head; the eyes become red and animated: what of it! One presents the edifice one idolizes" (1:919).

In both chapters, a particular *physical* vantage point is thus chosen to illustrate a *moral* point of view: as Mercier notes, "It is the moral that I was attentive to; only eyes are needed to see the rest" (1:34). While the bird's-eye view from the balcony allows him to criticize the dangers of Paris streets for the pedestrians who seem to slip through the crisscrossing wheels, the close-up view of the "beautiful" woman's insalubrious coiffure sets up a moral contrast with the clean and healthy habits of a village woman. A similar relationship between physical and moral points of view is illustrated in the chapter "Physionomie de la grande ville" (Physiognomy of the Big City), which begins with a topographical description of Paris viewed from the top of Notre-Dame—"Do you want to judge Paris physically? Climb the towers of Notre-Dame"—and ends with a bold critique of the king's abuse of his hunting privileges: "Princes are inexorable, on the subject of hunting, and exert a veritable tyranny" (1:34, 1:36). The distant view of Paris as a physical topography serves to introduce this moral and political critique, as Mercier moves without transition from a description of the outskirts of Paris to an evocation of the hunting rules in effect there.

Thus Mercier's "fractured aesthetic" is a function not only of the contrasting physical points of view from chapter to chapter, but also of the contrasting moral judgments about Parisian life. The multiplication of points of view within a single *tableau* means that he can open his tenth volume with a chapter entitled "Erreur rectifiée" (Corrected Error), in which he retracts his earlier claim that Paris was disproportional to the rest of France: "When one has made a mistake, one must correct oneself. No, Paris is not at all an overly large head, and disproportionate to the kingdom. This figure of rhetoric, which I had adopted, is not accurate" (2:776). The tension between the single *tableau* and the multiple viewpoints contained within it thus allows Mercier to judge and suspend judgment at the same time, leaving certain essential questions about the moral fiber of Parisian life unanswered even as he promises to resolve them before the "end" of his work.

One such question is posed in the first volume of the *Tableau de Paris,* when Mercier tentatively suggests that life in Paris is preferable to the state of nature, since even the poorest Parisians profit from the influence of the arts. But should the reader believe this claim? In concluding his chapter with "I thought that. Wait, reader, until the end of the book to know if I still think the same way," Mercier leaves the question wide open, for he himself does not yet know when or how his work will end (1:42). How, indeed, can he offer a definitive judgment about the possibilities for human happiness in a city where the material sources of oppression are undergoing constant transformation, in which "it is hardly possible that the painting of this year resemble next year?" (2:1309). Here, the question of point of view becomes inextricable from that of historical change: in citing the urban reforms mentioned earlier (cemeteries, houses on bridges, city gates) and in calling for others, Mercier again asks his readers to wait and see, but this time in order to know what other positive changes may come to pass: "What do you say, readers? . . . Have patience" (2:1033).

A similar connection between the suspension of definitive moral judgment and the passage of time can be seen in Mercier's comparison between Paris and Theseus's ship, of which the parts were gradually replaced until none of the original material remained:

> The ship that Theseus boarded when he liberated the Athenians from the tribute of Minos was kept until the time of Demetrius of Phaleron, that is to say, for a period of nine hundred years. As the ship got older, the rotten pieces were replaced with pieces of new wood; such that it was disputed later whether it was the same ship, or whether it was another one. The city of Paris somewhat resembles this ship. So many pieces have been added that nothing remains of its original construction. (1:425)

With this comparison, Mercier questions the constancy of the city's identity in the face of continual change. As long as Paris is changing, and as long as his work is contributing to that change, he cannot tell his readers definitively whether the poorest Parisians are better off in the city or in the state of nature. As in the footnote that recorded the rapid succession from *dos et ventre de puce* to *boue de Paris,* Mercier expresses the essential indeterminacy of the city's identity by multiplying the signs of indeterminacy within his own text: "But let us not anticipate the article about *Versailles,* which

I will or will not write," he remarks, thereby attributing to his text an identity no more stable than that of Paris itself (1:342).

In the face of this indeterminacy and perspectival fragmentation, readers of the *Tableau de Paris* are invited to assume an active role in composing
and recomposing a coherent view of Paris: as Mercier himself put it in another work, "The book is nothing; it is the reader who makes the book."[31]
This emphasis on the role of the reader in the elaboration of the *Tableau
de Paris* is consistent with Mercier's preference for sketches over completed
paintings, which he explains as a function of their increased possibilities for
imaginative participation: "I give my preference to sketches, to those studies where my soul flies out in front of the painter's, where I recognize his
look of love that swept across the paper."[32] But in addition to completing
or composing an image initiated by the describer, readers of the *Tableau de
Paris* are also encouraged to become active observers of the world around
them, comparing their impressions with Mercier's descriptions and potentially supplementing or even rewriting them: "The reader will rectify on
his own what the writer has seen badly, or what he has painted badly; and
the comparison will perhaps give him a secret wish to see the object again
and to compare it" (1:15). As a description, the *Tableau de Paris* is thus in
no sense intended as a substitution for the firsthand observation of Paris
itself; on the contrary, the work as a whole is a summation to go out and
see for oneself. When Mercier writes of Paris "one must see it, explore it,
study what it contains," he incites his readers to imitate his own trajectory
through the city streets, and at the same time to explore the *Tableau de Paris*
as a constantly shifting physical and moral topography (1:15).

Writing with Legs

Far from respecting the third of the three unities, the principle of spatial
unity, Mercier invents a *tableau* that covers as many different spaces as can
be observed by a constantly moving describer. He himself underscores the

---

31. Mercier, *Bonnet de nuit*, 1556.
32. Mercier, "Musées," *Nouveau Paris*, 978. On Mercier's preference for sketches over paintings, see Enrico Rufi, *Le rêve laïque de Louis-Sébastien Mercier entre littérature et politique*, Studies
on Voltaire and the Eighteenth Century 326 (Oxford: Voltaire Foundation, 1995), 173.

importance of movement in the genesis of the *Tableau de Paris* when he writes: "I ran so much to make the *Tableau de Paris* that I can say I made it with *my legs;* thus I learned how to walk on the paving stones of the capital in an agile, lively, and prompt manner. It's a secret that must be possessed to see everything [tout voir]" (2:1309). This emphasis on the describer's legs adds another layer to the creative process of description, which Mercier associated in his preface with his eyes and his understanding. In order to see all aspects of Parisian life and achieve his goal of global representation, Mercier must invent a new way of walking, and with it a new way of seeing and describing, specifically designed for the city and the representational challenges it poses.

The possibilities for spatial and textual expansion in the *Tableau de Paris* are further augmented by another special mode of observation and description, afforded by post-chaise travel. Unlike the stationary, framed perspective of a painting, the window of the post chaise offers a moving vantage point, a perpetually expanding frame that matches the immense frame of nature: "When our vision has become accustomed after some time to a crowd of moving objects of which the frame is immense, that is to say, when one has traveled for a few months, and above all in a post chaise, it is impossible to view the sky of a painter as anything other than a grotesque imitation."[33] By combining movement and the passage of time, this new kind of frame allows Mercier to observe a moving and changing sky, just as the promenades and years over which the *Tableau de Paris* is written present him with a moving and changing city. Thus in a crucial comment that links the temporal urgency of his project to the principle of spatial expansion, Mercier writes: "Let us see the world, if possible, before leaving it; the most fortunate of inventions is the post chaise" (2:1451). The post chaise is particularly suited to Mercier's urgent drive to see all aspects of Paris (and potentially the world beyond), because it "stops whenever you want, and rapidly passes over what doesn't merit being seen" (2:1451–52). This back-and-forth between rapidly covering space and stopping to observe in greater detail corresponds perfectly to Mercier's own technique as a describer, as he alternates between global and close-up views.

So great is Mercier's tendency toward spatial and textual expansion and accumulation that he alludes to the possibility of concluding the *Tableau de*

---

33. Mercier, *Polygraphe,* 214.

Paris with a description of London. The project of comparing the two cities, only partially realized in his posthumous *Parallèle de Londres et de Paris,* was to provide either a conclusion *or* a supplement to the *Tableau de Paris:*

> London, neighbor and rival, inevitably becomes the pendant to the painting I have traced, and the parallel presents itself naturally. The two capitals are so close and so different, although resembling each other in many respects, that, to complete my work, it is necessary that I fix my gaze on the *equal* [*émule*] of Paris. I will go, I swear by Newton and by Shakespeare, I will go to the banks of the Thames, to salute the temple of liberty, of which Cromwell was the terrible architect, and to see this famous island that proved the possibility of a good government; and if this second *tableau* is not too much beyond my strength, I will take it on, attempting to compensate, with the calmest attention and the most exact impartiality, for the other talents that heaven has refused to me. (2:1312)[34]

This passage reflects various tensions at play in the constant reworkings of Mercier's project: between singular and plural *tableaux,* and between a finished product and an open-ended work. Is Mercier's treatment of London to be a second *tableau* or a conclusion for the first? And how can it possibly serve as a conclusion given that it opens the *Tableau de Paris* beyond the confines of Paris and suggests the possibility of an ever more universal representation? The implication, consistent with Mercier's critique of painting and the pictorial frame, is that any "conclusion" to the *Tableau de Paris* must necessarily open out onto new areas of observation and description, thereby transforming the very idea of what it means to conclude a work.

A Moral Topography

In its resistance to pictorial framing and the three unities, the *Tableau de Paris* illustrates the novelty of Mercier's concept of the *tableau* as a model for the descriptive writer. His ideal of an unframed *tableau* frees him from the methodological difficulties faced by Buffon and Daubenton: he sees no need to impose limits on description, nor does he express any fear that an

---

34. See also Louis Sébastien Mercier, *Parallèle de Paris et de Londres,* ed. Claude Bruneteau and Bernard Cottret (Paris: Didier Érudition, 1982).

accumulation of detail may threaten the immediacy or coherence of the mental images formed by the reader. On the contrary, as the city changes— as the cemeteries are moved to the outskirts of the city, as the houses on the bridges of the Seine are destroyed, as the city gates of Saint-Antoine, Saint-Honoré, and La Conférence are demolished—Mercier's description grows, spilling outside of its frame just as Paris itself expands beyond the confines of the tollgates designed by the architect Claude Nicolas Ledoux. This expansion, as we have seen, makes room for the multiple perspectives on Paris that Mercier claims to offer, including contradictions and reformulations of previous images when necessary, and revisiting topics already treated in previous volumes. In a work written as much with the legs as with the eyes, these contradictions and repetitions correspond not only to the progress of time but also to the multiple angles perceived by a constantly moving describer. The principle of accumulation, which Charles identifies as an essential aspect of Mercier's "fractured aesthetic," is from the point of view of descriptive practice the very counterpoint of his contemporaries' struggles to limit and frame their descriptions. To this important shift corresponds Mercier's rejection of painting as a model for the descriptive writer, and his elaboration of a new topographical model more suited to the ideal of an unframed, global *tableau.*

In the opening pages of the *Tableau de Paris,* Mercier warns his reader not to expect a topographical description of the city: "If someone expected to find in this work a topographical description of squares and streets, or a history of previous facts, he would be disappointed in his expectations. I was concerned with the moral and its fleeting nuances" (1:14). Vidler has suggested that this rejection of topographical description reflects Mercier's aesthetic priorities, in particular his quest for a totalizing form of observation and description: "Rejecting the most common genres of description—topographies, inventories of monuments, catalogs of curiosities, histories—where the city was fragmented into many individual and static objects, he consciously pursues the path of totalizing observation."[35] But Mercier himself presents his rejection of topographical description not so much in terms of an opposition between totalizing and fragmentary forms of representation, as between physical and moral description. His admiration of three-dimensional relief maps—such as the "Tableau en

---

35. Vidler, "Mercier urbaniste," 237.

relief de la Suisse" (Relief Map of Switzerland) and the "Ville de Paris en relief" (City of Paris in Relief), described in *Mon bonnet de nuit* and *Le nouveau Paris* respectively—suggests that topography was in fact an important model for Mercier, serving to replace the model of painting favored by previous Enlightenment describers.[36]

Mercier begins his description of François-Louis Pfiffer's "Tableau en relief de la Suisse" by proclaiming its superiority over two-dimensional maps and landscape paintings: "Geographical maps show us on paper the respective placement of different countries; the painter puts before our eyes an extended landscape and makes us guess the distant objects that his paintbrush couldn't render; but in these arts, it is only by imagination that one perceives the unevenness of the ground: it is a relief map [tableau en relief] that renders and imitates nature perfectly" (958). This comparison may seem somewhat surprising given Mercier's preference for sketches over completed paintings, which, as we have seen, was a function of the increased possibilities for imaginative participation afforded by the sketch. In this case, paradoxically, Mercier sees the immense detail and exhaustive completeness of Pfiffer's relief map as facilitating the viewer's imaginative participation in the work. This participation takes the form of a trajectory through the space of the relief map, which Mercier expresses alternately as actual physical displacement ("you turn around these masses"; "you spend three hours traveling on a table twenty-two feet long"; "I visited the peak of the highest boulders"), as a function of the eye's movement ("the eye makes an incursion into these valleys; it plunges, it comes back up, it turns around the great chains of mountains; it throws itself into the gorges where hunters pursue their prey"), and as a function of the imagination's movement ("the imagination, in contemplating these pyramidal boulders descends little by little in the eternal region of ice"; "your imagination descends and traverses these majestic sinuosities") (959–60). In its combination of meticulous visual accuracy and multiple possibilities for imaginative participation, Pfiffer's relief map sets up a new relationship between description and imagination; as Mercier remarks, "I saw everything by the eye of

---

36. See the chapters "Tableau en relief de la Suisse," Mercier, *Bonnet de nuit,* 958–67; and "Ville de Paris en relief," Mercier, *Nouveau Paris,* 478–95. I will discuss the Parisian relief map in more detail in chapter 6. Subsequent references to the "Tableau en relief de la Suisse" chapter appear parenthetically in the main text.

the imagination" (965). The confluence of vision and imagination, and the combination of physical, optical, and imaginative exploration that Mercier sees in Pfiffer's relief map, reflect the descriptive ideal of the *Tableau de Paris,* as readers are invited to follow Mercier's trajectory through Paris, to adopt his various vantage points, and to compose a coherent vision of Paris in their imaginations.

The impression of physical trajectory created by the relief map is in part, according to Mercier, a function of Pfiffer's tireless exploration of the Swiss mountains in preparing it. Like the *Tableau de Paris,* Pfiffer's relief map is a work "made with the legs": "The author traversed these mountains as a great painter, and what vigor must he have needed in the shins and the head to complete this composition?" (961). Pfiffer's trajectory is also part of what makes his relief map a global representation, and as such, a model for Mercier's ideal of a totalizing description. Like the *Tableau de Paris,* Pfiffer's relief map incorporates multiple viewpoints, observations, and measurements into a single *tableau,* in which "nothing is forgotten," "everything is before your eyes," and "everything makes a painting [tout fait tableau]" (958, 959, 960). Because these multiple viewpoints are contained within twenty-two square feet, the viewer can experience a breadth of vision that encompasses an entire portion of the globe, "embrac[ing] its] backbone" (959). And although the relief map is clearly framed to the extent that the space of representation is limited by the table on which it rests, Mercier is so impressed by the meticulous order within that space that he experiences the world beyond it as chaos: "This unique *tableau* made me perceive a portion of the physiognomy of the globe. It carries I don't know what imprint of order, so much so that the edge of the table seemed to me chaos" (961). Rather than isolating objects from the universe—Mercier's habitual critique of the pictorial frame—these chaotic borders give the viewer the sense that no coherent universe can exist beyond the one represented on the table. The relief map is thus a world in and of itself, framed only to the extent that it is surrounded by the disorder of the outer reaches of the universe.

The impression of optical and imaginative trajectory, on the other hand, is elucidated when Mercier plays a series of optical and proportional games in order to place himself within the miniature universe. First, he imagines himself reduced in size and the objects around him enlarged—"all that is necessary is to make oneself smaller and magnify the surrounding objects, then one finds oneself thrust into the midst of the astonishing decor"—and then he imagines himself flying over the landscape with a microscope attached to his eye: "It seemed to me that a microscope was attached to my eye; I saw objects being magnified; for a moment I believed I was high in the region of thin air, and soaring comfortably over the great monuments of nature" (960, 964). In its combination of microscopic precision and vertiginous shifts in proportion and perspective, Pfiffer's relief map offers an experience that is both concrete and imaginative, scientific and poetic. Mercier highlights this combination of multiple levels of descriptive meaning when he remarks: "It was not granted to me to see this great *tableau* as a physicist, or as a naturalist; but I saw it as a poet, and perhaps as a political thinker" (964). And it is indeed the confluence of these three levels of meaning—physical, poetic, and political—that makes Pfiffer's relief map an aesthetic model for Mercier.

On a purely physical level, the geological and geographical accuracy of Pfiffer's relief map will, according to Mercier, allow future generations to perceive the evolutions of the earth's surface: "The future changes of the globe will be able to be compared with this monument; if some disruptions occur, they will be compared with this relief map: if a similar one had been made, three thousand years ago, today we would be able to appreciate the revolutions of the globe with less incertitude" (959). Pfiffer's relief map thus resembles Mercier's *Tableau de Paris,* of which he writes in his preface: "If near the end of each century a judicious writer had made a general *tableau* of what existed around him; if he had depicted, just as he had seen them, the mores and customs [les moeurs et les usages]; this series would today constitute a curious gallery of objects of comparison" (1:18). Like the *Tableau de Paris,* Pfiffer's relief map is doubly inscribed in the process of historical change: on the one hand, it allows the contemporary viewer to imagine the transformations of previous generations—"one has the impression of reading the history of the ancient revolutions of the globe"—and on the other hand, it serves as a stable point of comparison for generations to come (959).

Yet, as we have seen, Mercier attributes a significance that is both physical, and moral and political to Pfiffer's relief map; as he puts it, "After having embraced the physical, you can embrace, as it were, the moral and the political" (962). He thus includes in his description of the relief map a political reading of the Swiss landscape, which is influenced by Rousseau's depiction of Switzerland in *La nouvelle Héloïse* and *La lettre à d'Alembert sur les spectacles*. Borrowing from Rousseau the notion that it is the topographical isolation of the Swiss people that guarantees their moral purity, Mercier writes: "Here one sees again that physical circumstances determined the size of each political body: if the most appropriate form for the constitution of a country is subordinate to the measurement of its borders, these mountain ranges suspended in the air seem to be the refuge of democracies; here happiness is not purchased at the expense of others" (962–63). The belief that every physical topography contains a moral and political one is indeed fundamental to Mercier's thought and reflects his orientation in the *Tableau de Paris*. As a social critic, Mercier attacks the physical and visible structures that support and sustain moral abuses and political oppression. He interprets the structure of Parisian apartment buildings, for example, as a source of social and economic inequality—"in the human *hive*, the *cells* are prodigiously unequal"—since the poor pay more for water and firewood because they live in the less desirable rooms on the upper floors.[37] Thus, despite Mercier's claim that the *Tableau de Paris* is not a topographical description, his work can be interpreted as a physical and visible topography to the extent that physical description has moral and political implications.

Mercier ends his description of Pfiffer's relief map with a *coup de théâtre*: once the reader's eyes and imagination have become accustomed to the scale of the miniature representation, perceiving the mountains as immense and himself as tiny, the relief map's maker suddenly bursts into the landscape, stomping through forests and lakes and destabilizing the viewer's perceptions by mixing the world represented with the chaos surrounding it: "When you have admired all these details that seem so fragile to you, the author suddenly thrusts himself onto his work; you let out a cry of terror: there is nothing to fear; the author walks on the cottages, the trees, the forests, the lakes that he imitated: a new subject for surprise and admiration" (966). What Mercier admires here is not only the durability of the materials used in the construction of the relief map, but also the intrusion of the world beyond the frame into the space of the model, an intrusion that grants him a dizzying shift in perspective and scale similar to what he had experienced when "flying" over the topography in his imagination. Pfiffer's intrusion

---

37. Mercier, *Tableau de Paris*, 2:1033.

into his own work also gives new meaning to the notion of a *tableau* "made with the legs." For with this ending, the author's tireless hiking in the Swiss mountains is mirrored by his tireless walking across the *tableau,* as he continually seeks to perfect the detail and accuracy of his representation: "Since the author always has something to correct, he walks there without support; his only precaution is to take care that a pointed steeple doesn't pierce his foot. The author has been working on this monument for twenty years without anything being broken, and he regards it as an extremely durable work; he works on it relentlessly, and in a spry old age, his legs do not refuse to him the service needed to tend to the premises [lever le local]" (967). Despite the spatial limitations imposed by the table on which it rests, Pfiffer's relief map is, like the *Tableau de Paris,* an open-ended work, perpetually calling for the further accumulation of descriptive detail. As a final tribute to its author's remarkable effort, Mercier writes his description of the relief map "the very evening of the day I saw it," leaving it "intentionally uneven," in the image of the surfaces described by Pfiffer himself (967).

An Open Urban Stage

Mercier takes the model of topography to yet another level in the *Tableau de Paris* when he depicts an innovative form of theatrical representation, purportedly practiced in China, that "consists of representing cities on a small scale within a quarter league" (2:943). For Jean-Claude Bonnet, this theatrical model contains "the secret formula of the aesthetic of the *Tableau,* which mixes 'description' and 'representation' in an imaginary choreography that far surpasses the capacities of theater."[38] Mercier describes this theatrical model, called the *foire comique chinoise,* or Chinese comic fair, in a series of three chapters on the Palais-Royal, thereby drawing an analogy between one of his favorite observation posts in Paris and the curious Chinese spectacle. Although the Chinese fair is, like the Swiss relief map, a miniaturized reproduction, it has the advantage of being veritably animated by live actors who play the roles of various city inhabitants: "All the trades, all the din, all the comings and goings and even the pranks, are imitated by a crowd of actors; one is a merchant, the other an artisan; this

---

38. Bonnet, introduction, in Mercier, *Tableau de Paris,* 1:xlix.

one a soldier, that one an officer" (2:943). The Chinese fair represents all the activities of daily life, with an eye for sociological detail that mirrors Mercier's own attentiveness to the trades of water carriers and wigmakers in chapters such as "Porteurs d'eau" (Water Carriers) and "Boutique de perruquier" (Wigmaker's Shop).[39]

Mercier's attention to the objects of everyday life in the *Tableau de Paris*—as Bonnet puts it, "the simple attention to the things of life, this immensely interesting and precious aspect of the bourgeois culture of the eighteenth century"—is also an important aspect of the Chinese fair, which takes theatrical realism to new heights by incorporating multiple props into its representation.[40] It is a vast theatrical market, in which "the shops are opened, the wares are displayed; buyers are figured; one sees an area for silk, another for cotton, a street for porcelain, another for pottery: you find clothing, furniture, feminine finery; further along, books for the curious and for the learned" (2:943). Just as the realism and intricate detail of Pfiffer's relief map facilitated the imaginative participation of the viewer, the use of actual objects in the Chinese fair serves to draw the audience into the "fictive" space of the representation. As the spectator surveys the various wares displayed in this theatrical market, "clothes dealers pull on your sleeve and harass you to buy their wares" (2:943). Thus the Chinese fair is a form of theatrical representation consistent with Mercier's emphasis on reader participation in the reception of a descriptive text. If "it is the reader who makes the book" in the *Tableau de Paris,* it is the spectators who compose their own theatrical experience in the Chinese fair, by exploring streets and buildings, interacting with actors, and examining the various wares for sale.

In fact, there is almost no difference between the Chinese fair and the actual experience of city life, except the reduced scale of the city, the participation of actors, and the farcelike techniques used to "beat" troublemakers: "People quarrel, they fight; archers stop the quarrelers; they are taken before a judge, and the judge sentences them to a beating: when this amusing sentence is executed, the actors are touched in an insensible manner,

---

39. See Mercier, *Tableau de Paris,* 1:134–35 and 1:1340–45. Nonetheless, Jeremy Popkin notes that Mercier "had little interest in the densely populated working-class faubourgs on the eastern side of the city or in the productive activities that went on in their workshops." Popkin, *Panorama of Paris,* 7.

40. Jean-Claude Bonnet, "La littérature et le réel," in Bonnet, *Hérétique,* 25.

and the fake criminal imitates the cries of a torture victim, in a manner that delights the spectators" (2:943–44). This blurring of the lines between theatrical representation and actual city life, between fiction and reality, is further reinforced when Mercier suggests that for Parisians the Palais-Royal may serve as a substitute for the Chinese fair: "The *Palais-Royal,* more than any other edifice in the city, could serve, I think, to offer people a piquant festival, and of the kind I am indicating here" (2:946). Like the Chinese fair, the Palais-Royal is a microcosm of the Parisian macrocosm, containing all aspects of Parisian life within a limited space: "It is called *the capital of Paris.* Everything can be found here.... This enchanted dwelling is a luxurious little city, enclosed within a big one.... Whatever you could desire, you are sure to find it here" (2:930–31). Like Paris itself, the Palais-Royal is "the universe in abbreviated form," a place where "one can see everything, hear everything, know everything," to such an extent that other neighborhoods pale by comparison: "It dries out the other quarters of the city, which already appear as desolate and uninhabited provinces" (2:935, 2:937). As such, the Palais-Royal represents a real-life version of the Chinese fair, and serves as a model for the *Tableau de Paris,* offering a global, all-encompassing representation of Paris that can be explored and experienced by an active observer.

Yet there is an important difference between the Palais-Royal and the Chinese fair, which makes Mercier's enthusiastic account of this innovative form of theatrical representation somewhat paradoxical. As we have seen, Mercier played various proportional games in surveying Pfiffer's relief map in order to adjust for the difference in scale between himself and the landscape. Although the adjustment in scale is not nearly as great for the Chinese fair (which measures "a quarter league" instead of the "twenty-two feet" of Pfiffer's relief map), it is similarly a miniaturized reproduction, in which the streets, buildings, vehicles, and objects are reduced from their actual size. This miniaturization is for Mercier part of the artistry of the Chinese fair; as he expresses it, "There would be an art of imitating all these objects on a smaller scale" (2:945). At the same time, just as there was a proportional gap between Mercier and the Swiss topography, there is a proportional gap between the crowd of life-size actors (and spectators) participating in the Chinese fair and the miniature spaces they inhabit, including bars, inns, boutiques, and tribunals. This paradox becomes particularly apparent when Mercier imagines a *coup de théâtre* to mark the end of the

Chinese fair: "When everyone is outside, rain would be imitated, and one would see everyone fleeing; struggles between the carriages, which are no longer called anything but *pine trees,* would be represented; the coachman with a mustache would appear alongside the coachman in a smock; coaches, carriages, cabriolets, carts, wagons, tipcarts, who would prevent all this from being painted true to nature?" (2:945). But the question is not so much *who* would prevent this painting of Parisian life from being realized, but rather *how* the life-size actors could fit into these numerous vehicles, given the proportional discrepancy between themselves and the "stage" on which they perform. This paradox suggests that a truly global and inclusive Chinese fair can never be realized in the form of a theatrical representation, but only as a virtual representation, or a description.

Hence the question of the relationship between the Chinese fair and the *Tableau de Paris* must be posed. To the extent that the Chinese fair is populated by the people of Paris and animated by their activities, it is far closer to the *Tableau de Paris* than the topographical model of Pfiffer's relief map. Thus, instead of distinguishing between physical and moral topography, Mercier suggests that the only real difference between the Chinese fair and the *Tableau de Paris* is that the first is a representation, and the second a description: "If one managed to imitate the confusion of the streets, what pleases us so much in a description would please us no less in a representation" (2:945). In other words, the description of Parisian traffic jams that so entertained Mercier's readers in the chapter "Balcons" would find a concrete, representational equivalent in the *coup de théâtre* that marks the end of the Chinese fair. Thus Mercier suggests that his work could serve as a sort of script for a Parisian equivalent of the Chinese fair: "If one wanted to carry out a similar festival, I dare to say that my book would not be entirely unhelpful" (2:944). But does this mean, as Bonnet claims, that the "secret formula of the aesthetic of the *Tableau*" lies in a mixture of representation and description? To the extent that Mercier himself characterizes the Chinese fair as representation—a theatrical equivalent of his description—what does it mean to say that the *Tableau de Paris* is not only a description but also a representation? Although not representational in the concrete sense (unlike the relief map and the Chinese fair, which can actually be touched, walked through, inhabited), Mercier implicitly attributes a representational dimension to his work by consistently comparing it to these concrete, literal reconstructions and reenactments.

But can readers of the *Tableau de Paris* stomp through this particular relief map, can they become actors in this version of the Chinese fair? As long as Paris still exists, they can and are in fact encouraged to revisit the physical and moral topography described by Mercier, and to compare object with description. That they may only be able to do so two hundred years after Mercier wrote the *Tableau de Paris* does not invalidate this representational aspect of the experience. Given that "it is hardly possible that the painting of this year resemble next year," Mercier had already predicted the gap between the Paris perceived by his readers and his own description of it. And even if Paris ceased to exist, Mercier's text would not become purely descriptive, to the extent that readers would be compelled to compare the lost city with the cities and villages of their time. In either case, the participatory dimension of the *Tableau de Paris,* the way it encourages its readers to become active observers of the world around them, can be seen to constitute the very mixture of description and representation to which Bonnet refers.

Finishing an Unframed Painting

Thus although the Chinese fair satisfies Mercier's desire for an animated topography, the addition of life-size actors makes the combination of miniaturization and intricate detail found in the Swiss topography unfeasible. The question then becomes how much space a representation must take up in order to include all of the detail and movement desired by Mercier, while at the same time allowing the viewer to obtain a global perspective (we may be reminded here of Jorge Luis Borges's story "On Exactitude in Science," which refers to a map so detailed that its size equaled that of the empire it represented).[41] This is indeed one of the crucial problems of the *Tableau de Paris* itself, a work that Mercier characterizes as "at the very same time too long and too short" (2:497). The *Tableau de Paris* is by its very nature too long and too short, inasmuch as it attempts to provide a global view of Paris, and at the same time to fill in as much detail as possible. While the work provides an opportunity for contrasts similar to those

---

41. Jorge Luis Borges, "On Exactitude in Science," in *Collected Fictions,* trans. Andrew Hurley (New York: Penguin Books, 1998), 325.

of the relief map, when Mercier zooms in on the forest of hairpins on the beautiful woman's head or zooms out for a bird's-eye view from Notre-Dame, it is too long in the sense that, unlike the relief map, these multiple and contrasting views cannot all be surveyed in three hours' time. At the same time, it is necessarily too short, since the work of describing Paris can come to its conclusion only with the cessation of abuses to be reformed, and in the absence of new angles from which to describe. It is in this context that Mercier's struggles with the problem of how to end the *Tableau de Paris* can be understood. In a certain sense, it is only with the Revolution that the problem of closure is "resolved"; as Charles observes, "In order to stop accumulating within a single space, to move from one work to another, from an always new Paris to *Le nouveau Paris,* nothing less than a revolution will be required."[42]

Within the *Tableau de Paris,* the only truly conclusive chapter is the last chapter in the eighth volume, "Vue des Alpes" (View of the Alps), which Mercier originally wrote as a conclusion before he decided to add another four volumes to his work.[43] In this chapter, he alludes to his departure from Paris for Switzerland in 1781 after the first two volumes of the *Tableau de Paris* were forbidden. Not returning to Paris until 1785, Mercier wrote much of his work from the distant perspective of Switzerland; as Jeremy Popkin describes it, "The Paris of words that he created was a substitute for the living reality of the city."[44] Thus in what was to have been his concluding chapter, Mercier offers a reflection on the necessity of obtaining a distant, and therefore global, perspective on his subject: "I left Paris to paint it better. Far from the object of my crayons, my imagination embraces it and represents it in its entirety" (2:496–97). This claim notwithstanding, it is remarkable that Mercier was able to describe with such precision from the distant perspective of his Swiss retreat. This aspect of the *Tableau de Paris* is often forgotten by those who suggest that the chapters are organized according to Mercier's actual trajectory through the city streets.

---

42. Shelly Charles, "Histoire du texte: Études pour un tableau," in Mercier, *Tableau de Paris,* 1:xciv.

43. See Charles, "Histoire du texte," in Mercier, *Tableau de Paris,* 1:lxxxvii-lxxxix, for a discussion of how Mercier transformed a 1775 article entitled "Montagnes," published in the *Journal des dames,* into the chapter "Vue des Alpes." Most significant in this transformation was the addition of a social dimension, which was absent from the initially more poetic article.

44. Popkin, *Panorama of Paris,* 15.

Yet the "Vue des Alpes" chapter is conclusive not only in its evocation of a distant, global perspective (which seems to allow for the possibility of a definitive judgment on Paris in a way that much of the rest of the work does not), but also in its negative conclusion about the possibility of effecting reform through writing. In contemplating the majestic Swiss landscape (the same landscape he so admires in Pfiffer's *tableau*), Mercier sounds an unusual note of pessimism with respect to his project as a social critic. Referring to himself in the third person, he writes:

> The more he senses, soon what he senses the best is his weakness, his smallness, his impotence. He sees political abuses invincibly linked to physical strength, to crushing strength.
>
> It is above his head. This avalanche rolling with the sound of thunder will engulf the observer, the reformer, and the generous projects. Weak and small, will he rather shake the physical ills? In this heart so warmly moved, what strength, what means will he find? What is he? What does he want? What can he do? (2:500)

With these questions, Mercier transforms his initially peaceful contemplation of the Swiss landscape into an anxious musing about the potential influence of his *Tableau de Paris*. His pessimistic sense that the reformer, the observer, and his generous plans may be engulfed by forces of political oppression—as overpowering as nature itself—can be seen in contrast to multiple passages in the *Tableau de Paris* that express great confidence in the power of the written word to influence public opinion and to effect change. Mercier's belief in the power of even the tiniest of individual voices to question and criticize the powers that be can indeed be seen in bold comments such as "The oath of kings, shouldn't it be the most inviolable of all? That is my little opinion, and I'm not a person of independent means [un rentier]....It is said that states don't have morals; I will respond boldly: '*Too bad for them.*'" (1:313). In the chapter "Vue des Alpes," on the contrary, Mercier appears to abandon his project of social criticism—"he wanted to reform men; he no longer knows how to do anything other than admire nature"—and the bold voice of this tiny individual falls silent in the face of the physical forces surrounding it: "The nature around him seems to cry out to him: I am big, and you are small; this horizon is immense, and your conception is limited [bornée]. This boulder saw the first days of the

universe; if it could talk, it would confound you. Be silent before these immense masses" (2:500). With a phrase reminiscent of Saint-Pierre's "Nature is infinitely immense; and I am a very limited man," Mercier seems
to reject the possibility of using description to effect social reforms. Still,
just as Saint-Pierre did not cease to pursue his ruined sketch, Mercier does
not fall silent after the "Vue des Alpes" chapter. Not content to observe
Paris from the distant perspective of his Alpine retreat, the observer and
reformer goes back to Paris with his generous projects and adds another
four volumes to a book both "too long and too short," thereby invalidat-
ing the conclusions of his "final" chapter. Thus as a conclusion, the "Vue
des Alpes" is fundamentally untrue to the *Tableau de Paris* as a whole, not
only because it clearly frames the work, but also because it abandons the
city and its inhabitants in favor of a Rousseauist retreat, because it favors
silence over the continued act of writing, and above all because it loses confidence in the power of a tiny voice to speak out against the forces of social
and political oppression.

A counterpoint to the closure and discouragement of the "Vue des Alpes"
chapter can be found in the chapter cited earlier from the last volume of the
Tableau de Paris, entitled "Messieurs Cupis père et fils" (Messieurs Cupis
Father and Son).[45] In this key chapter, Mercier makes a powerful association between description and pleasure, tracing the origins of his descriptive
project to the pleasure he took as a child in describing his dancing teacher
to his comrades: "In the evening, I made for my comrades the description
of M. Cupis from head to toe; without him I wouldn't have been a *descripteur;* he developed in me the seed that since then has made the *Tableau de
Paris.* I had to paint his grotesque physiognomy, his short arms, his pointy
head; and since that time I have amused myself with describing" (2:1479).
This account of the origins of the *Tableau de Paris* is significant in two
respects. First, it highlights the centrality of human subjects in Mercier's
descriptive project, in a way that reflects both the principles of the *Encyclopédie* and the author's admiration for Jean de La Bruyère's *Caractères.*[46]

---

45. See Mercier, *Tableau de Paris,* 2:1479–82.

46. See the chapter "Saint Joseph," Mercier, *Tableau de Paris,* 1:577, where Mercier expresses
his admiration for La Bruyère as follows: "It is a little succursal chapel, located in the rue Mont-
martre; but Molière and La Fontaine lie at rest there; and these two original writers please me
more, with Fénelon and La Bruyère, than all the other authors of the century of Louis XIV, whatever their names may be."

The importance of human subjects in the *Tableau de Paris* can be seen in Mercier's multiple portraits of Parisians, in his engagement with the social problems of his time, and in his emphasis on the active participation of his reader. As the subject of descriptive portraits, as the beneficiary of the social changes called for in the *Tableau de Paris,* and as the active contributor toward the composition of a meaningful *tableau* of Paris, the human subject is both the origin and the end point of the *Tableau de Paris.*

Second, in recounting this formative experience through which he learned conjointly to laugh and to describe (but not to dance)—"instead of teaching me to dance, [M. Cupis] taught me how to laugh"—Mercier suggests that his primary motivation in writing the *Tableau de Paris* was to provide amusement for himself and others (2:1479). While pleasure is certainly not the sole force propelling the writing of the *Tableau de Paris*—it is seconded, as we have seen, by Mercier's conviction that writing can contribute to the reform of social abuses and injustices—it is an important one and exists in its own right, removed from any utilitarian aim. It is thus that the "Messieurs Cupis père et fils" chapter contains no hint of the reformist and utilitarian preoccupations often taken to be characteristic of the *Tableau de Paris.* Bonnet has remarked upon this duality in Mercier's work: "From the beginning this vigilant gaze was always accompanied and doubled by a curiosity that was more detached from the demands of the present."[47] More than pure curiosity, however, it is the pleasure experienced by Mercier as he translates the most curious objects of the world—like M. Cupis with his grotesque physiognomy—into descriptions, and above all the pleasure he communicates to his readers in doing so that is one of the principal origins and ends of the *Tableau de Paris.*

The question of descriptive pleasure, divorced from any reformist aim, also has implications for the "conclusion" of the *Tableau;* for just as Mercier's reference to the "seed that has since made the *Tableau de Paris*" suggests that descriptive pleasure is the starting point for his descriptive project, so do we discover in the last paragraph of the *Tableau de Paris* that pleasure is also the only possible end point for this open-ended work. To invoke reform in the final pages of the *Tableau de Paris* would be to suggest that Mercier's work as a social critic is complete. To invoke the pleasure of writing, on the contrary, is to call for its continuation in the pleasure of reading,

---

47. Bonnet, "Littérature et réel," 25.

which Mercier hopes to instill in his reader: "I have known almost no boredom since I started composing books. If I have caused any to my readers, may they forgive me, for I have amused myself quite a bit. Man exists by thought alone, and the good Providence granted me this victorious weapon against the most cruel enemy of the human species" (2:1579). Between the "I amused myself by describing" of the "Messieurs Cupis père et fils" chapter and the "I have amused myself quite a bit" of this concluding paragraph, Mercier makes descriptive pleasure the final justification and the final word for the *Tableau de Paris*. This is, of course, a highly ambiguous way to end a book that is both too long and too short, leaving the reader to wonder why a work that gives so much pleasure to its author and to its reader should ever come to an end.

* * *

For both Delon and Charles, the *Tableau de Paris* is an essentially open-ended work, and it is only the upheaval of the Revolution that allows and obliges Mercier to move from the *Tableau de Paris* to *Le nouveau Paris*. In Delon's view, "The principle of a collection such as the *Tableau de Paris* was incompleteness, the call for continuation. The Revolution is a phenomenon of a scale that necessitates its rewriting."[48] As we have seen, Mercier's claim that the *Tableau de Paris* constitutes a unified work, and a single painting, in no way implies the construction of a singular, coherent perspective on its object. It is a writing of the present, but in which the immediate historification of that present is everywhere inscribed into the text. It is an individual voice convinced of its power to effect change and to rewrite the city, but at the same time lost in a multitude of overwhelming changes that it can neither control nor capture. And because the *Tableau de Paris,* in its innovative literary form, embraces the bewildering mass of impressions experienced in Paris, whether it be in the ephemeral world of fashion or in the rapid evolution of colloquial language, readers can easily get lost in this work, just as they can get lost in an unfamiliar city. The contrast between the overwhelming length of the work and the brevity and focus of each of its chapters means that although the *Tableau de Paris* can only be read from

48. Michel Delon, introduction to *Paris le jour, Paris la nuit,* by Louis Sébastien Mercier and Restif de la Bretonne, ed. Michel Delon and Daniel Baruch (Paris: Robert Laffont, 1990), 13.

cover to cover over a long period of time and on multiple occasions, readers can nevertheless get an almost immediate impression of some particular detail or aspect of Paris. Like Mercier himself, readers of the *Tableau de Paris* are both near and far, caught in the present and the past, inside and outside the painting. This structure gives them a remarkable freedom to navigate within the work, comparing articles, noticing contradictions, perceiving echoes and resonances, and in the end composing their own individual perspective on the work and the city it describes. Thus if the *Tableau de Paris* is an anti-*tableau,* it is above all because it allows for this immense circulatory and interpretative freedom, in a way that for Mercier, painting could never do.

6

Description in Revolution

Beneath the current Paris, the former Paris is distinct,
like the old text between the lines of the new.

Victor Hugo, "Paris" (1867)

Mercier published the last volume of his *Tableau de Paris* in 1788, just
one year before the Revolution he later claimed to have prophesied in
1771 in his best-selling futuristic novel, *L'an 2440*. Ten years later, in 1798
or 1799, he published his account of revolutionary Paris, *Le nouveau Paris.*
Although Mercier presented this work as a companion piece to the *Tableau
de Paris,* he emphasized the tremendous gulf that separated the old Paris
from the new. He also suggested, significantly for an author who had previously eschewed autobiography, that in the space of that turbulent decade,
he himself had changed as much as Paris.[1] "May *Le nouveau Paris* enjoy
the same success as the old *Tableau de Paris!*" he wrote in his preface, "but
the brushstrokes, alas! are quite different, since the model and the painter
have been struck by the most tempestuous times and circumstances" (26).

---

1. On Mercier's reluctance to create "a personal mythology" in his work, see Jean-Claude Bonnet, introduction, in Mercier, *Tableau de Paris,* 1:xlv; and id., introduction, in Mercier, *Nouveau
Paris,* xlvi.

Like many others, Mercier had welcomed the Revolution eagerly and had lent his pen to its cause, founding the popular Paris daily the *Annales patriotiques et littéraires,* later taken up by Jean-Louis Carra, and publishing *De Jean-Jacques Rousseau, considéré comme l'un des premiers auteurs de la Révolution* (On Jean-Jacques Rousseau, Considered as One of the First Authors of the Revolution) in 1791.[2] But he also embraced politics directly, becoming deputy to the Convention in 1792 and allying himself with the ill-fated Girondins. Remaining loyal to his "modérantisme" throughout the Revolution, Mercier's fate would be closely tied to that of the Girondins: as one of the seventy-some deputies who signed a petition protesting their arrest, Mercier was imprisoned in October 1793 and barely escaped execution during the Terror. He was released in October 1794, a few months after the fall of Robespierre, and resumed his political and literary activities: under the Directory, he was a member of the legislative Council of Five Hundred, and held positions in the Institut and the École centrale, the new academic and pedagogical institutions founded by the Convention. It was at this time, and from this perspective, that in 1797 Mercier began gathering articles from his journalistic writings to compose *Le nouveau Paris.*

Le nouveau Paris was thus an occasion for Mercier to ponder the strange gulf that separated the old Paris from the new. But it was also an occasion for him to reflect on the relationship between language and politics, after a decade of intense literary and political activism. In this, too, he was not alone. As Sophia Rosenfeld has shown, the revolutionaries inherited from Enlightenment epistemology a preoccupation with the social and political conflicts that could arise from the misuse of language (or *abus des mots,* as it was commonly called). But they also inherited from writers such as Condillac, Diderot, and Rousseau the corresponding belief that language could be reformed in the service of political and social harmony. Hence, as Rosenfeld notes, "Language became a major site of political controversy and experimentation, and politics became a key locus of linguistic controversy and experimentation, from the middle of the eighteenth century to the opening of the nineteenth."[3] Mercier's work reflected this tight connection between

---

2. On this work and the broader notion of Rousseau as "author" of the Revolution, see James Swenson, *On Jean-Jacques Rousseau: Considered as One of the First Authors of the Revolution* (Stanford: Stanford University Press, 2000).

3. Sophia Rosenfeld, *A Revolution in Language: The Problem of Signs in Late Eighteenth-Century France* (Stanford: Stanford University Press, 2001), 4–5.

language and sociopolitical reform: in the *Tableau de Paris,* as we have seen, he sought to effect change through the precise and evocative description of social and political ills. Nonetheless, in keeping with his iconoclastic pronouncements as a member of the Institut, Mercier's position on the relationship between language and politics during the Revolution departed significantly from the status quo. This idiosyncratic position was informed by Mercier's descriptive practice, which was transformed in *Le nouveau Paris,* along with Paris and Mercier himself.

The Fragmented Map of Paris

Mercier opens *Le nouveau Paris* by underlining the central role of memory in his account of revolutionary Paris, and the consequently complex intertextual relationship between this work and the *Tableau de Paris:* "I no longer walk through Paris except on what reminds me of what is no longer. [Je ne marche plus dans Paris que sur ce qui me rappelle ce qui n'est plus.] I did well to do my painting in twelve volumes. For if it weren't done, the model is so effaced that it resembles the faded portrait of a grandparent who died in a hospice, relegated to a garret [il ressemble au portrait décoloré d'un aïeul mort à l'hôpital et relégué dans un galetas]" (31).[4] As this intricate and grammatically contorted analogy suggests, the old Paris is to be found both in the *Tableau de Paris* and, in an effaced and buried form, in Mercier's memorial account of the new Paris. Hence even as Mercier asserts the strange newness of revolutionary Paris, he signals the persistence of the city's former self for those willing to disinter it.

Hugo's subsequent claim that Paris could be read "like the old text between the lines of the new" (comme le vieux texte dans les interlignes du nouveau) is thus a particularly apt characterization of *Le nouveau Paris.* (Not coincidentally, Hugo greatly admired the work and even borrowed liberally from it in composing his historical novel *Quatre-vingt treize*).[5]

---

4. The grammatical construction in French creates an ambiguity, difficult to reproduce in translation, between the grandparent, who died in a hospice, and the portrait, relegated to a garret.

5. See, for example, the beginning of the second part of the novel, entitled "Les rues de Paris dans ce temps-là." In addition to more direct borrowings, this chapter includes a sentence reminiscent of Mercier's rhythmic description of the Directory ball-goers: "People danced in the ruined cloisters, with lanterns [lampions] on the altar, in the vault two batons in a cross carrying four

Mercier's efforts to inscribe the old Paris within *Le nouveau Paris,* even as he represented a radically new city, can be seen in his decision to preserve the form of the *Tableau de Paris* in his account of revolutionary Paris. As we have seen, the *Tableau de Paris* was innovative, even revolutionary, in its form: by arranging his brief, titled chapters in no discernible order, Mercier gave his readers as much freedom to circulate within his text as he himself had to wander through the city. Hence, even before the Revolution, the *Tableau de Paris* re-created the "crossing of innumerable relations" that Baudelaire would later attribute both to the modern city and to his own prose poems.[6] At the same time, through patterns of repetition between various chapters written over a period of eight years, Mercier created a sense of time passing as Old Regime Paris seemed to change slowly before the readers' eyes.

As Mercier was well aware, the rapid changes and heightened contrasts of revolutionary Paris were of an entirely different order. One might thus expect that he would have introduced new formal innovations to reflect the "accelerated time" that Reinhart Koselleck has attributed to modernity.[7] Yet despite the title of his work, and despite his conviction that an entirely new work was needed to describe revolutionary Paris, Mercier adopted precisely the same form he had invented to describe Old Regime Paris: brief, titled chapters arranged in no discernible order served as a constant reminder that *Le nouveau Paris* was a continuation of the *Tableau de Paris.* At the same time, chapter titles such as "Têtes poudrées" (Powdered Heads) served as an eloquent reminder that formerly innocuous words and images were now frequently charged with violent and politically divisive meanings. Hence even as the formal continuity encouraged readers to glimpse the old Paris between the lines of the new, it also forced them to recognize that everything, including language itself, had changed irrevocably.

Mercier signaled this change pointedly with his new title, *Le nouveau Paris.* By dropping the term *tableau,* he erased the formerly clear distinction

---

candles, and tombs under the dance." Victor Hugo, *Quatre-vingt treize,* ed. Judith Wulf (Paris: Flammarion, 2002), 145. See also Mercier, *Nouveau Paris,* 401.

6. Charles Baudelaire, *Le spleen de Paris: Petits poèmes en prose,* ed. Robert Kopp (1973; repr., Paris: Flammarion, 1987), 74.

7. Reinhart Koselleck, "Modernity and the Planes of Historicity," in *Futures Past: On the Semantics of Historical Time,* trans. Keith Tribe (1985; repr., New York: Columbia University Press, 2004), 22.

between object and representation, in the same way that, as Koselleck has noted, the midcentury shift from *Historie* to *Geschichte* in the German language meant that history "converged as event and representation."[8] This erasure was reinforced by Mercier's inclusion of the definite article in his new title, Le *nouveau Paris,* which in contrast to his previous title, *Tableau de Paris* (with no article), suggested that both the city and the work were one of a kind. This subtle distinction between the two titles was picked up by subsequent literary tradition: unlike its revolutionary companion piece, the *Tableau de Paris* inspired numerous imitations with the same or similar titles throughout the first half of the nineteenth century, to such an extent that the "tableau de Paris" has even been considered by some critics as a minor literary genre.[9]

Hence the new title implied not just a change in Paris itself, but also a fundamental reorientation in Mercier's representational project. This is confirmed by a seminal chapter in *Le nouveau Paris* entitled "La ville de Paris en relief (monument qui se voit au Palais-Égalité)" (The City of Paris in Relief [Monument That Can Be Seen in the Palais-Égalité]). In this chapter, Mercier describes an intricately detailed relief map of Paris, made of wood and cardboard by a certain Citoyen Arnauld and displayed in the Palais-Égalité in 1797 (see figure 5). (The Palais-Égalité, formerly the Palais-Royal immortalized by Diderot's *Neveu de Rameau,* was a favorite observation post for Mercier before and during the Revolution.) Expressing deep admiration for this map, Mercier draws an explicit parallel between Arnauld's artistry and his own work of description in the *Tableau de Paris:* "He did in the physical for Paris what I tried to do in the moral with my *Tableau*" (Il a fait au physique sur Paris ce que j'ai tenté de faire au moral dans mon *Tableau*) (495). This remark suggests that the relief map can be interpreted as a metaphor for the *Tableau de Paris* embedded within *Le nouveau Paris,* providing us with a rare opportunity to see how Mercier viewed his earlier description of Paris from a revolutionary vantage point. Interpreted in this light, the chapter suggests that the *Tableau de Paris* can be revisited and reread from a revolutionary perspective, but also that the

---

8. Koselleck, "Historia Magistra Vitae," in *Futures Past,* 32.

9. See Karlheinz Stierle, "Baudelaire and the Tradition of the *Tableau de Paris,*" *New Literary History* 11, no. 2 (1980): 345–61.

Figure 5. Late eighteenth-century or early nineteenth-century relief map of Paris. The provenance and current whereabouts of the map are unknown, but it was probably part of Napoléon Bonaparte's collection. It was taken by the Prussians in 1815 and exhibited in the Zeughaus in Berlin. This photograph comes from Gaston Renault's mission to Berlin and shows the state of the relief map in 1949. The photograph is reproduced with permission of the Musée des Plans-Reliefs in Paris (no. inv. PR 1296.22-5).

Revolution has in important ways made it obsolete, thereby justifying the writing of *Le nouveau Paris.*

Like the *Tableau de Paris,* Arnauld's relief map attempts to achieve a unified representation of Paris that can nonetheless be viewed from many different perspectives. Mercier underlines this parallel when he urges spectators of the map to stand up on a chair and take a bird's-eye view, just as he had urged readers of the *Tableau de Paris* to climb to the top of Notre-Dame to see Paris from on high.[10] He also suggests that spectators use a magnifying glass to bring the map's miniature scale up to size, thereby mirroring his own tendency in the *Tableau de Paris* to zoom in on certain details like the hairpins sticking into an elegant lady's scalp.[11] Thus Mercier emphasizes that the spectators' perspective on the map is not controlled or oriented in any single direction: like the readers of the *Tableau de Paris,* they have the freedom to survey the topography of Paris from many different angles and in any order they choose.

Arnauld's relief map also provides an occasion for Mercier to reflect on how much, or rather how little, the physical topography of Paris has changed since the Revolution, in the face of dramatic social and political changes: "Such is this curious and instructive map that puts Paris before our eyes, as it was in 1789, without any deterioration, and in all of its successive expansions. One sees that the Revolution, even if it made thousands of heads fall, did not in any way damage its physical mass; that it is the same, absolutely the same, and this reflection that tells us that the bird passes and that the nest remains, becomes even deeper [se creuse encore] when one contemplates so many palaces and houses no longer inhabited by their owners, nor by their possessors who are still living" (491). As a physical entity, Mercier suggests, Paris has remained unchanged during the revolutionary decade, even as the lives of its inhabitants have changed drastically. What then can Arnauld's relief map, which describes solely physical structures, tell its spectators about the Revolution?

This is where revolutionary memory, one of the central themes of *Le nouveau Paris,* comes into play. According to Mercier, Arnauld's map allows each spectator to revisit his or her personal memories of the Revolution, in connection with the various places depicted on it. In fact, Mercier

---

10. Mercier, *Tableau de Paris,* 1:34.
11. Ibid., 1:918–21.

spends most of the chapter describing not the map itself, but rather the memories it evokes in a wide variety of spectators. What we see in the chapter, then, is an individuation and fragmentation of the viewing public. This becomes particularly apparent when one of the spectators, a *bonnet rouge* or radical revolutionary, is marginalized from the viewing public. His exclusion is orchestrated by a mysteriously disembodied pointer that suddenly materializes in the text, to designate the site where Sanson, an infamous executioner during the Terror, chopped off heads, or, as Mercier puts it, minted fresh coins: "The attentive observer...easily recognizes the secret or hidden feelings of the individuals, by the objects they consider most particularly; the former red cap [bonnet rouge] himself trembles when the tip of the pointer marks the place where Sanson minted coins [battit monnaie], where the statue of liberty became the idol of Moloch; and he moves off a bit to the side so as not to hear the ensuing remark, which concerns him" (483–84).[12] It now appears that there is an anonymous tour guide conducting an ideologically motivated tour of Arnauld's map: first with the pointer, then with a remark, this guide accuses, and thereby excludes, certain members of the viewing public.

The question then becomes whether Mercier's position in *Le nouveau Paris* is analogous to that of this disembodied, accusing tour guide. Such an overtly ideological position would seem to deny the circulatory and interpretative freedom characteristic of the *Tableau de Paris*. It cannot be denied that *Le nouveau Paris* is a work of political polemic; at times, it seems that Mercier's sole motivation in writing the work was to accuse the radical Montagnard deputies of having destroyed the ideals of the Revolution: "Thirty to forty villains even more inept than barbarous came and decomposed everything great and momentous that genius and courage had formed. These thirty to forty villains are the Montagnard leaders. That is what I will prove in the rest of this text" (32). For some critics, such overt expressions of political ideology make *Le nouveau Paris* "a decided disappointment" when compared to the *Tableau de Paris*.[13]

---

12. Mercier attributes the expression "Battre monnaie sur la place de la Révolution" (To mint coins on the square of the Revolution) to Barère de Vieuzac, a deputy closely allied with Robespierre during the Terror, and cites it as an example of the violent excesses of revolutionary rhetoric. Mercier, *Nouveau Paris,* 249.

13. For Priscilla Parkhurst Ferguson, "*Le Nouveau Paris* in 1798 has less to do with customs than with politics and is a decided disappointment after the *Tableau.*" Ferguson also refers to a

Yet such judgments miss the point Mercier is making in his description of the relief map. As Lynn Hunt argued in her influential analysis of revolutionary political culture, "One of the most fateful consequences of the revolutionary attempt to break with the past was the invention of ideology."[14] And what Mercier's discussion of the relief map illustrates is that the divisive political ideologies that emerged from the Revolution were deeply entwined with the personal memories of the individuals who had experienced the revolutionary decade. Mercier underlines this most forcefully when he includes a veiled but discernible reference to his own experience of imprisonment during the Terror: "There the wife of the ex-conventionnel shows her daughter the prison where her unfortunate father, abandoned by the entire nation, and still republican, waited for the death he had braved in the interest of liberty, and in hatred of anarchy, and waited for it for thirteen months at every instant of the day and night" (481–82). As Bonnet has noted, Mercier seldom referred to his imprisonment, preferring to preserve the "intimate and religious character" of his resolution to survive the Terror.[15] In this case, however, he alludes subtly to that most personal experience in order to underline the extent to which it informs both his political ideology and his description of revolutionary Paris. No longer can he play the role of the Enlightenment describer, stepping up onto a chair to "embrace Paris in a single glance" (486). Nor can he occupy the disembodied position of the anonymous tour guide, who accuses the *bonnet rouge* without situating himself within the revolutionary map. On the contrary, the fragmentation of the viewing public in "Ville de Paris en relief" chapter suggests that any view of revolutionary Paris will be partial and fragmentary, driven by the vagaries of memory and political ideology.

Blond Wigs and Fragile Ribbons

Just as Mercier represents Arnauld's relief map as a site of contrasting memories and divisive political ideologies, he represents revolutionary

---

contemporary rival of Mercier, J. B. Pujoulx, for whom *Le nouveau Paris* was, as Ferguson puts it, "the work of a political historian rather than a man of letters." Priscilla Parkhurst Ferguson, *Paris as Revolution: Writing the Nineteenth-Century City* (Berkeley and Los Angeles: University of California Press, 1994), 237 n. 6.

14. Hunt, *Politics, Culture, and Class,* 12.

15. Bonnet, introduction, in Mercier, *Nouveau Paris,* xliv.

language as a site of individual expression and political contestation. Of course, Mercier was not alone in recognizing the importance of language in revolutionary politics. As Rosenfeld has shown, many of Mercier's contemporaries believed that social and political conflict originated in miscommunication or the willful abuse of language. As a result, the late eighteenth century and especially the revolutionary decade were marked by "a range of projects and semiotic experiments aimed at transcending the problems and limitations associated with vernacular words."[16] Although these projects took various forms, ranging from the gestural to the ideographic, they all reflected a utopian ideal of linguistic transparency and stability. The answer to revolutionary conflict, in other words, was to eradicate linguistic instability and confusion by establishing a shared language of social and political consensus. Yet although Mercier participated in the widespread critique of revolutionary rhetoric, he did not share his contemporaries' aspiration toward an ideal, fixed language of social and political harmony. As Rosenfeld notes, in his dictionary of revolutionary neologisms, *La néologie,* Mercier mocked his contemporaries' efforts at linguistic reform: "And who would not laugh at a tribunal that said to you: I am going to fix the language. Stop, imprudent one! You are going to nail it down [and] crucify it!"[17] Yet this view was not simply, as Rosenfeld suggests, a symptom of the broader shift away from "enlightened sociolinguistic ideals" at the end of the Revolution.[18] It was also rooted in Mercier's pre-revolutionary practice of description. In the *Tableau de Paris,* Mercier had paid close attention to the tiny details of material and linguistic culture, and to their transformations over time. He was thus in a particularly good position to appreciate the way that symbols and rhetoric became, in Hunt's words, "a field of political struggle" during the Revolution.[19] Rather than seeking to stabilize revolutionary language, Mercier pursued his descriptive project by tracking the shifting meaning of symbols and rhetoric in the constantly changing field of revolutionary politics.

A good example of this effort can be found in a chapter entitled "Chevelures blondes" (Blond Tresses), a title that perhaps intentionally

---

16. Rosenfeld, *Revolution in Language,* 9.
17. Quoted in Rosenfeld, *Revolution in Language,* 225. On Mercier's *La néologie,* see Rosenberg, "Louis-Sébastien Mercier's New Words."
18. Rosenfeld, *Revolution in Language,* 8.
19. Hunt, *Politics, Culture, and Class,* 53.

recalls the more innocuous treatment of hairstyles in the *Tableau de Paris.*
Here, Mercier cites a Convention deputy's ironic claim that the counterrevolutionaries had formed a new sect, whose initiates showed their devotion to guillotine victims by making wigs out of their hair: "Toothless
women rush to buy [the hair] of guillotined young fops, and to wear this
cherished hair on their heads" (249). In response to this example of abu-
sive revolutionary rhetoric, Mercier asks: "Who would believe that such a
speech was made? It was at this time that the reign of blond wigs began, as
if women had wanted to brave the bloody irony with this reprisal" (250).
Although Mercier is generally hostile to counterrevolutionaries, he seems
in this case to admire the women's subversive response to the deputy's abu-
sive rhetoric. His characterization of the blond wigs as a reprisal further
suggests that symbols can serve as a powerful response, on the part of individual actors, to revolutionary violence. Although the women cannot
literally resurrect the guillotine victims, they create a powerful symbol of
resurrection by wearing the hair of the dead on their heads. At the same
time, they wrest control of revolutionary language from the Convention
deputy, co-opting his rhetoric to their own purpose. Hence the "Chevelures blondes" chapter allows us to witness the political struggles to control language and symbolism that marked the revolutionary decade. At
the same time, it illustrates how the descriptive heritage of the *Tableau de
Paris* is both pursued and subverted in *Le nouveau Paris:* whereas in the
earlier work, it was Mercier's own shifts in perspective that allowed us
to perceive the painful and unhygienic underpinnings of a fashionable
woman's chignon, here it is the political struggle to control revolutionary
language that creates two opposing perspectives on the blond wigs. Like
Arnauld's map, revolutionary language thus appears to be divided from
within, its divergent meanings a function of both political ideology and
personal expression.

Yet Mercier also emphasized the way in which the constant upheaval
of revolutionary politics could quickly change the meaning of even the
most powerful revolutionary symbols. This can be seen in a brief chapter
entitled "Rubans" (Ribbons), which begins with a dictionary-style definition of the ribbons used by royalty during the Old Regime to decorate and
honor their courtiers. Mercier then contrasts these servile Old Regime ribbons, likened to a harness on the king's subjects, with the tricolored revolutionary ribbons (or *cocardes*) that, as Hunt has shown, became a powerful

symbol of liberty in the first years of the Revolution.[20] Yet Mercier concludes the chapter by evoking a third ribbon, the symbolic meaning of
which is both powerful and perilously fragile. This was the long ribbon
strung outside the Tuileries palace to serve as a barrier between the king
and his people, in the tense weeks leading up to the 10 August 1792 insurrection that brought an effective end to the monarchy: "To separate the
garden of the Tuileries palace occupied by Louis the traitor, from the terrace of the Feuillants where the public gathered, the people strung along
this terrace a simple *ribbon,* and this barrier was respected; no one crossed
it. A cannon would not have produced this effect. It's that the people were
obeying a law they had imposed upon themselves" (288). Although the
chapter ends there, Mercier's evocation of the ribbon as a self-imposed law
is rich in implications, when one considers the fragile underpinnings of the
constitutional monarchy, and the looming threat of popular violence in the
final year of Louis XVI's reign. In the aftermath of the king's treasonous
flight to Varennes, the Assembly could no longer ignore the internal tensions within the constitutional monarchy and was forced to reconsider its
own legitimacy.[21] From a social perspective, the king's flight had created a
widespread climate of suspicion and unrest that persisted until the aboli-
tion of the monarchy; indeed, the Assembly opened the Tuileries garden
to the public in response to popular pressure. In this context, the Tuileries
ribbon appears above all as a symbol of the increasing fragility of political
institutions, and the heightened risk of popular insurrection, at this deci-
sive moment in the Revolution's history.

    This interpretation is confirmed by Germaine de Staël, who makes an
explicit analogy between the Tuileries ribbon and the weakness of the Assembly in her *Considérations sur la Révolution française,* published posthu-
mously in 1818: "The constituent Assembly always believed, quite wrongly,
that there was something magic in its decrees, and that one would stop, in
everything, right at the line it traced. But its authority in this respect resembled that of the ribbon that had been strung up in the Tuileries garden
to prevent the people from approaching the palace: as long as opinion was

---

    20. Ibid., 57–59.

    21. Mona Ozouf, "Varennes," in *A Critical Dictionary of the French Revolution,* ed. François
Furet and Mona Ozouf, trans. Arthur Goldhammer (Cambridge, Mass.: Belknap Press/Harvard
University Press, 1989), 162.

favorable to those who had strung this ribbon, no one thought of going beyond it; but as soon as the people didn't want this barrier anymore, it no longer meant anything at all [elle ne signifia plus rien]."[22] As both de Staël and Mercier knew, the ribbon quickly proved the most fragile and illusory of barriers: on 10 August 1792, just a few weeks after the Tuileries garden was opened to the public, an insurrection in Paris and an attack on the Tuileries palace led to the dissolution of the monarchy, and, the following January, to the king's execution.

Mercier's position on the king's execution once again illustrates his sensitivity to the complex interplay between symbolism and politics during the Revolution. Although there was nothing particularly unusual about his position (as deputy to the Convention, he voted against death but in favor of lifetime imprisonment), what is striking is the extent to which he recognized what Mona Ozouf has called "the high symbolic stakes of the face-to-face confrontation between the king and the Revolution."[23] Like Jules Michelet after him, Mercier argued that Louis XVI's execution would risk turning him into a powerful symbol of the monarchy. The former king's lifetime imprisonment, in contrast, would reinforce the symbolic death of the monarchy that had already been effected by the laws of the nation: "I maintain that the king is dead, that he is buried; he no longer has a political existence.... Political laws have killed the political being.... The king is nothing more than a phantom; and having placed his head under the axe of the law, it's as if it had fallen" (316). This symbolic argument was reinforced by a more concrete, political calculation: as long as Louis XVI was alive, Mercier contended, the rulers of Europe would consider him the legitimate ruler of France and would not dare to take his place on the throne. In this way, the imprisoned former king would protect the fragile young Republic from the forces of reaction and counterrevolution. Hence Mercier's two-pronged argument acknowledged that in the king's trial, as Ozouf describes it, "political stakes were never distinct from symbolic and legal ones."[24] It also reflected his belief that at this moment of great political fragility, some measure of continuity between past and present was needed

22. Germaine de Staël, *Considérations sur la Révolution française,* ed. Jacques Godechot (Paris: Tallandier, 1983), 243.

23. Ozouf, "King's Trial," in Furet and Ozouf, *Critical Dictionary,* 95.

24. Ibid., 96.

to protect the progress of the Revolution; in this case, the preservation of the king's person would serve both to reinforce his symbolic death and to guarantee a smooth transition from the Old Regime to the new Republic.

Although Mercier opposed the king's execution, he accepted it after the fact to avoid a split in the Convention. In a chapter from *Le nouveau Paris* on the anniversary celebrations of the king's death, he wrote: "I did what was in me to save the last king from torture and from death; he is no longer; his ashes are insensible: if necessary, I will dance *politically* on his ashes" (750). But despite his political realism, Mercier signaled with this troubling image of dancing on the king's ashes his discomfort with the radical severance between past and present symbolized by the king's execution. Throughout *Le nouveau Paris,* in both his images (of women donning the hair of guillotine victims) and his political arguments (that the king's life must be spared to protect the young Republic), he insisted that the Revolution could not so easily dispense with its past. As a describer, he saw it as his role to bear witness to that past, and to grapple with the relationship between the old Paris and the new.

Lifting the Post-Thermidorian Curtain

Thus for Mercier a description of revolutionary Paris could not simply be a record of things seen: it had to reproduce the multilayered experience of walking through the new Paris while remembering the old. The emphasis on memory was in part a function of the genesis of *Le nouveau Paris:* while the initial project and some chapters date from the early years of the Revolution, it was only after his release from prison in 1794 that Mercier began a regular chronicle of revolutionary Paris in the newspaper *Les annales patriotiques et littéraires,* and only in 1797 that he began gathering articles to compose *Le nouveau Paris.* Thus, as Charles notes, the work exists not "in the mode of a chronicle ('I saw')," but "in the mode of memory ('I remember')."[25] But the emphasis on memory in *Le nouveau Paris* also reflects the specific political and social challenges facing the Revolution after the fall of Robespierre. After 9 Thermidor, as Bronislaw Baczko

---

25. Charles, "Histoire du texte: Des nouvelles de Paris au *Nouveau Paris,*" in Mercier, *Nouveau Paris,* clxxxvi-clxxxix.

explains, "the Revolution carried with it an unavoidable past of its own, which it could not jettison. It was obsessed, moreover, with memories of the immediate past: the Terror."[26] These preoccupations resurface repeatedly in *Le nouveau Paris,* which represents post-Thermidorian culture as a frenzied quest to hide memories of the Terror under a veil of decadent balls and feasts. As a describer, Mercier was thus faced with an important choice: Should he describe revolutionary violence in explicit, graphic terms, thereby unearthing painful memories that post-Thermidorian culture was attempting to bury along with the dead? Or should he rather depict the culture of pleasure that was created to obscure memories of revolutionary violence, but that could not seem to escape from its persistently resurgent images?

Despite his avowed reluctance, Mercier did not eschew the explicit and horrifying description of the popular violence he had witnessed prior to the institutionalization of violence under the Terror. In a chapter on the September 1792 massacres, he describes the brutal, sexualized violence to which the Princesse de Lamballe's corpse was allegedly subjected: "When Madame de Lamballe had been mutilated in a hundred different ways, when the assassins had divided up the bloody parts of her body among themselves, one of these monsters cut her virginal part and made himself a mustache from it, in the presence of spectators seized with horror and terror" (99). Despite Mercier's discomfort with such descriptions (he follows this one with "I no longer have the strength to write"), he presents them as a necessary antidote to the suppression of such memories in post-Thermidorian culture. Hence, in a passage that beautifully suggests how much description has become an act of unveiling, he writes: "If all the disastrous events are not forgotten amid our parties and pleasures, they are covered by a curtain that we are afraid to lift, or that we lift only rarely" (26).

Yet even the image of lifting a curtain to reveal hidden memories does not do justice to the subtlety of Mercier's approach to the description of violence. In some cases, it is the curtain itself that he chooses to describe, in a way that reveals the very horrors it was intended to hide. This can be seen in a chapter entitled "Les bals d'hiver" (Winter Balls), in which Mercier describes the frenzied dancing, gastronomic excess, and unchecked

---

26. Bronislaw Baczko, "Thermidorians," in Furet and Ozouf, *Critical Dictionary,* 409.

lubricity that overtook men, and especially women, in the aftermath of 9 Thermidor:

> They dance in the *Carmelites* where throats were slit; they dance in the *noviciate of the Jesuits;* they dance in the *convent of the Carmelites in the Marais;* they dance in the *seminary of Saint-Sulpice;* they dance in the *Filles de Sainte-Marie;* they dance in three ruined churches of my section, and on the paving stones of all the tombs that haven't yet been removed: the names of the dead are under the feet of the dancers who don't notice them, and who forget that they are trampling on sepulchers. (401)

When faced with descriptions such as this one, we may be inclined to ask whether such balls actually existed. In his discussion of the notorious victims' balls (at which dancers purportedly paid homage to their guillotined relatives with hairstyles and dance steps that evoked images of decapitation), Ronald Schechter argues that "despite the common agreement of historians over a period of more than 160 years, there is little if any contemporary evidence that the *bals des victimes* in fact existed."[27] Schechter thus interprets the persistent myth of the victims' balls as a collective aide-memoire that helped post-Thermidorian culture make sense of the Terror.

In his own chapter on the victims' balls, Mercier wonders, significantly in light of Schechter's claim, whether posterity will believe that a phenomenon so incredible actually existed (339). But regardless of whether such balls took place, Mercier's depiction of the swirling dancers reflects his broader view of post-Thermidorian culture: by dancing wildly in churches and convents, the ball-goers trample their ancestors' tombs, thereby erasing the collective memory of the dead traditionally preserved by religious institutions. Unlike Mercier, who traverses Paris in order to remember, the ball-goers turn ceaselessly upon themselves, seeking to forget the past through the rapid movement of their feet. Like so many other pleasure seekers in *Le nouveau Paris,* they seek to negate time itself, "forgetting the past, killing the present, not thinking about the future" (423). In this respect, Mercier's rhythmic depiction of the dancers reflects his view that the Jacobins set the Revolution on a fatal course by attempting to negate

---

27. Ronald Schechter, "Gothic Thermidor: The *Bals des victimes,* the Fantastic, and the Production of Historical Knowledge in Post-Terror France," *Representations* 61 (1998): 78–94.

the past: "Inept men had said *that in revolution, one must never look back.* This maxim is very wrong. Revolutions are conducted and brought to completion by those who measure and compare what is done, and what remains to be done" (18). With this remark, Mercier underscores the post-Thermidorian preoccupations of *Le nouveau Paris:* neither of the two essential problems facing the revolutionaries after 9 Thermidor—how to move beyond the Terror and how to end the Revolution—could be resolved without attention to the Revolution's newly constituted past. It is in this context that the formal resemblance between the *Tableau de Paris* and *Le nouveau Paris* takes on its full significance: it was, for Mercier, a symbolic means, however fragile, of resisting the revolutionary forces of erasure (of the past, of his memories, of the dead, and of the old Paris itself), even as he welcomed the progress of revolution.

The Kaleidoscope of Perspectives

Le nouveau Paris can thus be read as an attempt to set the revolutionary future into relation with its past. It is a work that explores what Koselleck has called the "historical experience of time."[28] One might ask, then, to what extent *Le nouveau Paris* marks a shift from description to something that might more properly be called history. Certainly, the work bears witness to the new historical plane of modernity, whose future, according to Koselleck, "is characterized by two main features: first, the increasing speed at which it approaches us, and second, its unknown quality."[29] This can be seen in the distinct shift in Mercier's position as an observer. As we have seen, Mercier claims in the *Tableau de Paris* to have written the work with his legs. Although he emphasizes the rapid, agile step that is needed to cover the entire city and "see all," this claim nonetheless suggests the image of a relatively stable city that can be traversed and explored in its entirety by a single observer. In *Le nouveau Paris,* in contrast, Mercier is confronted by such a rapid and unexpected succession of events that he can no longer choose the trajectory of his description: "How to paint so many

---

28. In addressing the historical experience of time, Koselleck focuses on works that "deal with the relation of a given past to a given future." Koselleck, *Futures Past,* 3.

29. Koselleck, "Modernity," in *Futures Past,* 22.

facts and events? I will say what I saw. Carried along on all the stormy tor-
rents, not having missed a gust of wind, my eye made out in the tempest a
few particular accidents" (32). Although Mercier retains both the principle
of firsthand observation and the metaphor of writing as painting, he can
no longer keep pace with the "accelerated time" and the unexpected succession of events that constitute the Revolution. Instead of traversing the
city and composing his description, he allows himself to be carried along
by the Revolution and attempts to make out a few details (however incidental) amid the turbulence. Hence the "newness" of *Le nouveau Paris* is
a factor not only of changes in the city itself but also of changes in the observer's historical experience of time.

Mercier offers explicit reflections on the relationship between description and history in a key chapter entitled "Tout est optique" (Everything
Is Perspective). In keeping with its title, much of this chapter suggests that
distance, whether spatial or temporal, inevitably distorts one's view of the
Revolution: "From nearby, how different things are from what we judge
them to be from afar! Everything has its deceptive appearances. One imagines Paris turned upside down with each political commotion, and children
roasted on a spit by the cannibals who took over the Bastille and the Tuileries palace. It is the wind that carries the noise of the cannon far away: right
next to it one doesn't hear it as well" (878). Here, Mercier appears simply to
be asserting the value of his firsthand perspective on revolutionary events,
as a necessary corrective to the inevitable distortions of history.

Yet Mercier immediately undercuts his initial assertion "Tout est optique," in the chapter title, with the opening phrase of the chapter, "Ou jeu
d'optique" (Or the interplay of perspectives) (878). After a detailed, evocative description of the Convention session that determined the king's fate
(which was subsequently picked up by Michelet), Mercier concludes: "Of
everything I saw there, nothing can be retold as it happened; it is impossible to represent things as they are; history will never be able to reach it"
(880).[30] Mercier is not merely suggesting here that there is an inevitable divergence between the describer's and the historian's perspectives. If he cannot describe revolutionary events as they really were, it is because his own

---

30. On the theatrical dimension of the king's trial, and on Mercier's account of it, see Marie-
Hélène Huet, *Rehearsing the Revolution: The Staging of Marat's Death, 1793–1797,* trans. Robert
Hurley (Berkeley and Los Angeles: University of California Press, 1982), 1–9.

perspective has already changed; indeed, when the events were actually happening, he had no idea of their significance in the history of the Revolution. Like Fabrice in Stendhal's *La chartreuse de Parme,* who finds himself at the battle of Waterloo without even realizing he is on a battlefield, Mercier was present for some of the most memorable days of the Revolution without realizing it until after the fact: "It's the same for all the memorable days; I was there, and I never knew where I was, that is to say, understood the peril I was in, or the singularities that surrounded me" (880).[31] Indeed, the very fact that Mercier calls 13 Vendémiaire (the day a young general named Bonaparte suppressed a royalist insurrection against the Thermidorian Convention) a memorable day signals the interplay of firsthand description and retrospective analysis in *Le nouveau Paris.* In a similar way, Mercier admits that he was initially too close to the Montagnards to believe in their "insolent and bloodthirsty audacity," thereby revealing that the ideological perspective of *Le nouveau Paris* does not necessarily reflect his firsthand perceptions and judgments (880).

However inevitable it may be, the accretion of historical distance poses a threat to Mercier's project in *Le nouveau Paris.* The myopic perspective of the describer proves particularly valuable in the context of the Revolution, when tiny, apparently incidental details can have a determining impact on the course of history: "Since revolutionary crises are composed of the *infinitely small* [sont composées d'*infiniment petits*], these form the essential basis of all events" (881). Precisely because he cannot sift the essential from the accidental, the describer is in a good position to understand the role of chance in the Revolution, such as the fact that "the cannonball that broke the chain of the drawbridge at the Bastille, twelve hours earlier or later, remained without effect" (882). With examples like this one, Mercier does not just assert the value of firsthand perspectives on the Revolution. He underscores the value of his own particular perspective as a describer, as someone who had already cultivated in the *Tableau de Paris* a fine-grained attention to the very kinds of details that would become so momentous in the revolutionary decade.

Yet Mercier is also aware that the "infiniment petits" of revolutionary times, and their causal relationship to the progress of history, necessarily remain elusive for even the most practiced describer. On the whole, the

---

31. Stendhal, *La chartreuse de Parme,* ed. Henri Martineau (Paris: Garnier Frères, 1961), 43.

chapter "Tout est optique" is deeply skeptical about the possibility of writing any coherent account of the Revolution, either from the point of view of the describer or from that of the historian: "How can such a history be written if one fails to grasp the sequence [enchaînement] of each day? For a given event was produced in such an unexpected manner that it seems to have been created and not engendered" (882). As the chapter progresses, it becomes clear that the interplay of perspectives is not merely a function of the competing temporal perspectives at work in the *Le nouveau Paris.* It is also a function of the Revolution itself, which creates a bewildering conjuncture of perspectives that cannot be organized into a coherent interpretation or representation: "How will the historian extract himself from this labyrinth? How will he avoid the empire of his own opinion, when the men most practiced in observation had trouble capturing a point of view, and fixing on an object in this extreme and continual mobility of perspectives [mobilité d'optique]?" (882). In characterizing the Revolution as a "mobilité d'optique" (or "jeu d'optique"), Mercier perfectly captures the poetics of *Le nouveau Paris:* rather than a unified painting of revolutionary Paris, *Le nouveau Paris* is a site where multiple perspectives, both temporal and spatial, are refracted and juxtaposed to form a bewildering kaleidoscope whose images can never be stabilized.

Hence in "Tout est optique," Mercier asserts that there is no ideal vantage point from which to view the Revolution. This sets him apart from the political thinker and historian Alexis de Tocqueville, who would claim some fifty years later to occupy "the precise point from which this great object can best be perceived and judged. Far enough from the Revolution to feel only weakly the passions that obscured the vision of those who accomplished it, we are close enough to it to be able to enter into the spirit that conducted it and to understand it."[32] Tocqueville adopted an approach closer to Mercier's in his *Souvenirs,* where he offered both an "objective" account of the 1848 Revolution and a more chaotic, personal account based on his own experience.[33] In *Le nouveau Paris,* however, the interplay of perspectives is worked into the very fabric of the text. Mercier's contemporary perceptions of revolutionary events are intermingled with his subsequent

---

32. Alexis de Tocqueville, *L'Ancien Régime et la Révolution,* ed. J.-P. Mayer, Collection Folio/Histoire (Paris: Gallimard, 1967), 61.

33. Alexis de Tocqueville, *Souvenirs,* ed. Luc Monnier (1964; repr., Paris: Gallimard, 1978).

interpretations of them. Tiny details are recorded alongside what have since been deemed the most memorable days of the Revolution, and no hierarchical structure allows the reader to distinguish the historic from the trivial. Personal memories of the most intimate nature are placed alongside public events and are seen to have the same significance for understanding the Revolution as a whole. It is thus no wonder that some readers have been disconcerted, and even disappointed, by *Le nouveau Paris,* for they are confronted with a work that tests the limits of representational coherence, and that takes its meaning from a profoundly disorienting fragmentation of perspectives.

* * *

It should now be possible to gauge the distance separating the *Tableau de Paris* from *Le nouveau Paris,* both in terms of Mercier's conception of Paris, and in terms of his representational project. The Enlightenment model of a unified *tableau* of Paris has clearly been abandoned, as the describer is no longer in a position to guarantee coherence. Unlike the spectator of Arnauld's relief map, Mercier can no longer step up onto a chair and "embrace Paris in a single glance" (486). Although he remains loyal to the principle of firsthand observation and to the metaphor of writing as painting, his perspective is now partial and subject to internal fragmentation. In a similar way, the principle of description appears, like revolutionary language itself, to be divided from within and pulled in several opposing directions. Description can no longer be distinguished clearly from history, as Mercier's contemporary perceptions of events are immediately set into (a relative) historical perspective. Yet this is not to say that *Le nouveau Paris* can be read in isolation from the *Tableau de Paris.* As Mercier asserts in his discussion of Arnauld's relief map, it is the city of Paris itself that remains stable amid the revolutionary turmoil: "At the heart of the tempests of the revolution and of the bloody anarchy, [Paris] maintained a stable position [a gardé une assiette immobile]; her own furors, the Jacobite excesses, couldn't destroy her, and the countless armies of plotting kings who wanted to devour her passed like a shadow; their distant fortresses have fallen, and Paris remains in her entirety" (493–94).[34] If Paris has indeed

---

34. With the term "jacobites," Mercier appears to be playing on words to reflect his belief that some Jacobins were counterrevolutionaries plotting with the English to restore the French

on a certain level remained the same, the *Tableau de Paris* subsists as the backdrop against which the disorienting perspectives of *Le nouveau Paris* must be understood. To read the two works together is to perceive both the concrete, unified representation of Paris proposed by Arnauld's relief map, and the fragmentation of perspectives effected by the revolutionary public's view of it.

There is, however, a more essential difference between the old Paris and the new that signals the obsolescence of both Arnauld's relief map and Mercier's *Tableau de Paris*. Whereas Mercier perceived the old Paris as a relatively stable entity to be traversed and described, he perceives the new Paris as an agent of revolutionary change. Thus in a portrait that prefigures the personification of Paris in nineteenth-century literature, Mercier characterizes Paris as a mental and physical force that propelled the Revolution forward:

> There, is the powerful brain that creates, forms, and disseminates republics, that will make them sprout from the land oppressed by kings and oligarchs; there, is the arm that will execute the most daring projects, that will cast a bridge from the Seine to the Thames; it has already changed the feudal face of Europe, and the more resistance there is to the rights of man and liberty, the larger the expanse that will be covered by the regenerating torrent. Like a rock in the middle of the ocean seeing waves arriving from the pole, it pushes them back; they roll in from the edge of the horizon, and it resists their efforts. It is attached to the foundations of the world, it will see a thousand shipwrecks and will remain in all its glory, in that glory granted by the force of thought and the courage of arms. (494)

This passage strikingly prefigures Victor Hugo's homage to Paris written for the Universal Exhibition of 1867.[35] Like Mercier, Hugo depicts Paris as a force of historical change that far surpasses individual men and their governments: "To be always wanting: that is the way of Paris. You think it is sleeping; no, it is wanting. The permanent will of Paris, that is what transitional governments are not sufficiently aware of. Paris is always in a

---

monarchy and were thus analogous to the English Jacobites who sought to restore the House of Stuart to the throne after the Glorious Revolution of 1688.

35. On Hugo's preface to the *Paris-Guide,* see Ferguson, *Paris as Revolution,* 69–75. On the important intertextual relationship between Hugo and Mercier, see Patterson, *Poetic Genesis.*

state of premeditation. It has the patience of a star slowly ripening a fruit. Clouds pass over its fixity. Then one fine day, it is done. Paris decrees an event. France, abruptly ordered to comply, obeys."[36] In 1867, in the midst of what had become the century of revolutions, Hugo warned transitional governments of the city's enduring will to effect change. For him, the agency of Paris provided a simple answer to the complicated question of historical causality: in answer to the question "Who made 14 July?" he responded simply: "Paris."[37]

For Priscilla Parkhurst Ferguson, Hugo's 1867 homage to Paris is a revolutionary text that "alters the very conception of the city" through its "assimilation of Paris and the Revolution."[38] It is thus striking to see how much this text, written during the Second Empire, after nearly a century of political upheaval, owes to *Le nouveau Paris.* Yet although this heritage underscores the modernity of *Le nouveau Paris,* it should not be forgotten that Mercier's initial project of describing the changing moral and physical topography of Paris grew out of the encyclopedic and descriptive aspirations of the Enlightenment. If *Le nouveau Paris* can serve as a bridge between the literatures of the Old Regime and the new, it is because this work remains attached, by its formal resemblance to the *Tableau de Paris,* to the literary and social ideals of an age made obsolete by the Revolution. At the same time, *Le nouveau Paris* is clearly much more than an end point. In addition to transforming the representation of the city for modern times, it embodied a revolution in the individual writer's position within the city and capacity to represent it. Whereas prior to the Revolution Mercier saw Paris as an object of description, in *Le nouveau Paris* he sees the city as a force that takes over his own representational goals: it is Paris that preserves memories of the past, it is Paris that assures the continuity between the Old Regime and the new, and it is Paris that is reflected in the kaleidoscope of revolutionary events that confound the individual observer. Rather than a total description of Paris, *Le nouveau Paris* is a testament to the city's ability to surpass the limitations of individual perception and representation: it is Paris seen as it can no longer be described.

---

36. Victor Hugo, "Paris," in *Oeuvres complètes,* vol. 10, *Politique,* ed. Jean-Claude Fizaine (Paris: Robert Laffont, 1985), 21.

37. Ibid., 22.

38. Ferguson, *Paris as Revolution,* 73.

CONCLUSION

Virtual Encyclopedias

One way of concluding this book would be to trace the literary heritage of Enlightenment descriptive practices into the nineteenth century. One might show, for example, how Honoré de Balzac looked to Buffon as a model for his encyclopedic compendium of social types, writing in the preface to his *Comédie humaine:* "If Buffon made a magnificent work by attempting to represent in one book the whole of zoology, wasn't there a work of this kind to be made for society?"[1] Or one might evoke the "big work" on *Le nouveau Paris* that Charles Baudelaire claimed to be preparing in a letter to his mother and trace Mercier's influence on the modern urban poetics of the prose poem.[2] Although it might be a harder case to make, one might even argue that descriptive poetry paved the way for

---

1. Honoré de Balzac, "Avant-Propos," in *Comédie humaine,* ed. Pierre-Georges Castex, Bibliothèque de la Pléiade 26 (Paris: Gallimard, 1976), 1:8.
2. On Baudelaire's admiration for *Le nouveau Paris,* see Bonnet, introduction, in Mercier, *Nouveau Paris,* i-ii. Popkin notes that "more than half a century before Baudelaire defined the *flâneur,* Mercier exemplified the concept." Popkin, *Panorama of Paris,* 14.

romantic poetry (notwithstanding Sainte-Beuve's claim that "the victory of the new school is proved at the very least by the complete ruin of the old") by dismantling classical poetics and carving out a space for the poet at the center and origin of poetic creation.[3]

But to conclude in this way would be to suggest that the true realization of the Enlightenment's descriptive project lies in nineteenth-century masterpieces that have been consecrated by literary history, at least in part because of their consummate use of description. This would go against the purpose of this book, which has been to show how description became, during the Enlightenment, a site of methodological tensions and competing truth claims that resulted in epistemological and linguistic experimentation and transformation. If many of the works studied here, and most notably descriptive poetry, have not been consecrated by literary history, it is precisely because they did not resolve those tensions. Like the "failed" project of descriptive poetry, the project of Enlightenment description, broadly conceived, was encyclopedic not just by virtue of its attempt to describe so many things in the world, but also because it relied on such a broad and multifarious concept of description. The preceding chapters have highlighted the moments when this broad concept started being fragmented from within: already in 1767, Buffon excised Daubenton's "deadly" anatomical descriptions from the *Histoire naturelle,* thereby paving the way for his own subsequent reception as an eloquent but nonscientific writer.[4] In a similar way, in his most ambitious poem, *Les trois règnes de la nature,* Delille called upon Cuvier and other scholars from the Institut (a revolutionary institution whose much debated disciplinary divisions reflected the shifting epistemological landscape) to contribute the prose notes that formed a little encyclopedia around his poem.[5] With this division of labor,

---

3. Sainte-Beuve, "Delille," 392–93.

4. For an account of the ways that scientific discourses constitute themselves by excluding the literary, with a reference to Georges Cuvier's treatment of Buffon, see Vincent Debaene, preface to *Oeuvres,* by Claude Lévi-Strauss, Bibliothèque de la Pléiade 543 (Paris: Gallimard, 2008), xxii–xxxi.

5. After various proposals, the Institut national des sciences et des arts, founded in 1795, was initially divided into the First Class of Mathematical and Physical Sciences, the Second Class of Political and Moral Sciences, and the Third Class of Literature and the Beaux-Arts. On the language politics of the Institut, see Rosenfeld, *Revolution in Language,* 193–226. On the various propositions and their relationship to Enlightenment encyclopedism, see Martin Staum, *Minerva's Message: Stabilizing the French Revolution* (Montreal: McGill-Queen's University Press, 1996), 33–55.

he signaled the limits of his own scientific knowledge and gestured toward the split between poetic and scientific description that would make descriptive poetry unreadable for subsequent generations.

When viewed in this light, the descriptive projects discussed in this book appear to witness and incarnate the outer limits of the Enlightenment's encyclopedic relationship to knowledge. The internal fragmentation of these works, and the emergence of the describer within them, can thus be seen as symptoms of the deep epistemological transformations that would soon make the Enlightenment's descriptive project obsolete. In a certain sense, the catastrophic revolution Diderot imagined in his "Avertissement" (best understood as a warning, and not just a foreword) to the eighth volume of the *Encyclopédie* did in fact occur, but it took the form of an epistemological earthquake rather than a natural disaster or barbarian attack.[6] As early as 1800, Germaine de Staël excluded the natural sciences from her still quite broad definition of literature, in a way that would have been unthinkable for Diderot or any of the encyclopedists only a few decades earlier.[7] Diderot's own literary reputation suffered from this split, in marked contrast to that of Rousseau, whose ambivalent attitude toward the sciences prefigured the modern antagonism between literature and science. But above all, it was Enlightenment description that fell between the fault lines of the new epistemological landscape: Saint-Pierre, mocked for his theory of natural harmonies, was remembered only as the author of *Paul et Virginie,* while descriptive poetry, once the source of Delille's fame, suffered the complete ruin Sainte-Beuve had predicted for it.

Nonetheless, the resurgence of interest in eighteenth-century description suggests that the Enlightenment's descriptive project has once again become relevant to us. Bender and Marrinan explain this timeliness in terms of the new computer technologies, such as the mapping of the human genome, that are allowing us to map and diagram our knowledge of nature in new and unprecedented ways.[8] To this one might add the more obvious point that we are once again in an age of encyclopedia, in an age of increased interconnectedness and access to knowledge, but also in an age

---

6. Diderot, "Avertissement" in *Encyclopédie,* ARTFL, 8:i–ii.
7. Germaine de Staël, *De la littérature considérée dans ses rapports avec les institutions sociales,* ed. Paul Van Tieghem (Geneva: Droz, 1959), 1:18.
8. Bender and Marrinan, *Regimes of Description,* 2–4 and 6–7.

where our exposure to knowledge is becoming increasingly fragmented. With the new institutions of Wikipedia and Google Books, we have so much information at our fingertips that our relationship to knowledge curiously resembles that of the Enlightenment describer: as individuals, we find ourselves cobbling together multiple fragments of a virtual encyclopedia that is collectively constituted but individually experienced by each of us in isolation.

When the ARTFL project at the University of Chicago unveiled its digital version of the *Encyclopédie* on the Internet in 1998, and Redon began marketing a relatively inexpensive CD-ROM version of the work, scholars of the Enlightenment were quick to draw analogies between features of Diderot and d'Alembert's project—notably the system of cross-references—and the new resources of digital technology (with titles such as "Diderot a-t-il inventé le Web?" [Did Diderot invent the Web?]).[9] But they were just as quick to point out that eighteenth-century readers did not consult the *Encyclopédie* in the same way, or for the same reasons, that we do today, and that the virtual encyclopedia was a new object, and one that created, as Philippe Roger described it, "an exceptional epistemological situation."[10] Roger emphasized in particular the fact that the "users" of the new virtual *Encyclopédie* would lose the "pedestrian trajectory, sometimes laborious and often disconcerting, suggested by the cross-references," because this path would be superimposed by that of search engines, whose procedures are programmed in a way that runs counter to the ideals of the encyclopedists.[11]

Paradoxically, then, Roger suggested that the virtual *Encyclopédie* would limit the circulatory freedom and subversive readings that Diderot and d'Alembert sought to facilitate. Above all, he suggested that the broad avenues of programmed readings would inevitably replace the tortuous,

9. Jean-François Bianco, "Diderot a-t-il inventé le Web?" *Recherches sur Diderot et sur l'"Encyclopédie"* 31–32 (2002): 17–25. This volume presents the proceedings of a conference on digital versions of the *Encyclopédie,* held at the Université de Paris 7—Denis Diderot in November 2000. See also Pierre Chartier's summary of the conference findings, "Présentation," in *Recherches sur Diderot et sur l'"Encyclopédie"* 30 (2001): 6–16; and the proceedings of another conference on the same topic, held at the École des hautes études en sciences sociales in June 1998: Philippe Roger and Robert Morrissey, eds., *L'"Encyclopédie": Du réseau au livre et du livre au réseau* (Paris: Honoré Champion, 2001).

10. Roger and Morrissey, *"Encyclopédie": Du réseau au livre,* 8.

11. Ibid., 16.

labyrinthine paths of individual readings. To this one might add that virtual readings of the *Encyclopédie* do not force us to grapple with the gargantuan proportions of the work, or with its evolution over time.[12] By appearing to cut through the mass and reveal the underlying systems of human knowledge that structure the *Encyclopédie,* virtual readings thus mask the difficulties Diderot experienced both as an editor and as a describer: How could he establish an adequate system of cross-references without having the entire work at his disposal? How could he keep pace with the changes in technology and language in the mechanical arts? How could he sustain his readers' interest in the long, technical descriptions necessary to reveal the mechanisms, genius, and language of the mechanical arts?

I make this point not to be antiquarian, but on the contrary because the problems Diderot faced, particularly with respect to the tension between rapid technological progress and slow, labor-intensive description, resemble the challenges posed by our own rapidly changing epistemological landscape. As Robert Darnton has emphasized, we know that Google Books and other such innovations will dramatically change our relationship to books and libraries, and even to knowledge itself.[13] But the technological innovations that led to Google Books continue apace, while the courts' attempts to work out their implications for copyright law and public access lag behind. Paradoxically, the current impact of copyright law on Google Books is such that we are often confronted with fragments rather than complete books. While this might encourage us to seek out the complete work in book form at a library or bookstore, it might just as well favor the practice of reading in snippets that is already cultivated by the Internet. Darnton underscores this risk when detailing the implications of Google's commitment to make 20 percent of all of its scanned books available at no charge on the Internet: "By clicking around, [readers] can jump to more disconnected, five-page segments, but only up to a fifth of the text and, in the case of fiction, nothing in the last fifteen pages. This leap-frogging

---

12. Pierre Chartier addresses the issue of the *Encyclopédie*'s temporal dimension being obscured in its digital versions. Chartier, "Présentation," 15.

13. See Robert Darnton, "Google & the Future of Books," *New York Review of Books,* February 12, 2009, http://www.nybooks.com/articles/22281; and id., "Google & Books: An Exchange," *New York Review of Books,* March 26, 2009, http://www.nybooks.com/articles/22496.

around in texts cannot be equated with serious reading. It is exactly the kind of reading many of us want to discourage among our students."[14]

Despite obvious historical differences, eighteenth-century writers were not altogether unfamiliar with such issues. In the last decade of the Old Regime, Mercier predicted that his contemporaries would soon be unwilling to read anything longer than the sentences inscribed on fireplace screens.[15] In a certain sense, he welcomed this trend and contributed to it through his prodigious journalistic output. Yet he also elaborated an innovative approach to description that depended both on a close attention to detail and on the sprawling dimensions of the *Tableau de Paris* for its meaning. Without a sustained and indeed *literary* reading of the work, we cannot appreciate the way Mercier incorporated change into a global, shifting *tableau* of Paris, or the way he sought to effect change through the precise and repeated description of social and political abuses. In a similar way, if descriptive poetry is reprinted without its prose notes, or in short excerpts, we lose any sense of its encyclopedic ambitions, and any appreciation for the ways it manipulated formal devices, such as circumlocution and imitative harmony, in the service of those ambitions. We lose, in other words, the rich epistemological and literary tensions that animated Enlightenment description and gave it meaning.

As both Darnton and Roger suggest, the success of our virtual encyclopedias will hinge on their relationship to the "real" world of books, libraries, and people. Will Google Books create a virtual library that is richer and more expansive than any we have ever seen, or will it simply endanger our current library system without providing an adequate replacement for it? Will it encourage us to engage in more sustained reading than ever before, or will it fragment our reading practices in a way that is antithetical to the advancement of knowledge? In a similar way, the success of the Enlightenment's descriptive project hinged on its capacity to open language out onto the world of animals, plants, machines, cities, and the people inhabiting them. The attempt to do just that can be seen in the back-and-forth movement between verse and prose notes in descriptive poetry, in Saint-Pierre's analogical language of flower petals, and in Mercier's invitation to his readers to climb to the top of Notre-Dame and judge for themselves

---

14. Darnton, "Google & Books."
15. Mercier, *Tableau,* 1:350.

whether the "head" of Paris was in fact too big for the "body" of France. Most of all, it can be seen in Mercier's attempt to put description in the service of social and political reform, and in his injunction to his readers to alter their perspectives and habits in response to his descriptions. Yet Enlightenment describers also cultivated a fine-grained attention to the materiality of language itself, as exhibited by Diderot's evocation of the *barre fendue* and the *barre fondue,* de Piis's alphabet of imitative harmony, and Mercier's fondness for the fleeting vocabulary of fashion jargon. The greatest challenge, then, in reading and interpreting Enlightenment description is to do justice to both sides of the equation, to avoid partial readings that treat description either as a mine for historical information or as a self-contained literary discourse.

So, in the end, this book is intended both as a chapter in the history of ideas and as a defense of literary studies. As I suggested in the introduction, we are at a critical juncture, when literature is no longer being treated as an autonomous category of discourse, and when other fields are borrowing the tools of textual analysis for their own purposes. From the rhetoric of science to historical epistemology, there is a new awareness that the science and literature of describing are inseparable from each other. The body of criticism that has emerged at this critical juncture has been instrumental in allowing me to contextualize my own study of Enlightenment description. Still, the attention to context must not come at the expense of extended analyses of the formal and stylistic properties of works that sought to incarnate and transform the relationship between knowledge and language. Above all, I hope to have demonstrated that some historical questions, about the Enlightenment relationship to knowledge or about the epistemological status of description cannot be adequately answered without a deep and sustained attention to language, style, and literary form. Even for works that lie outside the standard genres and categories of literary history and that are themselves deeply fragmented, we cannot read in fragments if we wish to recover views of knowledge and literature that are different from our own, but that may suddenly regain a new relevance as we experience our own epistemological and literary revolutions.

BIBLIOGRAPHY

N.B.: For multivolume works available online through Gallica, the electronic library of the Bibliothèque nationale de France, I have provided the URL for the first volume only. Subsequent volumes can be easily located using the bibliographic information provided.

Primary Sources

Aristotle. *Poetics.* In *Ancient Literary Criticism: The Principal Texts in New Translations,* edited by D. A. Russell and M. Winterbottom, translated by M. E. Hubbard, 85–132. Oxford: Oxford University Press, 1972.

Balzac, Honoré de. "Avant-Propos." In *Comédie humaine,* edited by Pierre-Georges Castex, vol. 1, 7–20. Bibliothèque de la Pléiade 26. Paris: Gallimard, 1976.

Baudelaire, Charles. *Le spleen de Paris: Petits poèmes en prose.* Edited by Robert Kopp. 1973. Reprint, Paris: Flammarion, 1987.

Bernardin de Saint-Pierre, Jacques-Henri. *Études de la nature.* 5 vols. Rev. ed. Paris: Imprimerie de Crapelet, 1804. Gallica. http://gallica2.bnf.fr/ark:/12148/bpt6k29313q.

———. *Les études de la nature.* Edited by Colas Duflo. Saint-Étienne: Publications de l'Université de Saint-Étienne, 2007.

———. *Paul et Virginie.* Edited by Robert Mauzi. 1966. Reprint, Paris: Flammarion, 1992.

Boileau-Despréaux, Nicolas. *Art poétique.* In *Satires, Épîtres, Art poétique,* edited by Jean-Pierre Collinet, 225–58. Paris: Gallimard, 1985.

Breton, André. *Manifeste du surréalisme.* In *Oeuvres complètes,* edited by Marguerite Bonnet, vol. 1, 309–46. Bibliothèque de la Pléiade 346. Paris: Gallimard, 1988.

Buffon, Georges-Louis Leclerc de. *Discours sur le style, suivi de "L'art d'écrire" du même et de "Visite à Buffon" d'Hérault de Séchelles.* Paris: Climats, 1992.

———. *Histoire naturelle des oiseaux.* Vol. 1. Paris: Imprimerie Royale, 1770. Gallica. http://gallica2.bnf.fr/ark:/12148/bpt6k97505m.

———. *Oeuvres.* Edited by Stéphane Schmitt. Bibliothèque de la Pléiade 532. Paris: Gallimard, 2007.

———. *Oeuvres philosophiques.* Edited by Jean Piveteau. Paris: Presses Universitaires de France, 1954.

Buffon, Georges-Louis Leclerc de, and Louis-Jean-Marie Daubenton. *Histoire naturelle, générale et particulière, avec la description du Cabinet du Roy.* 15 vols. Paris: Imprimerie Royale, 1749–67. Gallica. http://gallica2.bnf.fr/ark:/12148/bpt6k97490d.

Chateaubriand, François-René de. *Génie du christianisme.* Edited by Pierre Reboul. 2 vols. Paris: Garnier-Flammarion, 1966.

Condillac, Étienne Bonnot de. *Traité des sensations.* Corpus des oeuvres de philosophie en langue française. Paris: Fayard, 1984.

D'Alembert, Jean. *"Discours préliminaire des éditeurs" de 1751 et articles de l'"Encyclopédie."* Edited by Martine Groult. Paris: Champion, 1999.

Delille, Jacques. *Les géorgiques.* In *Les oeuvres de J. Delille,* vol. 2. Paris: L. G. Michaud, 1824.

———. *L'homme des champs, ou Les géorgiques françaises.* Paris: Levrault, Schoell et Cie, 1804. Gallica. http://gallica.bnf.fr/ark:/12148/bpt6k5445687m.

———. *Les trois règnes de la nature, par Jacques Delille; avec des notes par M. Cuvier, de l'Institut, et autres savants.* 2 vols. Paris: Frères Mame, 1808.

Dictionnaire de l'Académie française. 1st ed. 1694. ARTFL Dictionary Project. http://www.lib.uchicago.edu/efts/ARTFL/projects/dicos.

Diderot, Denis. "Bas." In *Oeuvres complètes,* edited by Herbert Dieckmann, Jacques Proust, and Jean Varloot. Vol. 6, *Encyclopédie II (Lettres B-C),* edited by John Lough and Jacques Proust, 27–126. Paris: Hermann, 1976.

———. *Choix d'articles de l'"Encyclopédie."* Edited by Marie Leca-Tsiomis. Paris: Comité des travaux historiques et scientifiques, 2001.

———. "Encyclopédie." In *Oeuvres complètes,* edited by Herbert Dieckmann, Jacques Proust, and Jean Varloot. Vol. 7, *Encyclopédie III (Lettres D-L),* edited by John Lough and Jacques Proust, 174–262. Paris: Hermann, 1976.

———. *Essais sur la peinture.* In *Oeuvres,* edited by Versini, 467-516.

———. *Oeuvres.* Edited by Laurent Versini. Vol. 4, *Esthétique-Théâtre.* Collection Bouquins. Paris: Robert Laffont, 1996.

———. "Prospectus." In *Oeuvres complètes,* edited by Herbert Dieckmann, Jacques Proust, and Jean Varloot. Vol. 5, *Encyclopédie I,* edited by John Lough and Jacques Proust, 83–104. Paris: Hermann, 1976.

———. *Salon de 1767.* In *Oeuvres,* edited by Versini, 517–819.

Diderot, Denis, and Jean d'Alembert, eds. *Encyclopédie, ou Dictionnaire raisonné des sciences, des arts et des métiers.* University of Chicago: ARTFL Encyclopédie Project,

Winter 2008 edition, general editor Robert Morrissey. http://encyclopedie.uchicago. edu/.

Féraud, Jean-François. *Dictionaire [sic] critique de la langue française.* 2 vols. Marseille: Mossy, 1777–78.

Flaubert, Gustave. *Dictionnaire des idées reçues.* In *Bouvard et Pécuchet,* edited by Claudine Gothot-Mersch, 485–555. Paris: Gallimard, 1979.

Grammaire et littérature. Vol. 1. In *Encyclopédie méthodique.* Paris: Panckoucke, 1782. Gallica. http://gallica2.bnf.fr/ark:/12148/bpt6k505847.

Le grand Robert de la langue française. 2nd ed. 9 vols. Paris: Dictionnaires Le Robert, 1985.

Hérault de Séchelles, Marie Jean. "Visite à Buffon." In Buffon, *Discours,* 43–87.

Horace. *The Art of Poetry.* In *Ancient Literary Criticism: The Principal Texts in New Translation,* edited by D. A. Russell and M. Winterbottom, translated by D. A. Russell, 279–91. Oxford: Oxford University Press, 1972.

Hugo, Victor. *Oeuvres poétiques.* Edited by Pierre Albouy. Vol. 2. Bibliothèque de la Pléiade 195. Paris: Gallimard, 1967.

———. "Paris." In *Oeuvres complètes.* Vol. 10, *Politique,* edited by Jean-Claude Fizaine, 1–43. Collection Bouquins. Paris: Robert Laffont, 1985.

———. *Quatre-vingt treize.* Edited by Judith Wulf. Paris: Flammarion, 2002.

———. "Réponse à un acte d'accusation." In *Oeuvres poétiques,* vol. 2, 494–500.

Johnson, Samuel. *The Lives of the Most Eminent English Poets, with Critical Observations on Their Works.* 3 vols. London: John Murray, 1854.

Lessing, Gotthold Ephraim. *Laocoön: An Essay on the Limits of Painting and Poetry.* Edited and translated by Edward Allen McCormick. 1962. Reprint, Baltimore: Johns Hopkins University Press, 1984.

Locke, John. *An Essay Concerning Human Understanding.* Edited by Kenneth Winkler. Indianapolis: Hackett, 1996.

Marmontel, Jean-François. *Éléments de littérature.* Edited by Sophie Le Ménahèze. Paris: Desjonquères, 2005.

Maunde, John. *Rural Philosopher; or, French Georgics: A Didactic Poem, Translated from the Original of the Abbé Delille; Entitled "L'homme des champs."* London: G. Kearsley, 1801.

Mercier, Louis Sébastien. "Conseil des Cinq Cents, séance du 28 frimaire." *Journal de Paris,* Nonidi 29 Frimaire l'an V—lundi 19 décembre 1796 vieux style.

———. *Dictionnaire d'un polygraphe: Textes de L. S. Mercier.* Edited by Geneviève Bollème. Paris: Union Générale d'Éditions, 1978.

———. *Mon bonnet de nuit, Du théâtre.* Edited by Jean-Claude Bonnet. Paris: Mercure de France, 1999.

———. *Néologie.* Edited by Jean-Claude Bonnet. Paris: Belin, 2009.

———. *La néologie, ou Vocabulaire de mots nouveaux, à renouveler, ou pris dans des acceptations nouvelles.* Vol. 1. Paris: Moussard-Maradan, 1801. Gallica. http://gallica2.bnf. fr/ark:/12148/bpt6k50792d.

———. *Le nouveau Paris.* Edited by Jean-Claude Bonnet. Paris: Mercure de France, 1994.

———. *Panorama of Paris: Selections from "Tableau de Paris."* Based on the translation by Helen Simpson. Edited and with a new preface and translations of additional articles by Jeremy D. Popkin. University Park: Pennsylvania State University Press, 1999.

——. *Parallèle de Paris et de Londres.* Edited by Claude Bruneteau and Bernard Cottret. Collection Études Critiques 2. Paris: Didier Érudition, 1982.

——. *Tableau de Paris.* Edited by Jean-Claude Bonnet. 2 vols. Paris: Mercure de France, 1994.

Michaud, Joseph-François. "Quelques observations sur la poésie descriptive." In *Printemps d'un proscrit, suivi de mélanges en prose,* 7–36. Paris: Giguet et Michaud, 1808.

Novalis. *Notes for a Romantic Encyclopaedia: Das Allgemeine Brouillon.* Edited and translated by David W. Wood. Albany: State University of New York Press, 2007.

Perrault, Claude. *Mémoires pour servir à l'histoire naturelle des animaux.* Paris: Imprimerie Royale, 1676.

Piis, Pierre-Antoine-Augustin de. *L'harmonie imitative de la langue française, poème en quatre chants.* Paris: Ph.-D. Pierres, 1785. Gallica. http://gallica2.bnf.fr/ark:/12148/bpt6k826195.

Pluche, Noël-Antoine. *Le spectacle de la nature, ou Entretiens sur les particularités de l'histoire naturelle.* 8 vols. Paris: Frères Estienne, 1764–70.

Rousseau, Jean-Jacques. *Lettre à Mr. d'Alembert sur les spectacles.* Edited by M. Fuchs. Geneva: Droz, 1948.

——. *Lettres sur la botanique.* In *Oeuvres complètes,* edited by Bernard Gagnebin and Marcel Raymond, vol. 4, 1149–97. Bibliothèque de la Pléiade 208. Paris: Gallimard, 1969.

——. *Rêveries du promeneur solitaire.* Edited by Henri Roddier. Paris: Garnier, 1960.

Sainte-Beuve, Charles-Augustin. "Delille." In *Portraits littéraires,* edited by Gérald Antoine, 392–420. Collection Bouquins. Paris: Robert Laffont, 1993.

Saint-Lambert, Jean-François de. *Les saisons.* In *Oeuvres de Saint-Lambert,* vol. 1. Clermont, Fr.: Pierre Landriot, 1814.

Saint-Pierre, Jacques-Henri Bernardin de. See Bernardin de Saint-Pierre, Jacques-Henri.

Staël, Germaine de. *Considérations sur la Révolution française.* Edited by Jacques Godechot. Paris: Tallandier, 1983.

——. *De la littérature considérée dans ses rapports avec les institutions sociales.* Edited by Paul Van Tieghem. Geneva: Droz, 1959.

Stendhal. *La chartreuse de Parme.* Edited by Henri Martineau. Paris: Garnier Frères, 1961.

Thomson, James. *The Complete Poetical Works of James Thomson.* Edited by J. Logie Robertson. London: Oxford University Press, 1908.

Tocqueville, Alexis de. *L'Ancien Régime et la Révolution.* Edited by J.-P. Mayer. Collection Folio/Histoire. Paris: Gallimard, 1967.

——. *Souvenirs.* Edited by Luc Monnier. 1964. Reprint, Paris: Gallimard, 1978.

Zola, Émile. "De la description." In Hamon, *Description littéraire,* 155–61.

Secondary Sources

Alpers, Svetlana. *The Art of Describing: Dutch Art in the Seventeenth Century.* Chicago: University of Chicago Press, 1983.

——. "Describe or Narrate? A Problem in Realistic Representation." *New Literary History* 8 (1976): 16–24.

Anderson, Wilda. *Diderot's Dream*. Baltimore: Johns Hopkins University Press, 1990.
———. "Encyclopedic Topologies." *Modern Language Notes* 101, no. 4 (1986): 912–29.
Atran, Scott. *Cognitive Foundations of Natural History: Towards an Anthropology of Science*. Cambridge: Cambridge University Press, 1990.
"Avertissement des éditeurs." In *Études de la nature, extraits, Paul et Virginie*, by Jacques-Henri Bernardin de Saint-Pierre, 7. La Renaissance du livre. Paris: Mignot, n.d.
Baczko, Bronislaw. "Thermidorians." In Furet and Ozouf, *Critical Dictionary*, 400–13.
Barthes, Roland. "De la science à la littérature." In *Le bruissement de la langue*, 13–20. Paris: Éditions du Seuil, 1984.
———. "L'effet de réel." In Genette and Todorov, *Littérature et réalité*, 81–90.
———. "Les planches de l'*Encyclopédie*." In *Le degré zéro de l'écriture, suivi de Nouveaux essais critiques*, 89–105. Paris: Seuil, 1972.
Bates, David W. "Cartographic Aberrations: Epistemology and Order in the Encyclopedic Map." In Brewer and Hayes, *Using the "Encyclopédie*," 1–20.
———. *Enlightenment Aberrations: Error and Revolution in France*. Ithaca, N.Y.: Cornell University Press, 2002.
Baudry, Janine. "Un aspect mauricien de l'oeuvre de Bernardin de Saint-Pierre: La flore locale." *Revue d'histoire littéraire de la France* 5 (1989): 782–90.
Beaujour, Michel. "Genus Universum." In *The Strasbourg Colloquium: Genre, A Selection of Papers*, edited by Samuel Weber, 15–31. Glyph Textual Studies 7. Baltimore: Johns Hopkins University Press, 1980.
———. "Some Paradoxes of Description." In Kittay, "Towards a Theory of Description," 27–59.
Becq, Annie. *Genèse de l'esthétique française moderne 1680–1814*. Paris: Albin Michel, 1994.
———. "La réflexion sur la poétique en France au XVIIIe siècle." In *Histoire des poétiques*, edited by Jean Bessière, Eva Kushner, Roland Mortier, and Jean Weisgerber, 219–39. Paris: Presses Universitaires de France, 1997.
Bender, John, and Michael Marrinan, eds. *Regimes of Description: In the Archive of the Eighteenth Century*. Stanford: Stanford University Press, 2005.
Bender, John, and David E. Wellbery, eds. *The Ends of Rhetoric: History, Theory, Practice*. Stanford: Stanford University Press, 1990.
Benrekassa, Georges. "Décrire, écrire, instruire: L'ensemble 'Épingle-Épinglier' dans l'*Encyclopédie*." In *Le langage des Lumières: Concepts et savoir de la langue*, 201–31. Collection Écriture. Paris: Presses Universitaires de France, 1995.
Bessière, Jean, ed. *L'ordre du descriptif*. Paris: Presses Universitaires de France, 1988.
Bianco, Jean-François. "Diderot a-t-il inventé le Web?" *Recherches sur Diderot et sur l'"Encyclopédie"* 31–32 (2002): 17–25.
Biographie universelle, ancienne et moderne. Edited by M. M. Michaud. 45 vols. 2nd ed. Paris: Louis Vivès, [1880].
Bloom, Harold. *The Anxiety of Influence: A Theory of Poetry*. Oxford: Oxford University Press, 1973.
Bollème, Geneviève. "L'écriture, cet art inconnu." In Mercier, *Polygraphe*, 7–83.
Bonnet, Jean-Claude. Introduction. In Mercier, *Nouveau Paris*, i-lxxiii.
———. Introduction. In Mercier, *Tableau*, 1:i-lxxii.

———. "La littérature et le réel." In Bonnet, *Hérétique,* 9–32.

———, ed. *Louis Sébastien Mercier (1740–1814): Un hérétique en littérature.* Paris: Mercure de France, 1995.

———, ed. *Le Paris de Louis Sébastien Mercier, Cartes et index.* Paris: Mercure de France, 1994.

Brewer, Daniel. *The Discourse of Enlightenment in Eighteenth-Century France: Diderot and the Art of Philosophizing.* Cambridge Studies in French 42. Cambridge: Cambridge University Press, 1993.

———. "Language and Grammar: Diderot and the Discourse of Encyclopedism." *Eighteenth-Century Studies* 13 (1979): 1–19.

———. "1751: Ordering Knowledge." In *A New History of French Literature,* edited by Denis Hollier, 447–55. Cambridge, Mass.: Harvard University Press, 1989.

Brewer, Daniel, and Julie Candler Hayes, eds. *Using the "Encyclopédie": Ways of Knowing, Ways of Reading.* Studies on Voltaire and the Eighteenth Century 2002:5. Oxford: Voltaire Foundation, 2002.

Buffon 1788–1988. An exhibition catalog. Paris: Imprimerie Nationale, 1988.

Buisson, Georges. "Le déclassement de la poésie du XVIIIe siècle sous l'influence de Sainte-Beuve." *Oeuvres et critiques* 7, no. 1 (1982): 117–30.

Cameron, Margaret. *L'influence des "Saisons" de Thomson sur la poésie descriptive en France (1759–1810).* Paris: Honoré Champion, 1927.

Caplan, Jay. *Framed Narratives: Diderot's Genealogy of the Beholder.* Minneapolis: University of Minnesota Press, 1985.

Cassirer, Ernst. *The Philosophy of the Enlightenment.* Translated by Fritz C. A. Koelln and James P. Pettegrove. 1951. Reprint, Princeton: Princeton University Press, 1979.

Charles, Shelly. "L'écrivain journaliste." In Bonnet, *Hérétique,* 83–120.

———. "Histoire du texte: Des nouvelles de Paris au *Nouveau Paris.*" In Mercier, *Nouveau Paris,* clxxix–ccxvi.

———. "Histoire du texte: Études pour un tableau." In Mercier, *Tableau,* 1:lxxiii–xciv.

Chartier, Pierre. "Présentation." In *Recherches sur Diderot et sur l'"Encyclopédie"* 30 (2001): 6–16.

———, ed. *Recherches sur Diderot et sur l'"Encyclopédie"* 31–32 (2002). Proceedings of a conference on digital versions of the *Encyclopédie,* held at the Université de Paris 7—Denis Diderot in November 2000.

Cherni, Amor. *Buffon: La nature et son histoire.* Collection Philosophies. Paris: Presses Universitaires de France, 1998.

Chouillet, Jacques. *L'esthétique des Lumières.* Paris: Presses Universitaires de France, 1974.

———. *La formation des idées esthétiques de Diderot.* Paris: Armand Colin, 1973.

———. "La promenade Vernet." *Recherches sur Diderot et sur l'"Encyclopédie"* 2 (1987): 123–63.

Citron, Pierre. "À propos des mots interdits." In *Delille est-il mort?* 213–25.

Clark, William, Jan Golinski, and Simon Schaffer, eds. *The Sciences in Enlightened Europe.* Chicago: University of Chicago Press, 1999.

Cook, Alexandra. "Rousseau and the Languages of Music and Botany." In *Musique et langage chez Rousseau,* edited by Claude Dauphin, 75–87. Studies on Voltaire and the Eighteenth Century 2004:08. Oxford: Voltaire Foundation, 2004.

Darnton, Robert. *The Business of Enlightenment: A Publishing History of the "Encyclopédie."* Cambridge, Mass.: Belknap Press/Harvard University Press, 1979.

———. *Édition et sédition: L'univers de la littérature clandestine au XVIIIe siècle.* Paris: Gallimard, 1991.

———. "Google & Books: An Exchange." *New York Review of Books,* March 26, 2009. http://www.nybooks.com/articles/22496.

———. "Google & the Future of Books." *New York Review of Books,* February 12, 2009. http://www.nybooks.com/articles/22281.

———. "Philosophers Trim the Tree of Knowledge: The Epistemological Strategy of the *Encyclopédie.*" In *The Great Cat Massacre and Other Episodes in French Cultural History,* 191–213. New York: Basic Books, 1984.

Daston, Lorraine. "Description by Omission: Nature Enlightened and Obscured." In Bender and Marrinan, *Regimes of Description,* 11–24.

———. "The Disciplines of Attention." In *A New History of German Literature,* edited by David E. Wellbery, 434–40. Cambridge, Mass.: Harvard University Press, 2004.

Daston, Lorraine, and Peter Galison. *Objectivity.* New York: Zone Books, 2007.

Daston, Lorraine, and Katharine Park. *Wonders and the Order of Nature, 1150–1750.* New York: Zone Books, 1998.

Dawson, Virginia P. "The Limits of Observation and the Hypotheses of Georges Louis Buffon and Charles Bonnet." In *Beyond History of Science: Essays in Honor of Robert E. Schofield,* edited by Elizabeth Garber, 107–25. London: Associated University Presses/Lehigh University Press, 1990.

Debaene, Vincent. Preface to *Oeuvres,* by Claude Lévi-Strauss, ix–xlii. Bibliothèque de la Pléiade 543. Paris: Gallimard, 2008.

Debray Genette, Raymonde. "Narration et description." In *Métamorphoses du récit: Autour de Flaubert,* 209–311. Paris: Seuil, 1988.

"Le décrit." Special issue, *Littérature* 38 (1980): 1–128.

Delille est-il mort? Collection Écrivains d'Auvergne. Clermont-Ferrand, Fr.: G. de Bussac, 1967.

Delon, Michel. Introduction to *Anthologie de la poésie française du XVIIIe siècle,* 7–31. Collection Poésie. Paris: Gallimard, 1997.

Delon, Michel, and Daniel Baruch, eds. *Paris le jour, Paris la nuit.* By Louis Sébastien Mercier and Restif de la Bretonne. Collection Bouquins. Paris: Robert Laffont, 1990.

Demoris, René. "La peinture et le 'temps du voir' au siècle des Lumières." In Bessière, *Ordre du descriptif,* 47–61.

Deneys-Tunney, Anne. *Écritures du corps: De Descartes à Laclos.* Collection Écriture. Paris: Presses Universitaires de France, 1992.

Didier, Béatrice. "Senancour et la description romantique." *Poétique* 12 (1982): 315–28.

Dieckmann, Herbert. "L'*Encyclopédie* et le fonds Vandeul." *Revue d'histoire littéraire de la France* 51, no. 3 (1951): 318–32.

———. "An Interpretation of the Eighteenth Century." Review of *Die Philosophie der Aufklärung,* by Ernst Cassirer. *Modern Language Quarterly* 15 (1954): 295–311.

Duchet, Michèle. *Anthropologie et histoire au siècle des Lumières.* Bibliothèque de l'Évolution de l'Humanité. 1971. Reprint, Paris: Albin Michel, 1995.

Duflo, Colas. "Le hussard et l'inscription." In *Études de la nature,* by Bernardin de Saint-Pierre, 7–28.

Eddy, John H., Jr. "Buffon's *Histoire naturelle:* History? A Critique of Recent Interpretations," *Isis* 85 (1994): 644–61.

Ehrard, Jean. *L'idée de nature en France dans la première moitié du XVIIIe siècle.* Bibliothèque de l'Évolution de l'Humanité. 1963. Reprint, Paris: Albin Michel, 1994.

Fabre, Jean. *Lumières et romantisme: Énergie et nostalgie de Rousseau à Mickiewicz.* 2nd ed. 1963. Paris: Klincksieck, 1980.

——. "On ne peut oublier Delille." In *Lumières et romantisme,* 259–83.

——. "Paul et Virginie pastorale." In *Lumières et romantisme,* 225–57.

——. "Variations sur les nuages: En marge de 'Pan Tadeusz' et de la poésie descriptive." In *Lumières et romantisme,* 285–301.

Farber, Paul Lawrence. "Buffon and Daubenton: Divergent Traditions within the *Histoire naturelle.*" *Isis* 66 (1975): 63–74.

——. *Discovering Birds: The Emergence of Ornithology as a Scientific Discipline, 1760–1850.* 1982. Reprint, Baltimore: Johns Hopkins University Press, 1997.

Fellows, Otis E., and Stephen Milliken. *Buffon.* New York: Twayne, 1972.

Ferguson, Priscilla Parkhurst. *Paris as Revolution: Writing the Nineteenth-Century City.* Berkeley and Los Angeles: University of California Press, 1994.

Folkierski, Wladyslaw. *Entre le classicisme et le romantisme: Étude sur l'esthétique et les esthéticiens du XVIIIe siècle.* Paris: Honoré Champion, 1969.

Foucault, Michel. *Les mots et les choses: Une archéologie des sciences humaines.* Collection Tel. Paris: Gallimard, 1966.

——. *The Order of Things: An Archaeology of the Human Sciences.* 1971. Reprint, New York: Vintage-Random, 1973.

Frängsmyr, Tore, J. L. Heilbron, and Robin E. Rider, eds. *The Quantifying Spirit in the 18th Century.* Berkeley and Los Angeles: University of California Press, 1990.

Frantz, Pierre. *L'esthétique du tableau dans le théâtre du XVIIIe siècle.* Paris: Presses Universitaires de France, 1998.

Fried, Michael. *Absorption and Theatricality: Painting and Beholder in the Age of Diderot.* Chicago: University of Chicago Press, 1980.

——. Foreword to *Laocoön,* by Lessing, vii–viii.

Fumaroli, Marc, ed. *Histoire de la rhétorique dans l'Europe moderne, 1450–1950.* Paris: Presses Universitaires de France, 1999.

Furet, François, and Mona Ozouf, eds. *A Critical Dictionary of the French Revolution.* Translated by Arthur Goldhammer. Cambridge, Mass.: Belknap Press/Harvard University Press, 1989.

Galand-Hallyn, Perrine. *Le reflet des fleurs: Description et métalangage poétique d'Homère à la Renaissance.* Geneva: Droz, 1994.

Genette, Gérard. "Frontières du récit." In *Figures II,* 49–69. Paris: Seuil, 1969.

——. *Introduction à l'architexte.* Collection Poétique. Paris: Seuil, 1979.

Genette, Gérard, and Tzvetan Todorov, eds. *Littérature et réalité.* Paris: Seuil, 1982.

Guitton, Édouard. "À propos du projet 'descriptif' de Rousseau dans les *Rêveries.*" In *Rêveries sans fin: Autour des "Rêveries du promeneur solitaire,"* edited by Michel Coz and François Jacob, 89–97. Références 10. Orléans, Fr.: Paradigme, 1997.

——. *Jacques Delille (1738–1813) et le poème de la nature en France de 1750 à 1820.* Paris: Klincksieck, 1974.

———. "La poésie en 1778." *Dix-huitième siècle* 11 (1979): 75–86.

Guy, Basil. "Bernardin de Saint-Pierre and the Idea of 'Harmony.'" *Stanford French Review* 2 (1978): 209–22.

Hamon, Philippe, ed. *La description littéraire: Anthologie de textes théoriques et critiques.* Paris: Macula, 1991.

———. *Du descriptif.* 4th ed. Paris: Hachette, 1993. First published in 1981 as *Introduction à l'analyse du descriptif.*

———. "Qu'est-ce qu'une description?" *Poétique* 12 (1972): 465–85.

———. "Rhetorical Status of the Descriptive." In Kittay, "Towards a Theory of Description," 1–26.

Hayes, Julie Candler. *Reading the French Enlightenment: System and Subversion.* Cambridge Studies in French 60. Cambridge: Cambridge University Press, 1999.

Heffernan, James A. W. *Museum of Words: The Poetics of Ekphrasis from Homer to Ashbery.* Chicago: University of Chicago Press, 1980.

Heller-Roazen, Daniel. *The Inner Touch: Archaeology of a Sensation.* New York: Zone Books, 2007.

Herval, René. "Saint-Pierre (Jacques Henri Bernardin de)." In *Dictionnaire des lettres françaises,* edited by Georges Grente. *Le XVIIIe siècle,* edited by François Moureau, 1197–1202. 1960. Reprint, Paris: Fayard, 1995.

Hobson, Marian. *The Object of Art: The Theory of Illusion in Eighteenth-Century France.* Cambridge: Cambridge University Press, 1982.

Hofer, Hermann. "'Mercier devant la Révolution." In *L'écrivain devant la Révolution 1780–1800,* edited by Jean Sgard, 205–16. Grenoble: Université Stendhal, 1990.

Horrent, Jacques. "Le réalisme descriptif dans la tempête de *Paul et Virginie.*" *Cahiers d'analyse textuelle* 11 (1969): 7–26.

Huet, Marie-Hélène. *Rehearsing the Revolution: The Staging of Marat's Death, 1793–1797.* Translated by Robert Hurley. Berkeley and Los Angeles: University of California Press, 1982.

Hunt, Lynn. *Politics, Culture, and Class in the French Revolution.* 20th anniv. ed. 1984. Berkeley and Los Angeles: University of California Press, 2004.

Jardine, N., J. A. Secord, and E. C. Spary, eds. *Cultures of Natural History.* Cambridge: Cambridge University Press, 1996.

Jordanova, L. J., ed. *Languages of Nature: Critical Essays on Science and Literature.* London: Free Association Books, 1986.

Kadish, Doris. *The Literature of Images: Narrative Landscape from Julie to Jane Eyre.* New Brunswick: Rutgers University Press, 1987.

King, Amy M. *Bloom: The Botanical Vernacular in the English Novel.* Oxford: Oxford University Press, 2003.

Kittay, Jeffrey. "Descriptive Limits." In Kittay, "Towards a Theory of Description," 225–43.

———, ed. "Towards a Theory of Description." Special issue, *Yale French Studies* 61 (1981).

Koselleck, Reinhart. *Futures Past: On the Semantics of Historical Time.* Translated by Keith Tribe. 1985. Reprint, New York: Columbia University Press, 2004.

Krieger, Murray. *Ekphrasis: The Illusion of the Natural Sign.* Baltimore: Johns Hopkins University Press, 1992.

Kuhn, Thomas S. *The Structure of Scientific Revolutions.* 2nd ed. 1962. Chicago: University of Chicago Press, 1970.

Labio, Catherine. *Origins and the Enlightenment: Aesthetic Epistemology from Descartes to Kant.* Ithaca, N.Y.: Cornell University Press, 2004.

Lafon, Henri. *Les décors et les choses dans le roman français du dix-huitième siècle de Prévost à Sade.* Studies on Voltaire and the Eighteenth Century 297. Oxford: Voltaire Foundation, 1992.

———. "Sur la description dans le roman du XVIIIe." *Poétique* 12 (1982): 303–13.

Laissus, Yves. "*L'histoire naturelle.*" In *Buffon 1788–1988,* 73–89.

Lanson, Gustave. *Histoire de la littérature française.* 18th ed. 1895. Paris: Hachette, 1924.

Larson, James L. *Interpreting Nature: The Science of Living Form from Linnaeus to Kant.* Baltimore: Johns Hopkins University Press, 1994.

Laudan, Larry. *Science and Hypothesis: Historical Essays on Scientific Methodology.* Dordrecht: D. Reidel Publishing Company, 1981.

Lee, Rensselaer W. *Ut Pictura Poesis: The Humanistic Theory of Painting.* New York: W. W. Norton, 1967.

Logé, Tanguy. "Chateaubriand et Bernardin de Saint-Pierre." *Revue d'histoire littéraire de la France* 5 (1989): 879–90.

Lovejoy, Arthur O. "Buffon and the Problem of Species." In *Forerunners of Darwin: 1745–1859,* edited by Bentley Glass, Owsei Temkin, and William L. Straus, Jr., 84–113. Baltimore: Johns Hopkins University Press, 1959.

Loveland, Jeff. "Louis-Jean-Marie Daubenton and the *Encyclopédie.*" *Studies on Voltaire and the Eighteenth Century* 2003:12, 173–219. Oxford: Voltaire Foundation, 2003.

———. *Rhetoric and Natural History: Buffon in Polemical and Literary Context.* Studies on Voltaire and the Eighteenth Century 2001:3. Oxford: Voltaire Foundation, 2001.

Lukács, Georg. "Narrate or Describe?" In *Writer and Critic and Other Essays,* edited and translated by Arthur Kahn, 110–48. London: Merlin Press, 1970.

Lyon, John, and Phillip R. Sloan, eds. *From Natural History to the History of Nature: Readings from Buffon and His Critics.* Notre Dame: University of Notre Dame Press, 1981.

Mantoux, Paul. *The Industrial Revolution in the Eighteenth Century: An Outline of the Beginnings of the Modern Factory System in England.* Translated by Marjorie Vernon. 1928. Reprint, New York: Routledge, 2006.

Mauzi, Robert. *L'idée du bonheur dans la littérature et la pensée françaises au XVIIIe siècle.* 1960. Reprint, Paris: Armand Colin, 1979.

May, Gita. *Diderot et Baudelaire critiques d'art.* Geneva: Droz, 1967.

McDonald, Christie V. "The Utopia of the Text: Diderot's 'Encyclopédie.'" *The Eighteenth Century: Theory and Interpretation* 21, no. 2 (1980): 128–44.

Menant, Sylvain. *La chute d'Icare: La crise de la poésie française (1700–1750).* Geneva: Droz, 1981.

Mitchell, W. J. T. *Iconology: Image, Text, Ideology.* Chicago: University of Chicago Press, 1986.

Molino, Jean. "Logiques de la description." *Poétique* 23 (1992): 363–82.

Mornet, Daniel. *Les sciences de la nature en France au XVIIIe siècle.* 1911. Reprint, New York: Lenox Hill-Burt Franklin, 1971.

———. *Le sentiment de la nature en France de Jean-Jacques Rousseau à Bernardin de Saint-Pierre: Essai sur le rapport de la littérature aux moeurs.* 1907. Reprint, Geneva: Slatkine Reprints, 2000.

Moscovici, Claudia. "Beyond the Particular and the Universal: D'Alembert's 'Discours préliminaire' to the *Encyclopédie.*" *Eighteenth-Century Studies* 33, no. 3 (2000): 383–400.

Moser, Walter. *De la signification d'une poésie insignifiante: Examen de la poésie fugitive au XVIIIe siècle et de ses rapports avec la pensée sensualiste en France.* Studies on Voltaire and the Eighteenth Century 94, 277–415. Banbury, Oxfordshire: Voltaire Foundation, 1972.

Mücke, Dorothea von. "Goethe's Metamorphosis: Changing Forms in Nature, the Life Sciences, and Authorship." *Representations* 95 (2006): 27–53.

Munsters, Wil. *La poétique du pittoresque en France de 1700 à 1830.* Geneva: Droz, 1991.

Ogilvie, Brian W. *The Science of Describing: Natural History in Renaissance Europe.* Chicago: University of Chicago Press, 2006.

O'Neal, John C. *The Authority of Experience: Sensationist Theory in the French Enlightenment.* University Park: Pennsylvania State University Press, 1996.

Ozouf, Mona. "King's Trial." In Furet and Ozouf, *Critical Dictionary,* 95–106.

———. "Varennes." In Furet and Ozouf, *Critical Dictionary,* 155–64.

Patterson, Helen Temple. *Poetic Genesis: Sébastien Mercier into Victor Hugo.* Studies on Voltaire and the Eighteenth Century. Geneva: Institut et Musée Voltaire, 1960.

Poovey, Mary. *A History of the Modern Fact: Problems of Knowledge in the Sciences of Wealth and Society.* Chicago: University of Chicago Press, 1998.

Popkin, Jeremy D. Editor's preface to *Panorama of Paris,* by Mercier, 1–19.

Potts, Alex. "Disparities between Part and Whole in the Description of Works of Art." In Bender and Marrinan, *Regimes of Description,* 135–52.

Pratt, Mary Louise. *Imperial Eyes: Travel Writing and Transculturation.* New York: Routledge, 1992.

Proust, Jacques. *Diderot et l'"Encyclopédie."* Paris: Armand Colin, 1962.

———. "La documentation technique de Diderot dans l'*Encyclopédie.*" *Revue d'histoire littéraire de la France* 57, no. 3 (1957): 346–48.

———. *L'Encyclopédie.* Paris: Armand Colin, 1965.

———. "De l'*Encyclopédie* au *Neveu de Rameau:* L'objet et le texte." In *Recherches nouvelles sur quelques écrivains des Lumières,* edited by Jacques Proust, 273–340. Geneva: Droz, 1972.

———. *Marges d'une utopie: Pour une lecture critique des planches de l'"Encyclopédie."* Cognac, Fr.: Le temps qu'il fait, 1985.

———. "Questions sur l'*Encyclopédie.*" *Revue d'histoire littéraire de la France* 72 (1972): 36–52.

Reill, Peter Hanns. *Vitalizing Nature in the Enlightenment.* Berkeley and Los Angeles: University of California Press, 2005.

Reynaud, Denis. "Pour une théorie de la description au XVIIIe siècle." *Dix-huitième siècle* 22 (1990): 347–66.

Ricardou, Jean. *Problèmes du Nouveau Roman.* Paris: Seuil, 1967.

Riffaterre, Michael. "Descriptive Imagery." In Kittay, "Towards a Theory of Description," 107–25.

——. "L'illusion référentielle." In Genette and Todorov, *Littérature et réalité,* 91–118.

——. "Interpretation and Descriptive Poetry: A Reading of Wordsworth's 'Yew-Trees.'" *New Literary History* 4 (1973): 229–56.

——. "Le poème comme représentation: Une lecture de Hugo." In *La production du texte,* 175–98. Collection Poétique. Paris: Seuil, 1979.

——. "Système d'un genre descriptif." *Poétique* 9 (1972): 15–30.

Riskin, Jessica. *Science in the Age of Sensibility: The Sentimental Empiricists of the French Enlightenment.* Chicago: University of Chicago Press, 2002.

Roger, Jacques. *Buffon: Un philosophe au Jardin du Roi.* Paris: Fayard, 1989.

——. *Les sciences de la vie dans la pensée française du XVIIIe siècle.* Paris: Armand Colin, 1963.

Roger, Philippe. "'Libre et despote': Mercier néologue." In Bonnet, *Hérétique,* 327–47.

Roger, Philippe, and Robert Morrissey, eds. *L'"Encyclopédie": Du réseau au livre et du livre au réseau.* Paris: Honoré Champion, 2001.

Rosenberg, Daniel. "An Eighteenth-Century Time Machine: The *Encyclopedia* of Denis Diderot." *Historical Reflections/Réflexions historiques* 25, no. 2 (1999): 227–50.

——. "Louis-Sébastien Mercier's New Words." *Eighteenth-Century Studies* 36, no. 3 (2003): 367–86.

Rosenfeld, Sophia. *A Revolution in Language: The Problem of Signs in Late Eighteenth-Century France.* Stanford: Stanford University Press, 2001.

Roudaut, Jean. "Les exercices poétiques au XVIIIe siècle." *Critique* 181 (1962): 533–47.

——. "La poésie du XVIIIe siècle lue au XXe siècle depuis 1950, réponses à un questionnaire." *Oeuvres et critiques* 7, no. 1 (1982): 139–50.

——. *Poètes et grammairiens du XVIIIe siècle, anthologie.* Paris: Gallimard, 1971.

——, ed. "Poetry and Poetics." In *Transactions of the Fifth International Congress on the Enlightenment,* vol. 4, 1571–1658. Studies on Voltaire and the Eighteenth Century 193. Oxford: Voltaire Foundation, 1980.

Rufi, Enrico. *Le rêve laïque de Louis-Sébastien Mercier entre littérature et politique.* Studies on Voltaire and the Eighteenth Century 326. Oxford: Voltaire Foundation, 1995.

Saint-Amand, Pierre. *Diderot: Le labyrinthe de la relation.* Paris: J. Vrin, 1984.

Schechter, Ronald. "Gothic Thermidor: The *Bals des victimes,* the Fantastic, and the Production of Historical Knowledge in Post-Terror France." *Representations* 61 (1998): 78–94.

Sermain, Jean-Paul. "Le code du bon goût (1725–1750)." In Fumaroli, *Histoire de la rhétorique,* 879–943.

Singy, Patrick. "Huber's Eyes: The Art of Scientific Observation before the Emergence of Positivism." *Representations* 95 (2006): 54–75.

Slaughter, M. M. *Universal Languages and Scientific Taxonomy in the Seventeenth Century.* Cambridge: Cambridge University Press, 1982.

Sloan, Phillip. "The Buffon-Linnaeus Controversy." *Isis* 67 (1976): 356–75.

——. "Buffon Studies Today." *History of Science* 32 (1994): 469–77.

——. "From Logical Universals to Historical Individuals: Buffon's Idea of Biological Species." In *Histoire du concept d'espèce dans les sciences de la vie,* edited by Jean-Louis

Fischer and Jacques Roger, 101–40. Proceedings of Colloque international Singer Polignac, May 1985. Paris: Fondation Singer-Polignac, 1987.

Smith, Pamela H. *The Body of the Artisan: Art and Experience in the Scientific Revolution.* Chicago: University of Chicago Press, 2004.

Spary, E. C. "Codes of Passion: Natural History Specimens as a Polite Language in Late 18th-Century France." In *Wissenschaft als kulturelle Praxis, 1759–1900,* edited by Hans Erich Bödeker, Peter Hanns Reill, and Jürgen Schlumbohm, 105–35. Göttingen: Vandenhoeck und Ruprecht, 1999.

———. *Utopia's Garden: French Natural History from Old Regime to Revolution.* Chicago: University of Chicago Press, 2000.

Staum, Martin. *Minerva's Message: Stabilizing the French Revolution.* Montreal: McGill-Queen's University Press, 1996.

Sternberg, Meir. "Ordering the Unordered: Time, Space, and Descriptive Coherence." In Kittay, "Towards a Theory of Description," 60–88.

Stierle, Karlheinz. "Baudelaire and the Tradition of the *Tableau de Paris. New Literary History* 11, no. 2 (1980): 345–61.

Swenson, James. *On Jean-Jacques Rousseau: Considered as One of the First Authors of the Revolution.* Stanford: Stanford University Press, 2000.

Thomas, Chantal. "'La sphère mouvante des modes.'" In Bonnet, *Hérétique,* 33–53.

Tison-Braun, Micheline. *Poétique du paysage: Essai sur le genre descriptif.* Paris: A. G. Nizet, 1980.

Trahard, Paul, and Édouard Guitton, eds. *Paul et Virginie,* by Bernardin de Saint-Pierre. Collection Classiques Garnier. 2nd ed. 1964. Paris: Bordas, 1989.

Vidler, Anthony. "Mercier urbaniste: L'utopie du réel." In Bonnet, *Hérétique,* 223–43.

Vouilloux, Bernard. "La description du tableau." *Poétique* 18 (1988): 27–50.

———. *La peinture dans le texte: XVIIe au XXe siècles.* Paris: CNRS, 1994.

Wall, Cynthia Sundberg. *The Prose of Things: Transformations of Description in the Eighteenth Century.* Chicago: University of Chicago Press, 2006.

Warnick, Barbara. *The Sixth Canon: Belletristic Rhetorical Theory and Its French Antecedents.* Columbia: University of South Carolina Press, 1993.

Watts, George B. "The *Encyclopédie* and the *Descriptions des arts et métiers." French Review: Journal of the American Association of Teachers of French* 25, no. 6 (1952): 444–54.

Webb, Ruth Helen, and Philip Weller. "Descriptive Poetry." In *The Princeton Encyclopedia of Poetry and Poetics,* edited by Alex Preminger and T. V. F. Brogan, 283–88. Princeton: Princeton University Press, 1993.

Williams, Roger L. *Botanophilia in Eighteenth-Century France: The Spirit of the Enlightenment.* Archives internationales d'histoire des idées 179. Dordrecht: Kluwer, 2001.

INDEX

Page numbers in *italics* refer to figures.